Donal O

ONE MINUTE A DAY

on the

Weekday Readings

VERITAS

First published 1995
by Veritas Publications
7-8 Lower Abbey Street
Dublin 1

ISBN 1 85390 223 3

**British Library Cataloguing
in Publication Data.
A catalogue record for
this book is available
from the British Library.**

Cover design by Bill Bolger
Printed in the Republic of Ireland by Betaprint Ltd, Dublin

Contents

Introduction

Each weekday in our churches many people put themselves out to celebrate the Eucharist. They come to sanctify their day, to be in touch with the Lord and receive his inspiration and guidance through his Word and through his Sacrament. They like a Mass that is meaningful and inspirational, where there is time to pray and reflect, before they have to rush off to their daily tasks. They have a great love for this important Sacrament and make it an integral part of their day. These are the special people of the parish. But there is the danger that they could become over-familiar with the Mass, that it could become very routine for them. However, though much of the Mass remains the same from day to day, the scripture readings change over a two-year cycle and so cannot become routine. Thus by carefully reading the two daily readings and reflecting on them, they can bring a good message away with them for their day.

There is not much time for a homily at these weekday celebrations, but a short explanation or reflection on the scripture readings can be very beneficial. Throughout the two-year cycle those who attend the Mass each day can deepen their knowledge of the essential features of the Word of God. They can learn about the relationship between God and his chosen people in salvation history. They can reflect on the spiritual thoughts and the wisdom of the prophets. They can listen more intently to the riches of St Paul and the apostles. Above all, they can be inspired by the actions and teachings of Jesus.

The short items in this collection are just starting-points for each day. They are not intended to be read out, but it is hoped that with a careful reading of the text of the day, they can help form short one-minute reflections. They can be used either as short homilies or introductions to the readings. Sometimes they may suggest lessons or practical guidelines for the day. Those for the Advent-Christmas and Lent-Easter cycles are simple reflections suitable for the season. During Ordinary Time a short introduction is included whenever a new biblical book is used and a little more detail is given about the background of the work. In general more emphasis is placed on the first readings, as the gospels need less elaboration.

Short sketches of the more important saints are also given. Where the readings are proper, reflections are included. It is recommended that the continuous readings be used for memorials that do not have their own texts.

The last section contains summaries of all the biblical books and a brief account of salvation history for reference purposes. The abbreviations of scripture references are those used in the *Jerusalem Bible*.

My thanks are due in no small way to Fr Lar O'Connor, St Peter's College, Wexford, Fr Paddy O'Brien, PP, Kilanerin, Fr Eltin Griffin O Carm, Gort Muire, Dublin, and Fiona Biggs, Veritas, for all their help and encouragement.

Donal J. Collins

First Week of Advent

Monday   **Is 2:1-5 [Yr A: Is 4:2-6] Mt 8:5-11**

During Advent we try to get into the spirit of the people of old waiting for the expected arrival of the Messiah. For the first few days we try to take on the spirit of the prophets who waited and longed for the Messiah, because he would free them from evil. Then, in the middle of next week, we go along with John the Baptist – 'Prepare ye the way of the Lord.' Finally, from 17 December, we get into the heart of our Lady, as she looked forward to the birth of her son.

For the first nine days we follow the very ancient custom of using special extracts from the prophet Isaiah. He really longed for the time of the Messiah. Today we look forward with him as he tells of his great vision of universal peace. The Lord has washed away the evil from us and has covered us with his glory.

[This oracle looks forward to the day when the people of God will be purified and experience the glory of God.]

For these first nine days the gospel readings have the same theme as the extracts from Isaiah. Christ came to establish the new world of peace. If we could but have faith, all the evils in us would be healed. Look at the great faith of the centurion.

Tuesday   **Is 11:1-10 Lk 10:21-24**

Isaiah foretells that one will come from God who will have the spirit of wisdom, insight, counsel, power, knowledge, and fear of the Lord, a man of integrity. He will bring great peace. That day, the root of Jesse, Jesus Christ, shall stand as a signal to the peoples.

Happy are the eyes that see what you see – the prophets wished for this. The Father knows the Son and the Son reveals this relationship to us.

Wednesday   **Is 25:6-10 Mt 15:29-37**

In the new order, there will be peace and plenty of good things. Death will be destroyed forever. The Lord will wipe away the tear from every cheek. We exult and rejoice that he has saved us.

Jesus foreshadows the land of plenty when he heals the many sick and feeds the multitude in the desert.

Thursday   **Is 26:1-6 Mt 7:2. 24-27**

Again Isaiah is extolling the great peace the Messiah will bring. Those who trusted in him will be saved. He will bring down the haughty. The Lord is the everlasting Rock.

It is important both to listen to the words of Jesus, and also to carry them out. In that way we can be a rock against any idea that is put in our way.

Friday   **Is 29:17-24 Mt 9:27-31**

In this new world of peace, the lowly will rejoice in the Lord, the poor will exult, and the blind will see. Scoffers, tyrants and gossipers will be eliminated. Stand in awe before the God, the holy one of Jacob.

The blind man saw again. We pray that any spiritual blindness that is in us will be healed so that we can accept the message of Christ in full.

Saturday   **Is 30:19-21.23-26 Mt 9:35-10:1.6-8**

Isaiah continues to sing about the new peaceful world brought about by the Messiah. Weep no more, he tells the people. The Lord knows what you need and will supply you with all good things. There will be good harvests.

The harvest is rich but the labourers are few. Jesus sends his disciples out to bring his Good News. The kingdom of heaven is at hand.

Second Week of Advent

Monday   **Is 35:1-10 Lk 5:17-26**

All this week Isaiah gives great messages of comfort and hope. Rejoice, have courage, do not be afraid. Your God is coming – he is coming to save you. The eyes of the blind shall be opened, the ears of the deaf unsealed, the lame shall leap like deers. There will be joy and gladness – sorrow and lament will be ended.

The people reflect the awe of the first reading – 'We have seen great things today.' Jesus carries out his mission of healing, when he cures the paralysed man. But faith is an important prerequisite.

Tuesday   **Is 40:1-11 Mt 18:12-14**

The time of deliverance has come – the people have suffered enough and their sin is atoned for. A voice cries: 'Prepare in the wilderness a way for the Lord. Shout with joy. Here is your God!' The Lord is coming with power. He is like a shepherd caring for his flock.

Even sinners can be part of the kingdom – the Lord goes after them just as a shepherd goes after the strays. He is forever trying to persuade them to repent.

Wednesday   **Is 40:25-31 Mt 11:28-30**

The Jews felt abandoned by God in exile. Isaiah gives them hope of deliverance. Look up and see the myriads of stars – all were created by God. That God is an everlasting God and gives strength to the weary.

Jesus has an encouraging message for those who feel overburdened by life. 'Come to me and learn from me and you will find peace.'

Thursday   **Is 41:13-20 Mt 11:11-15**

Again, Isaiah is trying to encourage the Jews. He speaks of God taking them by the hand and making them strong. Their land will become very fertile and all will see the hand of God in their lives.

Up to now we have been concentrating on the prophet's anticipation of the saviour. In the gospels for the next few days we work along with John, as he looked forward to the coming of the Messiah. Jesus mentions that he was to fulfil many of the prophecies we have heard over the past few weeks.

'I will teach you what is good for you – I will lead you in the way you must go. If only you had remained faithful you would be full of happiness.'

Jesus sees his generation like children crying out: 'We played the pipes and you won't dance....' If only they had not remained blind to the work of John, then they would have been able to take what Jesus had to say.

Saturday   **Si 48:1-4. 9-11 Mt 17:10-13**

We have a reference today to the prophet Elijah. Like John the Baptist, his job was to allay God's wrath before the fury broke. Some regarded John as Elijah come back again.

Jesus compares John to Elijah – just as Elijah was not recognised neither would John be. Like Elijah and John, Jesus himself would suffer at the hands of the people.

Third Week of Advent

Monday   Nb 24:2-7.15-17 Mt 21:23-27

For the next two days we move away from Isaiah. Today we hear two oracles from the Book of Numbers. These are very consoling because they both speak of a great leader who is to come to the house of Israel. All the people are to have this air of expectancy for their saviour. 'How fair your dwellings, Israel. A hero arises from their stock, he reigns over countless people.' We try to imbibe this spirit too as we look forward to the coming of Christ at Christmas.

We still hear of John the Baptiser and his work of preparing the way. The chief priests and elders tried to ensnare Jesus, but he turned the tables on them by asking them what they thought of the work of John. He condemns them for their spiritual blindness – if they had read the scriptures they would know who he was, and they would know about John's mission to prepare the way for him.

Tuesday   Zp 3:1-2.9-13 Mt 21:28-32

We have an extract from the prophet Zephaniah – he is looking forward to the day when the people are taken away from their sins and from sinful people. When the Messiah comes the insincere, the rebellious, the defiled, those who will not listen to the Lord, they will be taken away. God says, I will give the people lips that are clean; you will do no wrong, will tell no lies. You will be able to rest with no one to disturb you. Then there will be peace and contentment.

We hear about John once more. Again the chief priests and elders closed their eyes. They were like the son who said he would do what his father ordered, but did what he wanted instead. Sincerity of heart is what really counts. They were too blind to see that even public sinners repented after John's preaching; they would not accept John.

Wednesday   Is 45:6-8.21-26 Lk 7:19-23

We are back to Isaiah – he gives us a great poetic document. It was written to give consolation to the downtrodden Israelites. The good God will bring salvation to his people. He is a God of integrity and a saviour. 'Send victory like a dew, you heavens, and let the clouds rain it down. Let the earth open for salvation to spring up. Victorious and glorious through the Lord shall be all the descendants of Israel.'

John is again the topic of the gospel. To strengthen their faith he gets his disciples to meet Jesus and ask him about himself. He is fulfiling what the scriptures said of the saviour – curing the blind, the lame, the lepers, raising the dead to life, and proclaiming the Good News.

Thursday   **Is 54:1-10 Lk 7:24-30**

Isaiah brings more words of great joy and consolation – do not be afraid, but shout for joy, the saviour is coming to you. The mountains may depart, the hills may be shaken, but my love for you will never leave you, says the Lord, who takes pity on you. This is what the Messiah will bring. We can apply this message directly to ourselves as we look forward to Christmas.

Jesus speaks of John again and describes him as being greater than any of the prophets. He is the one who is the messenger to prepare the way before Christ, the saviour. How he looked forward to seeing the Messiah!

Friday   **Is 56:1-3.6-8 Jn 5:33-36**

Isaiah again reminds his people that salvation is soon to come. So they must act with justice and integrity. They will all be gathered together and will be joyful in his house of prayer.

John was there to prepare the way for Jesus. He comes to carry out the works of his Father. Let us see John, the lamp alight and shining, as we, like him, look forward to the coming of Jesus next week.

Fourth Week of Advent

17 December   Gn 49:2.8-10 Mt 1:1-17

These are special days when the thought of the expected Messiah gets very intense. The kingship will never pass from the house of Jacob into which Jesus will be born. Each of these days has a very special antiphon or short prayer appealing to the Lord to come. These are known as the 'O' antiphons. We use these each day to proclaim the gospel.

This week we try to get into the mind of Mary as she looked forward to the birth of her son. The Israelites were very conscious of their genealogy – today we have the genealogy for Jesus through Joseph, the husband of Mary. His line can be traced back to David, the greatest king of the Jews and then right back to Abraham, the father of the chosen people.

'O wisdom, you come forth from the mouth of the Most High. You fill the universe and hold all things together in a strong yet gentle manner. O come to teach us the way of truth.'

18 December   Jr 23:5-8 Mt 1:18-24

The days are coming, the prophet Jeremiah says, when the Lord will raise a virtuous branch for David and he will save Judah. 'In his days justice shall flourish and peace till the moon fails.'

The gospel gives us the fulfilment of the prophecy. Joseph is told about the conception of Mary's child. He is to name him Jesus. Think about Joseph's faith. 'O Adonai and leader of the house of Israel, you appeared to Moses in a burning bush and you gave him the Law on Sinai. O come and save us with your mighty power.'

19 December   Jg 13:2-7.24-25 Lk 1:5-25

The promise and birth of the famous Samson prefigures that of John. He was destined to save the people from the Philistines. John had the mission to prepare for Jesus who is to be a saviour on a much wider and more spiritual scale.

Zechariah couldn't grasp fully what the angel was telling him and so lost his power of speech until John was born. His faith was not as strong as Joseph's.

'O stock of Jesse, you stand as a signal for the nations; kings fall silent before you whom the people acclaim. O come to deliver us, and do not delay.'

20 December   Is 7:10-14 Lk 1:26-38

One of the Israelite kings is given a sign – a sign that he did not want. The maiden is with child and will soon give birth to a son whom she will call Emmanuel, a name which means 'God-is-with-us'. This is an obvious reference to the birth of Jesus.

Mary now freely becomes the mother of Jesus – 'I am the handmaid of the Lord, let what you have said be done to me.' What great faith she had.

'O key of David and sceptre of Israel, what you open no one else can close again; what you close no one can open. O come to lead the captive from prison; free those who sit in darkness and in the shadow of death.'

21 December   Sg 2:8-14 [Zp 3:14-18] Lk 1:39-45

We have a beautiful poem from the Song of Songs. Come, my beautiful one, the winter is passed; come out into the spring, show me your face and let me hear your voice.
[Shout for joy, daughter of Zion, Israel, shout aloud! Rejoice, exult with all your heart, you have no more evil to fear.]

In spite of her condition, Mary sets out to the hilly country to visit her cousin Elizabeth, the mother of John. 'Blessed is she who believed that the promise made her by the Lord would be fulfiled.'

'O rising Sun, you are the splendour of eternal light and the sun of justice. O come and enlighten those who sit in darkness and in the shadow of death.'

22 December   I S 1:24-28 Lk 1:46-56

Today the readings are full of thanks. Hannah gives thanks for the birth of her son, Samuel and presents him in the Temple.

Mary is visiting her cousin – the mother of John the Baptiser. She gives thanks to God – 'My soul proclaims the greatness of the Lord...'

'O king whom all the peoples desire, you are the cornerstone which makes all one. O come and save man whom you made from clay.'

23 December   Ml 3:1-4. 23-24 Lk 1:57-66

Before the Messiah will come, a prophet will be sent to prepare the way. He will purify the people.

That special person is John. Zechariah, his father, gets his power of speech back when he gives him the name given by the angel.

'O Immanuel, you are our king and judge, the One whom the people await and their Saviour. O come and save us, Lord, our God.'

24 December   I S 7:1-5. 8-11.16 Lk 1:67-79

David, the best of the kings of Israel, is reminded that his house and sovereignty will always last – as a spiritual kingdom.

After John's birth, Zechariah gave his great prayer of praise. 'Blessed be the Lord, the God of Israel. You, little child, shall go before the Lord to prepare the way for him.'

Octave of Christmas

26 December: St Stephen   Ac 6:8-10; 7:54-59 Mt 10:17-22

Stephen was filled with grace and power and worked signs among the people. His zeal and integrity annoyed many and eventually he gave his life for his faith.

Jesus tells his disciples that many will attack them because they are his followers. The Holy Spirit will enlighten them when necessary.

27 December: St John   I Jn 1:1-4 Jn 20:2-8

John gives strong testimony to the fact that he saw and related to Jesus. He wants others to share his joy in this.

John had more faith than Peter – as soon as he saw the empty tomb he immediately believed that Jesus had risen from the dead.

28 December: Holy Innocents   I Jn 1:5-2:2 Mt 2:13-18

God is light. If we live in light we will live in union with Jesus Christ. He will purify us from our sins – he was the sacrifice that took away our sins.

God in his providence looks after his chosen and saves Jesus from the wickedness of Herod. The children become special martyrs.

29 December   I Jn 2:3-11 Lk 2:22-35

During the octave we take the first reading from the first letter of St John. This was one of three letters, probably written by disciples of John, to encourage unity in the early Church, in which there were many divisions. This letter is very positive and loving in tone. We can be sure that we are in God only when we are living the same kind of life as Christ lived. We are now living in the light and must obey his Commandments.

We gave the touching story of the presentation in the Temple. 'Now Master, you can let your servant go in peace, just as you promised; because my eyes have seen the salvation which you have prepared for all the nations to see.'

30 December   I Jn 2:12-17 Lk 2:36-40

The love of the Father cannot be in any one who loves the world, because nothing the world has to offer could ever come from the Father but only from the world. Anyone who does the will of God remains for ever.

The story of the presentation continues. Anna was filled with the Holy Spirit and prophesied that the child would be the saviour of Jerusalem.

Many will come forward claiming to be Christ. Don't listen to them – you know the truth, you have been anointed by the Holy One.

The Word is God, the creator of the great world. The Word became flesh and dwelt amongst us. He has given us the power to become the children of God.

Second Week after Christmas

1 January: Solemnity of Mary Mother of God

'This celebration, assigned to January 1 in conformity with the ancient liturgy of the city of Rome, is meant to commemorate the part played by Mary in this mystery of salvation. It is meant also to exalt the singular dignity which this mystery brings to the "holy Mother ... through whom we were found worthy ... to receive the Author of life." It is likewise a fitting occasion for renewed adoration of the newborn Prince of Peace, for listening once more to the glad tidings of angels, and for imploring from God, through the Queen of Peace, the supreme gift of peace. For this reason we have instituted the World Day of Peace.' (*Marialis cultus* – 1974).

Nb 6:22-27 Ga 4:4-7 Lk 2:16-21

The Lord gave Moses a special blessing. It means more now that Christ is among us: 'May the Lord bless you and keep you; may the Lord let his face shine on you and be gracious to you; may the Lord uncover his face to you and bring you peace.'

God sent his Son, born of Mary, to enable us to become God's adopted children. We are no longer slaves, but have the same intimacy as a child with loving parents. We can actually say 'Abba, Father' to God.

Think of the thoughts and feelings of Mary as the shepherds departed. She treasured all these things and pondered them in her heart. She is the Mother of Jesus, the Son of God.

2 January   I Jn 2:22-28 Jn 1:19-28

We continue with John. To acknowledge the Son is to acknowledge the Father as well – to deny Christ is to deny the Father. Keep alive in you what you have been taught and you will live in the Son and in the Father – you will possess eternal life.

John the Baptist reminds his listeners that he was not the Christ, but came to prepare the way for him – the voice of one crying in the wilderness.

3 January   I Jn 2:29-3:6 Jn 1:29-34

Think of the love that the Father has lavished on us, by letting us be called God's children. We are already the children of God but what we are to be in the future has not yet been revealed – we shall be like him because we shall see him as he really is.

John the Baptist gives testimony that Jesus is the Messiah – he saw the Spirit descend upon him – he is the chosen one of God.

4 January   I Jn 3:7-10 Jn 1:35-42

Do not let anyone lead you astray; to live a holy life is to be holy just as God is holy. Anyone not loving his brother is no child of God's.

Some of John's disciples join Jesus. One of these was Andrew. He introduced his brother Simon to him – the man who was to be called Peter.

5 January   I Jn 3:11-12 Jn 1:43-51

John continues his treatise on love. Jesus gave up his life for us; we too, ought to give up our lives for our brothers. Our love is not to be just words or mere talk, but something real and active.

Philip is called to be a disciple of Jesus and he in turn gets Nathanael – who was without guile.

6 January [except Epiphany]*   I Jn 5:5-13 Mk 1:6b-11

The Spirit, the water and the blood are the three witnesses to the work of Christ. We accept God's testimony, given as evidence for his Son. God has given us eternal life and this life is in his Son.

We have the story referred to earlier in the week – the baptism of Jesus. The Holy Spirit descends on him like a dove and a voice from heaven said, 'You are my son, the beloved; my favour rests on you.'

7 January   I Jn 5:14-21 Jn 2:1-12

We are confident that if we ask the Son of God for anything and it is in accordance with his will, he will hear us. And, knowing that whatever we may ask, he hears us, we know that we have been granted what we asked of him. When we repent of our sins, we have just to ask for pardon and it will be given to us.

We see from the account of the wedding feast of Cana that Mary had a great influence on Jesus. We are now her children, so she will be just as dedicated to us.

---

*1. Where the Epiphany is celebrated on 6 January follow the dates in brackets on pp.18-19.

2 Where the Epiphany is celebrated on the Sunday between 2 and 8 January, use the readings above up to the Saturday and those on p.18 according to the days.

Weekdays of the Christmas Season

Monday [7 January] I Jn 3:22-4:6 Mt 4:12-17. 23-25

We continue with John's first letter. We know that he lives in us by the Spirit that he has given us. Whatever we ask of God, we shall receive, because we keep his Commandments and live the kind of life that he wants – we love one another as he told us to.

Jesus begins his mission. He is saddened by the lack of repentance and spirituality that he sees.

Tuesday [8 January] I Jn 4:7-10 Mk 6:34-44

Anyone who fails to love can never have known God, because God is love. God's love for us was revealed when he sent his only Son into the world so that we could have life through him.

The gospel story is an example of the kindness of Jesus. He fed them well, but he wanted to build up their faith. If he was able to do this, he could surely carry out the rest of his promises.

Wednesday [9 January] I Jn 4:11-18 Mk 6:45-52

God is love and anyone who lives in love lives in God and God lives in him. In love there can be no fear; fear is driven out by perfect love.

In the aftermath of the miracle of the loaves and fishes the faith of the apostles had not yet developed fully. 'Have courage, do not be afraid.'

Thursday [10 January] I Jn 4:19-5:4 Lk 4:14-22

Anyone who says that he loves God and hates his brother, is a liar – how can he love God whom he cannot see, when he refuses to love his brother?

While at Nazareth Jesus preaches in his own synagogue. He reminds them that he has been sent to bring the Good News to the poor as well as to do the other things the Messiah was expected to do.

Friday [11 January]   **I Jn 5:5-13 Lk 5:12-16**

The Spirit, the water and the blood are the three witnesses to the work of Christ. We accept God's testimony, given as evidence for his Son. God has given us eternal life and this life is in his Son.

We have one of the early miracles of Jesus. The man had faith in him, so Jesus was able to cure his leprosy.

Saturday [12 January]   **I Jn 5:14-21 Jn 3:22-30**

We are confident that if we ask the Son of God for anything which is in accordance with his will, he will hear us. And, knowing that whatever we may ask, he hears us, we know that we have been granted what we asked of him. When we repent of our sins, we have just to ask for pardon and it will be given to us.

John the Baptist reminds his listeners that he himself was not the Christ. He was only sent to prepare the way. That must have been a very hard thing to say.

Lenten Themes

The Season of Lent

W   Call to repentance
T   Obey the Commandments and follow Christ
F   Fast must be accompanied with justice
S   Share with the needy

First Week of Lent

M   Keep the Commandments – judgment
T   Our Father in heaven
W   Repentance – Jonah
T   Confidence in prayer – Esther
F   Sincere reconciliation
S   Be perfect as your heavenly Father is perfect

Second Week of Lent

M   Compassion
T   Sins are forgiven (white as snow)
W   Suffering and discipleship
T   Spiritual treasures (the rich man and Lazarus)
F   Joseph prefigures Jesus – salvation through suffering
S   Forgiveness – prodigal son

Third Week of Lent

M   Baptism – Naaman – prophet
T   Forgiveness – seventy-seven times
W   Obey the Commandments
T   Listen to God and follow his laws
F   Repent and trust in God's mercy
S   Sincerity

Fourth Week of Lent

M   Faith brings joy
T   Power of baptism
W   The Son represents the Father
T   Jesus is more influential than Moses with the Father
F   The righteousness of Jesus and his followers brings out the evil in us
S   Jesus will be led like a lamb to the slaughter

Fifth Week of Lent

M   Sin is condemned but the repentant sinner is forgiven
T   Salvation comes through Jesus being lifted up
W   Though Jesus will flow salvation
T   Before Abraham was, I am
F   Jesus is threatened for doing God's work
S   Salvation will come through the death of Jesus

Holy Week

M   The Messiah will bring true justice – the anointing prepares for his death
T   Peter's impulsive promise
W   The suffering Messiah

The Season of Lent

Ash Wednesday   **Jl 2:12-18 2 Co 5:20-6:2 Mt 6:1-6.16-18**

During Lent a number of themes is presented to us constantly – prayer, fasting and almsgiving; repentance, forgiveness and the mercy of God; baptism, dying to sin and rising to new life with Christ.

Today we are reminded that we are called to repentance – to make a complete conversion. God speaks to us and asks us to come back to him – let the change be internal as well as external. He is all tenderness and compassion, slow to anger, rich in graciousness, and ready to relent. We fast to help us make up for our sins and strengthen our will-power.

St Paul makes the appeal in Christ's name – be reconciled to God. Do not neglect the grace of God which you have received.

Give alms – but make sure it is done quietly. Similarly, with prayer and fasting. Your Father who sees all that is done in secret will reward you.

Thursday   **Dt 30:15-20 Lk 9:22-25**

Obey the Commandments of God and you will live. Let yourself be drawn from God and you will die – you will not receive God's promise.

Jesus refers to his passion and death: his followers, if they are true to him, will also find it tough. 'Take up your cross daily and follow me: do not be ashamed of me.'

Friday   **Is 58:1-9 Mt 9:14-15**

Fasting, no matter how public, is useless if it is accompanied by injustice toward others. You must also share your bread with the hungry and look after the needy. Then the Lord will listen to you.

The disciples of Jesus will fast when he is taken away from them.

Saturday   **Is 58:9-14 Lk 5:27-32**

If you avoid injustice, if you share with the needy, your light will rise in the darkness and the Lord will guide you. You will be like a spring that never runs dry, you shall find happiness in the Lord.

Jesus visits Levi, the tax collector. In spite of his profession, he has more real spirituality than the Pharisees and scribes.

First Week of Lent

Monday   **Lv 19:1-2.11-18 Mt 25:31-46**

The Lord speaks to us through Moses : Be holy, for I, the Lord your God, am holy. By keeping the Commandments, especially in regard to justice, you will become holy.

We have the scene of the last judgment. We will be judged on how we keep the Lord's Commandments – especially those that concern the welfare of others. 'As you did it to the least of these, you did it to me.'

Tuesday   **Is 55:10-11 Mt 6:7-15**

The word of God is somewhat like rain and snow. It comes from the heavens, waters the earth, gives growth and food and then returns to the heavens. The Word nourishes – it carries out God's will and so does not return empty-handed.

Jesus teaches us how to pray – 'Our Father in heaven, may you be called holy – forgive us our debts – save us from the evil one.'

Wednesday   **Jon 3:1-10 Lk 1129-32**

We have the climax of the famous story of Jonah. He tried to get away from God and the duty of preaching that he was given. That is why he found himself in the sea monster. After his preaching the people of the city fasted and repented.

All the signs the crowd need are to be found in the scriptures. Take the example of the Ninevites and Jonah and turn away from sin – remember, greater than Jonah is here.

Thursday   **Est 14:1.3-5.13-14 Mt 7:7-12**

We have the great prayer of Esther. Her courage came from her belief that God alone could save his people and her confidence that he would answer her prayers. Prayer needs fasting and alms-giving to accompany it to get a sense of hopelessness and dependence.

Jesus reminds us that we have only to trust in the goodness and providence of God and then ask him to give us what we need. As a result we must treat others well.

Friday   **Est 18:21-28 Mt 5:20-26**

What we decide to do and what we actually do will determine our future. We must repent and stay away from sin, and then we shall live. God's mercy cannot really reach into the unforgiving heart.

Our reconciliation must come from the heart – only then will our offering be effective and acceptable.

Saturday   **Dt 26:16-19 Mt 5:43-48**

Observe God's law – then you will be his people, consecrated to the Lord. He will be your God.

We have part of the Sermon on the Mount. To be children of our Father in heaven, we must do more for others than the pagans do. We must love our enemies, pray for those who persecute us, and we must be perfect as our heavenly Father is perfect.

Second Week of Lent

Monday   **Dn 9:4-10 Lk 6:36-38**

We have all sinned in many ways – we have done wrong, we have acted wickedly, we have betrayed God's Commandments. As a result we are full of shame. But mercy and pardon belong to the Lord.

Be compassionate, do not judge, give in good measure. Remember that God is compassionate.

Tuesday   **Is 1:10.16-20 Mt 23:1-12**

Cease to be evil, learn to do good, Trust in the mercy of God: 'Though your sins are like scarlet, they shall be as white as snow; though they are as red as crimson, they shall be like wool.'

Be careful to be sincere – do as your teachers teach you, but not necessarily what they do. Be the servant of all.

Wednesday   **Jr 18:18-20 Mt 20:17-18**

Jeremiah was persecuted in spite of his good work for the people in praying for them to God. Like Jesus he must suffer.

Jesus makes reference to his sufferings as he is going towards Jerusalem. We can accompany him and belong to his kingdom if we follow him in his suffering.

Thursday   **Jr 17:5-10 Lk 16:19-31**

If we put our trust in things of this world, we will become dry and empty – like a dead bush. If we trust in God we shall be like the plant growing near the water: full of life.

Jesus tells the story of Lazarus and the rich man. This develops the ideas of the first reading. The rich man trusted in his money and possessions and ended up with nothing. The poor man was blessed with eternal life.

Friday   **Gn 37:3-4 12-13.17-28**

Joseph, the favourite son of Jacob, was sold by his brothers because they were very jealous. But for Reuben, they would have killed him instead.

Jesus tells the parable of the unjust stewards. They went so far as to kill the owner's son, the heir. This prefigures Christ's death. Grace came through this death.

God will grant us his forgiveness, he will pardon our sins, he will take away our faults and show his mercy. Let us go to him with trust and ask for this forgiveness.

Jesus gives the great example of mercy in the story of the prodigal son. Like the father, God will welcome back the repentant sinner – he rejoices over his return to life. He reminds the older, good son of this.

Third Week of Lent

Monday   **II Kg:5:1-5 Lk 4:24-30**

We have the great story of Naaman, the leper, which prefigures baptism. In the early Church this story was used to prepare the catechumens on their way to their baptism at Easter. So we are reminded of the power of our God.

This is one of the stories Jesus refers to when he tells his own people in Nazareth that no prophet is without honour except in his own country.

Tuesday   **Dn 3:25.34-43 Mt 18:21-35**

The emphasis is on forgiving. We have the prayer of Azariah in the furnace: 'Do not abandon us forever: we are despised because of our sins. May the contrite soul and the humble spirit be acceptable to you.'

'Seventy-seven times' was the answer given by Jesus about forgiveness. Then he gives us the frightening and very telling parable about the ungrateful steward.

Wednesday   **Dt 4:1,5-9 Mt 5:17-19**

It is important for those who wish to be part of God's kingdom to obey all his Commandments. By doing this we can show God's greatness to the world.

Jesus tells his listeners to follow the law and encourage others to follow it as well. Make sure there is no scandal.

Thursday   **Jr 7:23-28 Lk 11:14-23**

Those who listen to God and follow his laws will be his people. But many refuse to listen and turn their backs on him, following the dictates of their own evil hearts.

Those who are close to God and who are with God can overcome the power of Satan.

Friday   **Ho 14:1-10 Mt 12:28-34**

Come back to your God – he will love you with all his heart when you do so. He will give you grace – like dew on the ground, full of freshness.

Jesus reminds us that those who are not with him are against him. Trust in his forgiveness.

We must try to have genuine love and repentance which will not disappear like the morning dew. 'What I want is love, not sacrifice.'

The Pharisee and the publican pray in different ways. We can all see the Pharisee in ourselves. Let's try to be sincere. If we claim to love God, let us show it by loving our neighbour.

Fourth Week of Lent

Monday   Is 65:17-21 Jn 4:43-54

Be glad and rejoice – I will create a new world, a world of joy and
gladness, a world without illness or hardship – the wolf and the lamb will
feed together. This is my promise to my people.

The second sign given by Jesus in Cana – the court official had a son
who was ill in Capernaum and wanted Jesus to come and cure him. All he
needed was faith and faith brought him joy.

Tuesday   Ezk 47:1-9.12 Jn 5:1-6

Today's reading gives us the opportunity of reflecting on the power of
baptism. The vision of the growing river and the fruit it produced reminds
us of the spiritual fruits of baptism.

In the gospel the water also brought healing. Jesus added the important
fruit of forgiveness. In Holy Week we die in baptism to the old person and
rise to a new being.

Wednesday   Is 49:8-15 Jn 5:17-30

Back to Monday's theme – you are my people, I will remember my
covenant with you. I will make your way safe – rejoice and be glad. A
woman does not forget her child: but even if she were to forget, I will
never forget you.

The Father has given the Son complete authority and influence and
power – he can give life to anyone he chooses. Whoever refuses to
honour the Son refuses to honour the Father.

Thursday   Ex 32:7-14 Jn 5:31-47

Moses makes an impassioned plea to God to forgive the sins of the
Israelites. Sin can always be forgiven when there is repentance.

Jesus tells his disciples that he does not have to depend on human
testimony – John first gave his testimony, but now his own works are
testimony. The scriptures bear this out – I have come in the name of my
Father. If you really believed in Moses you would believe in me too.

Righteous people are never popular among the evil doers – they show up their evil ways. Christ suffered because of his righteousness: so will we. Let's not be like the malicious who have no hope that holiness and blamelessness will be rewarded.

Jesus speaks to those trying to kill him – he reminds them that they really do not know where he comes from.

Jeremiah foreshadows the passion of Jesus – he is to be like a trustful lamb, led to the slaughterhouse.

There is a lot of discussion among the chief priests and Pharisees about who Jesus is. Even the police are impressed by him – much to the dismay of the Pharisees. Among the Pharisees, one sane voice is heard. Nicodemus reminds them that 'we cannot pass judgment on a man until we give him a hearing'.

Fifth Week of Lent

Monday   Dn 13:1-9.15-17.19-30.33-63 Jn 8:1-11

We have the famous story from Daniel of how the wickedness of the two old men was exposed! Through simple wisdom Daniel was able to save Susanna, who had refused to compromise her virtue.

Jesus is confronted with a woman taken in adultery. Although he condemns the sin, he ensures that the sinner is not judged, but pardoned.

Tuesday   Nb 21:4-9 Jn 8:21-30

We are again reminded of what the crucifixion will do for us. Those who looked at the bronze serpent on the standard were saved from poison. So those who look on Jesus, who will be lifted up, will be saved. Use the sign of the cross with respect and reflection.

Wednesday   Dn 3:14-20.91-92.95 Jn 8:31-42

Certain Jews refused to worship the statue made by Nebuchadnezzar and were thrown into a furnace. They survived and demonstrated the great power of the God they believed in.

Jesus was very maddening for the Pharisees – he is only to be with them for a short time. But through him would flow fountains of living water that would bring redemption and new life.

Thursday   Gn 17:3-9 Jn 8:51-59

Again we are reminded of the great covenant or pact which the Lord God made with Abraham. He is the father of the Jews and our forefather too.

The Jews of Jesus' time were more sceptical – they would not accept him and believed he was committing blasphemy when he said 'before Abraham ever was, I am'.

Friday   Jr 10:10-13 Jn 10:31-42

The people want to denounce the prophet. But no matter what happens he has the Lord God on his side – sing praise to God.

Jesus too is being threatened by the stone-throwing Jews. 'I am not blaspheming', he said. 'I am doing the work of my Father. Believe in the work I do.'

We have another reminder of the covenant that God made with his people. Salvation and peace will eventually come to them.

The high priests are discussing what to do with Jesus. Caiaphas prophesies that one man must die for the people – through this act salvation and peace will come.

Holy Week

Monday   Is 42:1-7 Jn 12:1-11

As we go from Palm Sunday to Holy Thursday we reflect quietly on Jesus the Messiah. The readings from Isaiah give us some of the characteristics of the great saviour. 'This is my specially chosen servant, who will not waver. He will bring true justice.'

The gospel tells us of the incidents during the last days of Jesus before the Passover. Today we hear that Mary, the sister of Lazarus and Martha, anoints Jesus – in preparation for his death – in spite of the protests of Judas, who saw it as a waste of money.

Tuesday   Is 49:1-6 Jn 13:21-33.36-38

'You are my servant in whom I shall be glorified. The Lord formed you in the womb – you will restore my people.'

We contrast Judas and Peter. Judas is greedy and his greed leads to disloyalty and betrayal. Jesus will be glorified through his actions. Peter is impetuous and makes unreasonable promises that he will later regret. But he will also repent of his mistakes.

Wednesday   Is 50:4-9 Mt 26:14-25

The Messiah was given a disciple's tongue, but would be insulted. 'I have offered my back to those who struck me, my cheeks to those who tore at my beard.'

There are many things to reflect on as we prepare for the three sacred days, beginning tomorrow. We have a description of the betrayal, the preparation for the Last Supper, the account of this supper and the institution of the Eucharist, and the forecast that the disciples would scatter in fear, in spite of their protestations of loyalty.

First Week of Easter

Monday   **Ac 2:14.22-32 Mt 28:8-15**

For the Easter season the first readings are taken from the Acts of the Apostles. This is really a great adventure story where we learn about the early work of the apostles. St Peter – the impetuous disciple – gives a very powerful talk about Jesus who was crucified. But unlike the patriarch, David, whose tomb is still there, Jesus has risen from the dead. 'You will not allow your holy one to experience corruption.'

In the gospel extracts this week we hear the various accounts of the appearance of the risen Christ. The women met Jesus after he rose and they told the rest of the disciples. So the guards' attempt to explain the disappearance of the body was made in vain.

Tuesday   **Ac 2:36-41 Jn 20:11-18**

The people were moved by Peter's powerful speech about the risen Jesus. They repented of their sins and received the gift of the Holy Spirit.

Jesus meets Mary who is so full of sadness that she does not recognise him at first. She too must spread the word of his resurrection.

Wednesday   **Ac 3:1-10 Lk 24:13-35**

The miracle of Peter and John at the Beautiful gate of the Temple. It was carried out in the name of Jesus Christ the Nazarene, who had risen from the dead.

Today we have the touching story of Jesus meeting his two disciples on the road to Emmaus. He was revealed to them partly through the scriptures and fully through the breaking of bread, or the Eucharist.

Thursday   **Ac 3:11-26 Lk 24:35-48**

Peter uses the miracle as an opportunity to preach about the crucified Christ who fulfiled the prophecies of the scriptures. The listeners must repent and then God will bless them.

After the Emmaus incident Jesus at last visits all his disciples. He showed them he was real by eating with them. Then he explained the scriptures, told them that they were witnesses to his resurrection and promised them the Holy Spirit.

Friday   Ac 4:1-12 Jn 21:1-14

The Sadducees did not believe in the resurrection of the dead and so
Peter's message about Jesus angered them. When arrested Peter and John
used the opportunity to preach their message to the high priests and pretty
well astounded them.

Jesus visited Peter and some of the other disciples and helped them
catch lots of fish. Again they were amazed at the power of this man – who
seemed to be more than a mere man: hence the question, 'Who are you?'

Saturday   Ac 4:13-21 Mk 16:9-15

The high priests were impressed and worried about Peter and John's
powerful statement: all they could do was quietly tell them to stop
preaching their message!

We have Mark's review of the first visits of Jesus to his friends and
disciples after his resurrection.

Second Week of Easter

Monday   Ac 4:23-31 Jn 3:1-8

The answer of Peter and John and the whole community to the admonition of the high priests was to offer a strong, heartfelt prayer to God – a prayer of praise and thanks for what he had done, a prayer asking for the strength and wisdom to continue their work.

For the rest of the Easter season we use various sections of St John's gospel, beginning with Jesus' discourse to Nicodemus. We must be spiritually reborn by baptism of water and the Holy Spirit.

Tuesday   Ac 4:32-37 Jn 3:7-15

The disciples continued their work of preaching about the risen Jesus. They were also learning to share what they had to make their work more efficient.

Still with Nicodemus, Jesus tells him that there must be great faith among his followers – like the salvation that came to those in the desert when they looked on the serpent staff, those who look to the risen eternal life would come to the crucified Christ.

Wednesday   Ac 5:17-26 Jn 3:16-21

The apostles find themselves arrested again – but they are saved by an angel. This causes great fear among the high priests and the soldiers. First Jesus and now this!

The central message of Christianity was given to Nicodemus: 'God sent his Son, not to condemn the world, but to bring light and salvation to those who believed in him.'

Thursday   Ac 5:27-33 Jn 3:31-36

The apostles were again brought before the authorities. They insisted that obedience to God comes before obedience to people. God raised Jesus from the dead to bring repentance and forgiveness of sins.

We jump to the work of John the baptiser – who is the forerunner of the Messiah. 'I must decrease; he must increase.' God gave his Son the Spirit and all who believe in him will have eternal life.

Friday   **Ac 5:34-42 Jn 6:1-15**

One voice of reason was heard among the high priests. Don't worry about their preaching: if its origin is human it will fade away. If it is from God, then we mustn't fight it.

For the next week and a half we have Jesus teaching about the Eucharist. He begins with the miracle of the loaves and fishes. Having given them physical food he wants the people to see the spiritual significance of this miracle.

Saturday   **Ac 6:1-7 Jn 6:16-21**

The Church was growing so fast that some sort of structure was needed for practical reasons. The disciples elected a number of deacons, including Stephen. The apostles would continue preaching while the deacons looked after the day-to-day practical details.

Jesus comes to the disciples on the water and calms the lake – another incident to prepare them for the doctrine of the Eucharist.

Third Week of Easter

Monday   **Ac 6:8-15 Jn 6:22-29**

Stephen preaches with great power and effect. The authorities found his wisdom too challenging so they concocted false statements against him and had him arrested. Stephen did not worry about the consequences of his preaching.

After the miracle of the loaves and fishes the people ran all over the place looking for Jesus. He tried to get them to see the spiritual significance of what he had done – 'work for food that endures to eternal life'.

Tuesday   **Ac 7:51-8:1 Jn 6:30-35**

We hear the end of Stephen's long sermon in which he tells the people how all the prophets were persecuted. Now they had done the same to the Just One, Jesus Christ. They took out their anger on him and stoned him to death. One of those who approved their action was Saul, who later became Paul.

The people wanted a sign like that of Moses who gave them manna in the desert. Jesus reminds them it is his Father who gives the true bread from heaven – bread that gives life to the world.

Wednesday   **Ac 8:26-40 Jn 6:44-51**

Stephen's death and Saul's persecution caused the disciples to scatter. Now we see Philip north of Jerusalem in Samaria where he had success healing many people.

Jesus continues to preach about the true bread from heaven that will give life to the world. He is this bread of life. Those who believe in him will be raised up on the last day – this is his Father's will. All will have eternal life through him.

Thursday   **Ac 8:26-40 Jn 6:44-51**

We jump to the fascinating account of the conversion of the Ethiopian court official by Philip. He was prepared for his baptism by his study of and reflection on the scriptures.

Jesus continues his discourse on the Eucharist. Listen to the teaching of the Father as foretold in the scriptures. 'I am the bread of life – and unlike the manna in the desert – this bread gives eternal life.' He finishes with the most unusual statement that 'this bread is my flesh'.

Saul was still persecuting the Christians and had got documents to pursue this even further. Then it happened. Jesus spoke to him on the road to Damascus and changed his whole life.

In spite of their amazement, Jesus continues to elaborate on his flesh and blood being real food and drink – food that will lead to eternal life – 'the bread of life'.

We are back to Peter again. He is now in the town of Jaffa by the sea, and we see him curing people and even raising people from the dead in the name of Jesus.

Many of Jesus' followers could not stomach what Jesus had to say about eating his flesh and drinking his blood. But if he was able to feed the multitudes from a few loaves, he should be able to give his flesh as food. The close apostles went along with Peter – 'Lord, who shall we go to? You have the message of eternal life.'

Fourth Week of Easter

Monday   **Ac 11:1-18 Jn 10:1-10**

Right from the beginning there was tension among some Christians who
believed that one had to become a Jew before becoming a Christian. They
criticised Peter, but he had the answer. The vision of the animals showed
that all God's creatures are good. This vision was immediately followed
by the experience of seeing the Holy Spirit come on the pagans who had
come to him.

Jesus is the good shepherd. He knows the sheep by name and they
know his voice. He also used the image of himself as the gate of the
sheepfold.

Tuesday   **Ac 11:19-26 Jn 10:22-30**

The scattering after Stephen's death brought the apostles to different parts
of the Greek world, where they converted the pagans. They were first
called Christians at Antioch. We also see Saul, after his conversion,
receiving instruction and training.

'My sheep listen to my voice: I know them, they follow me, and I will
give them life. They shall not be taken from me. The works I do in my
Father's name are my witness.'

Wednesday   **Ac 12:24-13:5 Jn 12:44-50**

Having completed his novitiate Saul was chosen by the Holy Spirit to go
off with Barnabas on the first missionary journey.

'I am the light of the world – whoever believes in me will not be in the
dark – they see me and they see the one who sent me. I speak what the
Father has told me.'

Thursday   **Ac 13:13-25 Jn 13:16-20**

Paul, as he was now called, travelled to Cyprus and later went on to
Pamphylia and Antioch. Here we have him preaching his first great
sermon in which he points out that scripture showed that the saviour
would come from David and the saviour is Jesus.

For the rest of the Easter season we take extracts from the Lord's
discourse to the apostles at the Last Supper – we could regard this as his
last will and testament. 'Whoever welcomes the one I send welcomes me,
and whoever welcomes me, welcomes the one who sent me.'

Friday   **Ac 13:26-33 Jn 14:1-6**

Paul continues the sermon we began yesterday. The people of Jerusalem did not realise that Jesus was the promised saviour and they crucified him. But God raised him from the dead. This is the Good News.

Jesus promises to look after his faithful followers. 'There are many rooms in my Father's house. I am going to prepare a place for you. I am the Way, the Truth, the Life.'

Saturday   **Ac 13:44-52 Jn 14:7-14**

Many Jews were converted as a result of Paul's sermon. Others tried to turn the people against him, so he spoke to the pagans who were very glad to hear that God had chosen them. Eventually he left because of the rejections by the Jews.

Jesus gives us an important message: 'I am in the Father and the Father is in me. Whoever believes in me will perform the same works as I do myself.'

Fifth Week of Easter

Monday   **Ac 14:5-18 Jn 14:21-26**

Paul and Barnabas moved to Iconium and Lycaonia and there they cured a
cripple. As a result many of the people thought they were gods. Paul tried
to get them to turn from their many pagan gods to the one living God.

Jesus reminds his disciples that the condition for loving him and thus
being loved by his Father is to keep his Commandments. He promises the
Advocate, the Holy Spirit, to teach them all things.

Tuesday   **Ac 14:19-28 Jn 14:27-31**

The Jews, who were angry with Paul in the cities he had already visited,
now tried to stone him. So Paul and Barnabas went back to Antioch,
encouraging their people to remain firm in their faith.

Jesus bequeaths a special peace to his disciples – one the world cannot
give. So they must not let their hearts be troubled. He is not going to
desert them but go to his Father.

Wednesday   **Ac 15:1-6 Jn 15:1-8**

Some more Jews tried to cause trouble by suggesting that in order to
become a Christian one had first to become a Jew. So the apostles decided
to go back to Jerusalem to the first Council of the Church. Word preceded
them about the huge numbers of pagans who had been converted by them.

Jesus uses the analogy of the vine. We are all branches of that vine with
him. The Father prunes the vine and expects it to produce fruit: we can
only produce this fruit if linked to Jesus.

Thursday   **Ac 15:7-21 Jn 15:9-11**

At the Council of Jerusalem, Paul reminds the disciples that God gave the
Holy Spirit to many of the pagans. James quoted a scripture passage
which promised salvation to the pagans as well as the Jews. So they
decided not to make it difficult for the pagans. They would not have to
become Jews.

Jesus goes on to tell his disciples that his primary commandment is to
love one another. I want my joy to be in you and your joy to be complete.

Friday Ac 15:22-32 Jn 15:12-17

The apostles at the Council of Jerusalem issued a letter to be sent to all the churches telling the Christians that one did not have to become a Jew as well as a Christian. To avoid giving scandal they made some practical suggestions, including abstinence from meat that had been sacrificed to idols.

Jesus tells his disciples that they are not mere servants, but friends – friends for whom he will lay down his life: everything he had learned from his Father will be passed on to these, his friends, who were chosen by him. So love one another.

Saturday Ac 16:1-10 Jn 15:18-21

Paul set out on his second missionary journey. This time he recruited Timothy. They went to new territory, going over to Macedonia.

Jesus tells his disciples that they will suffer because they are his friends – they are not of the world – the world will persecute you too.

Sixth Week of Easter

Monday   **Ac 16:11-15 Jn 15:26-16:4**

Paul, on his second missionary journey, reaches Macedonia and goes to a town called Philippi, where they meet Lydia. This devout woman, who worked in the expensive purple dye trade, looked after them during their stay there.

Jesus again tells the disciples that the Advocate will be his witness. They will also be his witnesses and this will bring its own share of suffering.

Tuesday   **Ac 16:22-34 Jn 16:5-11**

Paul gets into trouble when he casts an evil spirit out of a fortune-teller. He was arrested, beaten and imprisoned. An earthquake was the cause of the jailer's conversion. The magistrates were horrified to learn that they had flogged a Roman citizen.

Jesus tells his disciples not to be sad because he is going. He will send the Advocate who will show the world about sin, about who was in the right, and about judgment.

Wednesday   **Ac 17:15.22-18:1 Jn 16:13-15**

Paul travels to the great city of Athens where he gives another great sermon. He tried to show the Athenians that their statue to the unknown god was really one to the true God. But when he spoke to them about Jesus rising from the dead many of them scoffed at him. Only a small number wanted to hear from him again.

The spirit of truth will lead you to the complete truth. He will glorify me and show you the Father.

Thursday [except Ascension Thursday]   **Ac 18:1-8 Jn**
16:16-20

In Corinth Paul tried first to preach to the Jews, but they turned against him. He then directed his teaching toward the pagans.

For a while, Jesus says, I am going away and you will be sad. But your sorrow will turn into joy.

Friday

The Lord reminded Paul that he would suffer for him. Some of the Jews had tried to bring him before the local Roman tribunal. The proconsul would have nothing to do with their legal quibbles.

Your sorrow will be turned into joy – just like the sorrow that turns into joy at childbirth. Your hearts will be full of joy that will not be taken from you.

Saturday

Over in Ephesus there was an energetic follower, Apollos, who only knew about the baptism of John the Baptist. He converted many of the people to the way of Jesus, but did not know about the Holy Spirit.

Jesus continues his great discussion to his disciples – ask for anything in my name and my Father will give it to you. Remember, in loving me you love the Father who loves you.

Seventh Week of Easter

Monday   **Ac 19:1-8 Jn 16:29-33**

Paul now comes on the scene in Ephesus, where many had been converted by Apollos, but did not know about the Holy Spirit. Paul laid hands on these and they were filled with the Holy Spirit.

Jesus reminds the disciples again that they will be scattered on his behalf. But do not fear, 'I have conquered the world.'

Tuesday   **Ac 20:17-27 Jn 17:1-11**

After many ups and down in Ephesus Paul now had to leave. He tells of the premonitions he has about being a prisoner for the Lord. But he must still bear witness to the Good News. Later he was to write a great letter to the Christians in Ephesus.

Jesus prays to his Father – the hour has come to glorify your son – I have glorified you on earth. He then prays for his disciples – 'they belong to you.'

Wednesday   **Ac 20:28-38 Jn 17:11-19**

Paul continues his farewell speech to the Ephesians. He asks the leaders to be on their guard for the flock – fierce wolves will invade you – many even from among your ranks will betray you. He reminds them to be generous, that 'there is more happiness in giving than in receiving'.

Jesus continues his prayer for his disciples: 'Keep them true to your name. I am not asking you to take them from the world, but to protect them from the evil one.' 'Consecrate them in the truth.'

Thursday   **Ac 22:30 23:6-11 Jn 17:20-26**

Paul returns to Jerusalem and is arrested. Many tried to kill him. He is given the opportunity of explaining what he was doing. He recounts the story of his conversion. He divides the Sadducees and the Pharisees – the Sadducees do not believe in the Resurrection so they will not accept that Jesus could rise. So there is a great row and Paul has to be rescued. The Lord tells him that he must also bear similar witness in Rome.

Jesus continues his prayer: 'I pray for those also who through their words will believe in me. May they all be one as you are in me and I am in you.'

Friday   **Ac 25:13-21 Jn 21:15-19**

The Jews continue to conspire against Paul and he is moved to Caesarea and later appeals his case to Rome. Felix, the Roman governor, told king Agrippa about Paul, and about the dispute he has had with the Jews, and told him how determined he was to get him to Rome. In this way Paul would fulfil the prophecy that he must bear witness to Jesus in the capital city.

We move to the end of John's gospel. Peter repeats 'I love you' for each time he denied Jesus earlier. He repents and is forgiven, and is told to 'follow me'.

Saturday   **Ac 28:16-20. 30-31 Jn 21:20-25**

Paul appealed to Rome and was eventually brought there. We skip all the details of his adventurous journey. He explains to the leading Jews in the city why he is there. Then he stayed for two years proclaiming the kingdom of God and teaching about Jesus Christ.

John denies that he was singled out not to die. But he vouches for the truth of all that he has written in his book – the testimony is true.

First Week in Ordinary Time

Monday   **Heb 1:1-6 Mk 1:14-20**

Hebrews, written circa 80AD, is used for four weeks. It begins with a powerful introduction. The Greeks thought of things as being copies or shadows of the real creation, and they looked for the real creation; the Jews saw the need for the perfect sacrifice. Both are now fulfiled in Jesus Christ. God sent his Son, the very expression of his essence, into the world. He made his great sacrifice and purified humankind and has now taken his royal seat at the right hand of the glory in the heights. In the past bits and pieces of this were revealed to people, but now we have it all.

For the first nine weeks of Ordinary Time we use the gospel of Mark and today we see the beginning of the public mission of Jesus. He calls the first of his disciples – 'he called them once'.

Tuesday   **Heb 2:5-12 Mk 1:21-28**

God created man a little less than himself. Because of sin we do not reach our full potential – we are subject to the world in many ways, even though the world should be subject to us. Jesus Christ came into this situation so that by his life, death and glory he might make us what we were meant to be.

It wasn't long after the beginning of his public ministry that Jesus began to make an impression. This was due to his style of teaching – he taught with authority, and he also had authority over the demons.

Wednesday   **Heb 2:14-18 Mk 1:29-39**

Through his suffering, Jesus identified with all humanity; he feels for us, he can sympathise with us, he can understand suffering. As a result of all of this he can help.

Jesus healed Simon Peter's mother-in-law and then went on to cure many others who were ill. But afterwards he went off to a quiet place to pray.

Thursday   **Heb 3:7-14 Mk 1:40-45**

The writer has been trying to prove the unique supremacy of Jesus Christ. He stops and exhorts his readers that they must not harden their hearts like the roving Jews in the desert. They must not refuse to give Jesus their obedient trust.

Today we see Jesus healing the leper – it was almost unheard of that a leper could be cured. Jesus tried to keep a low profile, but his listeners would not let him.

Friday   **Heb 4:1-5.11 Mk 2:1-12**

If you don't harden your hearts you will definitely enter into the place of rest with the peace of God, the real promised land. We must make sure that the word that is given to us is woven into the very fibre of our being through faith.

Jesus was not interested in merely healing the sick. There was always a spiritual message to be learned. We see the value of faith and the fact that Jesus had power to forgive sin. No ordinary person could have that power. These were the little references to the fact he was man and God – much of it went unnoticed at the time.

Saturday   **Heb 4:12-16 Mk 2:13-17**

The word of God is alive and active, effective and penetrating – it can see into our hearts. This is our faith. Through this faith we have Jesus Christ, the effective high priest, who was with both God and humankind and is capable of feeling our weaknesses with us.

The passage is a very consoling one for us. Jesus did not come to help those who believed that they were spiritually healthy. He came to help those who were striving to overcome sin in their lives, those who were genuine.

Second Week in Ordinary Time – 1

Monday   **Heb 5:1-10 Mk 2:18-22**

Every high priest can understand human weakness, and is appointed by God. He has to deal with things concerning God, and he must offer sacrifices for his own sins and for the sins of his people. Christ was appointed by God and could understand human weakness, even though he was not weak, and he did the things pertaining to God. He offered prayer and entreaty, aloud and in silent tears.

While the bridegroom is still at the party there will be no fasting. But when he goes the guests must fast. It is important to recognise the signs of the times.

Tuesday   **Heb 6:10-20 Mk 2:23-28**

God blesses those who are active for Christ and give service to God's dedicated people. God swore by himself – he is the greatest – that he might bless and multiply Abraham's descendants. The hope he gives to us is like an anchor.

We see again Jesus' horror of hypocrisy. He pointed out that the laws were made for people, and not people for the laws.

Wednesday   **Heb 7:1-3.15-17 Mk 3:1-6**

The whole chapter refers to the vague figure of Melchizedek. He was a priest to whom Abraham gave obedience. There is no reference to his birth or death, so he is said to be forever. He was superior to the Levite priests. In a sense he foreshadowed the great high priest, Jesus Christ, who is forever.

Jesus again shows his power. The Pharisees needed to know that Jesus promoted the Commandments. Faith is the essential characteristic.

Thursday   **Heb 7:25-8:6 Mk 3:7-12**

This high priest is holy, stainless, different from sinners, higher than the heavens. He does not need to offer sacrifices for himself. So Christ's ministry is not a shadow or copy, but the very essence.

Jesus is overwhelmed with the approach of all those looking for a cure. Faith was the essential requirement.

If the first covenant had worked there would be no need for the second. I will be their God and they shall be my people. I will forgive their iniquities and never call their sins to mind.

At this stage in his mission, Jesus picked his apostles from his chosen disciples. They were then sent out to complete the mission.

The writer thinks of the great ceremonies in the Tabernacle. Yet they are only a shadow, only copies of reality. The tabernacle of Jesus Christ is something special. The actions are not copies. He has won for us eternal redemption, not with the blood of goats and bulls, but through his own blood.

Jesus was under great pressure. Even his relatives misunderstood what he was about.

Third Week in Ordinary Time – 1

Monday   **Heb 9:15.24-28 Mk 3:22-30**

Jesus brings a new covenant, not a copy of reality. In his sacrifice he did not use a manufactured sanctuary modelled on the real one – it was heaven itself in the presence of God himself. So his sacrifice was far superior and never needs to be made again. We die once and go to judgment: Christ died, but rose, and will come back to judge.

The scribes were already trying to discredit Jesus – he works through the devil, they said. Jesus turned this back on them. He also reminds them that all their sins will be forgiven, if they go to the throne of grace and repent.

Tuesday   **Heb 10:1-10 Mk 3:31-35**

The old sacrifices were imperfect – they could only give a distant and spasmodic contact with God. So they were only a pale copy of what real worship ought to be – they could never bring humankind into a close relationship with God. Christ was fully obedient to the Father and so his sacrifice was perfect.

Jesus reminds his listeners that anyone who does the will of God can become his brother, sister and mother.

Wednesday   **Heb 10:11-18 Mk 4:1-20**

We continue the treatise on sacrifice. The Jewish priests had to offer sacrifice over and over again – every day. They could never fully take away sins. Jesus offered only one sacrifice – it was an act of perfect obedience and therefore the only perfect sacrifice. He now sits at the right hand of the Father.

Today's parable and explanation need no further elaboration. Just ask yourselves where you stand.

Thursday   **Heb 10:19-25 Mk 4:21-25**

We move from theology to practical exhortation. Jesus is the living way
to the presence of God. We have been purified and freed from our sins.
We are full of hope. Let us approach the presence of God and hold fast to
our creed and encourage one another.

   Whatever talents we are given in life, we are expected to use them to
the best of our ability. We should be the beacons of virtue in the
community.

Friday   **Heb 10:32-39 Mk 4:26-34**

Because you belong to Christ you have had your struggle, you have been
involved in persecution. 'Be what you were at your best.' Keep up the
struggle. We need to keep our hope before us, we need fortitude.

   Some further parables on a difficult question – how is the that the evil
exist side-by-side with the good? The harvest will give the answer.

Saturday   **Heb 11:1-2.8-19 Mk 4:35-41**

Faith guarantees the blessings we hope for. It dictates all our conduct.
Look at the faith of Abraham – a faith ready for a tremendous adventure.
Look at the faith of his barren wife, Sarah. Look at Abraham's faith when
he was asked to sacrifice his son, Isaac.

   Jesus calms the waters – the disciples were trying to get away for some
quiet reflection and prayer. Having faith is essential. With faith Jesus can
calm our fears.

Fourth Week in Ordinary Time – 1

Monday   **Heb 11:32-40 Mk 5:1-20**

We are in the fourth and last week of the sermon to the Hebrews. The author continues on the theme of the need for faith, and refers to other great people of the Old Testament – Gideon, Samson, Barak, David and Samuel. Each one faced incredible odds in fighting for God and came out victorious. They were made strong out of weakness – just like the many women and children who suffered persecution because of their faith.

The strange story of the demons and the pigs – forbidden meat to the Jews. The power of Jesus is without limit.

Tuesday   **Heb 12:1-4 Mk 5:21-43**

We have a summary of the Christian life. First we have a goal – to become like Christ; we have an inspiration in the unseen cloud of witnesses; we have an example in Jesus himself; we have the presence of Jesus himself. How can you compare the suffering you have with that of Jesus?

Two great stories of the results of faith in the healing power of Jesus. Remember how close we are to Jesus in the Mass.

Wednesday   **Heb 12:4-7.11-15 Mk 6:1-6**

The author gives another reason why people should cheerfully bear affliction when it comes – the great saints of the past have borne it and it is also little compared to what Christ suffered. Bear the hardship – it is sent by God as a discipline which gives value to life.

We go from great faith to great doubt – Jesus was not accepted in his own community – the people found it hard to have faith in him.

Thursday   **Heb 12:18-19.21-24 Mk 6:7-13**

In the old covenant we just expected a God of lonely majesty, a complete separateness from God, a prostrating fear. Think of Moses before the burning bush. Christians have something different – the new glories of heaven with the joyful assembly of the angels and God's people; we have God the judge, but also Jesus the perfect high priest.

Jesus sends his disciples out on their first mission – this was to be their test of faith. They brought the healing power of Jesus.

Friday   **Heb 13:1-8 Mk 6:14-29**

Coming to the end of the sermon the author lists five essential practical qualities of the Christian life – brotherly love, hospitality, sympathy for those in trouble, purity in and respect for marriage, and contentment – free from the love of money.

We switch to the story of the beheading of John the Baptist. The power of women is greater than they realise!

Saturday   **Heb 13:15-17.20-21 Mk 6:30-34**

We finish Hebrews with a prayer. Let's offer God an unending sacrifice of praise and keep doing good works. 'I pray that the God of peace, who brought our Lord Jesus back from the dead to become the great shepherd of the sheep by the blood that sealed an eternal covenant, may make you ready to do his will in any kind of good action; and turn us all into whatever is acceptable to himself through Jesus Christ, to whom be glory for ever and ever, Amen.'

The apostles tried to get away to a quiet place to reflect after the death of John, but the crowds followed them. Jesus took pity on them for they were like sheep without a shepherd – they were hungry for knowledge.

Fifth Week in Ordinary Time – 1

Monday   **Gn 1:1-19 Mk 6:53-56**

We begin reading from the Book of Genesis, the first book in the Bible. The first part of Genesis consists of various traditions that were passed down from one generation to the next and were eventually written down. They were stories with a spiritual significance – each had a special message about God. It is important to remember that the people at the time had no interest whatever in how things had happened in the past. Today we have the first half of the story of creation. The message is that God made all things in the world out of nothing.

Jesus continues his healing mission. Spiritual healing was always a very important part of his work.

Tuesday   **Gn 1:20-2:4 Mk 7:1-13**

We continue the creation story. The story was presented in the style of a teacher of the time, having a pattern that was easy to remember. The point of the story is that God is all-powerful, that he made the world out of nothing. We are expected to acknowledge his greatness, and to rest one day of the week to do this.

The Pharisees and some of the scribes were critical of the fact that Jesus did not observe the various purification rites. He reminds them that sincerity and internal purification are what is really important.

Wednesday   **Gn 2:4-9.15-17 Mk 7:14-23**

We move on to the story of the creation of man. Man was made in the image of God – he is a special part of the great creation. God breathed into his form and gave him life. He was given special gifts and did not know evil.

Jesus continues his discourse on inner purity. What comes from the heart is either good or bad. If it is bad we have fornication, theft, murder, adultery, avarice, malice, deceit, indecency, slander, pride and folly.

Thursday   **Gn 2:18-25 Mk 7:24-30**

Today we have the story of the creation of woman. Again, a nice story is used to get across the message loudly and clearly that woman is equal in nature to man. This was revolutionary at the time, because people in that part of the world – and even today – regard women as being very inferior in nature to men.

We have a great example of the faith of a non-believing pagan. Faith was not confined to the Jews.

Friday   **Gn 3:1-8 Mk 7:31-37**

We have the story of the Fall. Humankind has always been subjected to evil – and that evil came about of our own doing. We inherited that evilness in the form of original sin. This occurred because we misused our freedom and disobeyed God – we thought we knew better than God.

This time Jesus uses a sign to carry out his healing – Ephphatha, be opened. It was like a forerunner to the sacraments.

Saturday   **Gn 3:9-24 Mk 8:1-10**

The consequence of our fall from grace is that people would suffer pain – evil would always remain in our lives. But there is also the hint, or even a promise of a saviour in future times.

We have an account of the multiplication of the loaves and fishes. This ultimately led to the establishment of the Eucharist – if Jesus was able to feed this number, he could give his flesh and blood as spiritual food.

Sixth Week in Ordinary Time – 1

Monday   **Gn 4:1-15.25 Mk 8:11-13**

We have the well-known story of Cain and Abel. It is an account of fratricide, of the conflict between the farmer and the stockgrazer, the settler and the nomad. Because humankind was bound by evil, we have people killing each other, which was never meant to be.

The Pharisees were getting touchy with Jesus – they were not able for his wisdom and insights. They wanted things to be too 'cut and dried'. Now they were looking for a sign.

Tuesday   **Gn 6:5-8.7:1-5.10 Mk 8:14-21**

We move on though Genesis to the story of Noah. This was to condemn the great violence and evil that people inflicted on one another. Only the good were saved – Noah and his family along with one pair from each animal species.

Jesus is getting a little annoyed with his disciples, who look on the material side all the time. Jesus tests their faith.

Wednesday   **Gn 8:6-13.20-22 Mk 8:22-26**

We continue the story of the flood (which lasted for forty days), how Noah knew it was over, and what happened after it had abated.

We have the miracle of Jesus giving sight to the blind man. This time the miracle occurred over a period of time.

Thursday   **Gn 9:1-13 Mk 8:27-33**

We come to the last part of the story of Noah. The God of Israel acted out of justice and in response to moral evil in humans, but still continued to love them and hold out the promise of blessing at the end.

We have Peter's proclamation of faith, followed by his criticism of what Jesus had to say about his future. At this stage he did not fully understand the spiritual message that Jesus was delivering.

Friday   **Gn 11:1-9 Mk 8:34-39:1**

We come to the final story in Genesis, the tower of Babel. This is told with humour and irony and makes a very pointed attack against pagan religious ideas. The people in the story wanted to be like God and tried to build a monument reaching up to heaven. But God confused them and they could not finish it.

Today Jesus gives people conditions for following him – they must renounce themselves and take up their cross daily.

Saturday   **Heb 11:1-7 Mk 9:2-13**

We leave Genesis and for one day go back to the letter to the Hebrews, to a section that was skipped when we were using it some time ago. The author makes reference to many of the accounts we have read over the past few days – Cain and Abel – and to the future, the faith and call of Abraham.

The disciples were given a unique experience, one which would strengthen their faith which was still so weak. Jesus was transfigured before them and they got a glimpse of him in his glory.

Seventh Week in Ordinary Time – 1

Monday   **Si 1:1-10 Mk 9:14-29**

We move on to Sirach or Ecclesiasticus, a book of moral guidance, containing many maxims. It is full of short essays addressing such topics as duties towards God, towards one's parents, and towards rulers. It begins with the statement that all wisdom comes from the Lord. Who can know the sand of the seashore, the drops of rain, the days of eternity? It is the Lord who created this wisdom. The beginning of wisdom is fear of the Lord.

Jesus casts out the difficult spirit – the kind which needs prayer.

Tuesday   **Si 2:1-11 Mk 9:30-37**

In serving the Lord be sincere of heart, committed, unshaken by adversity, forsake him not no matter what happens to you. You are to be tested like gold. Trust in the Lord and he will help you. This sums up some of the duties we have toward God.

Jesus speaks about his future sufferings and yet he finds his disciples talking about which of them was the greatest. 'You must be simple like a little child – that is the way to welcome me.'

Wednesday   **Si 4:11-19 Mk 9:38-40**

Wisdom is personified here. Her rewards are many – life, favour, glory, right judgement. Growth in wisdom comes by trusting her. Small, wise decisions will lead to a conviction that wisdom can be trusted. But to abandon wisdom is an evil, for she will abandon us and misery will be our lot.

Jesus gives a timely reminder to his disciples that anyone who is not against him must be for him.

Thursday   Si 5:1-8 Mk 9:41-50

When we rely too much on wealth and power we are abandoning wisdom. With wisdom we will realise that God's mercy and his anger are both in proportion to our actions. If we have strayed and sinned, we listen to wisdom so that we can return to the Lord. If we don't and rely on ourselves, we may miss the opportunity of God's mercy.

Two serious points – give a cup of cold water to a fellow human and it is given to Christ. Scandalise a young person and you are worse than useless – like insipid salt.

Friday   Si 6:5-17 Mk 10:1-12

Wisdom teaches us true friendship. Have plenty of acquaintances, but few advisers or really close friends. Gradually build up trust and friendship by testing the person. A true friend, who will stand by you in trouble, is a sure shelter, a rare treasure, beyond price, someone whose worth cannot be measured, and is the elixir of life. If you respect the Lord, then you will make true friends.

Jesus gives his disciples a strong warning that marriage must be protected, and that a proper marriage can never end in divorce.

Saturday   Si 17:1-15 Mk 10:13-16

We are given a reminder that God made us to rule over all the creatures of the earth, and to see the glory of God in them. So we must give thanks and praise to God. But we are also reminded that we must beware of any wrongdoing, for we have the facility to distinguish between good and evil.

Jesus gives a good practical example of how we are to be – like little children. Otherwise we shall not enter the kingdom of heaven.

Eighth Week in Ordinary Time – 1

Monday   **Si 17:24-29 Mk 10:17-27**

Through wisdom we learn that God hates sin and unjust living. We must turn away from these and repent, for God encourages those who were losing hope. 'How great is the mercy of the Lord, his pardon on all those who turn towards him!'

Jesus shows that the Commandments are only the basic rules of good living. He presents great ideals for us to follow as well. The rich man found these too hard – if we become too attached to riches we will never live up to the ideals of Jesus Christ.

Tuesday   **Si 35:1-12 Mk 10:28-31**

When we worship God it is important that we bring the best that we have; our offering must also be sincere. Remember that worship and the Commandments go hand in hand – we cannot have one without the other. We shall always be rewarded when we honour God with generosity.

Those who do try to follow the ideals of Jesus Christ and leave all to follow him, will definitely receive their reward. This reward will be greater than they can ever expect in this life – it will be eternal life.

Wednesday   **Si 36:1.4-5.10-17 Mk 10:32-45**

Today we have an intense prayer to God for mercy, for success in dealing with enemies, for compassion. It is a prayer for the time when the country will again be filled with songs of praise for God, a time when the world will know and acknowledge this one, everlasting God.

Suffering is to be the lot of Christians, just as it was the lot of Jesus. So too is service with generosity. The Son of Man did not come to be served, but to serve and to give his life as a ransom for many.

Thursday   **Si 42:15-25 Mk 10:46-52**

This is another great poetic prayer of praise. We can see the many varied works of the Lord. We can see his glory in them. In fact it is impossible to describe them all. But God knows them all and can even see into the depths of our hearts. 'How desirable are all his works, how dazzling to the eye!'

We have a great example of the power of faith. The blind man at the roadside refused to give up in spite of those trying to quieten him. As a result of his commitment he was cured.

Friday   **Si 44:1.9-13 Mk 11:11-26**

The piety of Israel's ancestors is now praised. Those who were heroes and who followed the law of the Lord are remembered. Their good works will not be forgotten. Thanks to them the glory of their children will remain forever.

Two lessons are given today. Respect the house of God. Have faith in God and your prayer will be heard. In your prayer always include one asking for forgiveness just as you forgive others.

Saturday   **Si 51:12-20 Mk 11:27-33**

The last section of the book of Ecclesiasticus or Sirach contains a poem in praise of wisdom. In the original Hebrew, each verse begins with a different letter of the alphabet. It tells of the search for wisdom and what wisdom has done for the author. He is determined to possess her and as a result has been able to keep the law scrupulously. 'I have directed my soul towards her, and in purity have found her.'

Jesus is too shrewd to be caught out by the chief priests, who were jealous of his influence. If they couldn't tell whether John's baptism came from heaven or from man, then he wouldn't tell them where his authority came from. Open your eyes and you will know the answer.

Ninth Week in Ordinary Time – 1

Monday   **Tb 1:1-2.2:1-9 Mk 12:1-12**

This is a fictional story of a dutiful servant son, Tobias, who is given miraculous help by an angel. It was written among the Jews of the Dispersion, possibly Egypt, around the beginning of the second century BC. Tobit was a very religious and law-abiding Jew. Among his good deeds was the burying of the dead, even in war.

Jesus tells the parable of the vineyard and the unjust stewards who were like the Jewish leaders. The crowds loved him for his story, the leaders were very angry, but could do nothing.

Tuesday   **Tb 2:9-14 Mk 12:13-17**

Tobit was blinded, which created problems for him, but he remained faithful to God – even trying to return the present of a kid that might have been stolen. His prayer is for forgiveness of sins.

The leaders now tried to catch Jesus out: 'Should we have to pay tax?' If his answer was 'no', the Romans would object; if 'yes', the Jews would object. He got out of the trap.

Wednesday   **Tb 3:1-11.16 Mk 12:18-27**

Tobit prays for forgiveness – he appeals to be allowed to go to his eternal home. We switch to Sarah who had her own misfortunes – seven dead husbands and now an outcast. She prayed. Both prayers were heard and now the setting for the story has been established.

The Sadducees, who had no belief in life after death, tried to set another trap. He got out of that too – marriage was to ensure life: it is not necessary in eternity.

Thursday   **Tb 6:11. 7:1. 9-14 Mk 12:28-34**

Tobias was asked by his father to travel to collect money that he had invested. Without realising it his companion was the angel Raphael. They stayed at Raguel's house, the father of Sarah. Tobias asked for the hand of Sarah in marriage and with much misgiving, Raguel agreed. Tobias and Sarah prayed for protection and were granted it.

They still questioned him about which are the greatest Commandments. He gave the answer that every good Jew should know.

Friday   **Tb 11:5-15 Mk 12:35-37**

Tobias was married, went off and got his father's money and eventually set off home. They received a great welcome. Tobias, on the advice of Raphael, used the gall of the fish they had caught on the outward journey and cured Tobit's blindness. He praised God.

Jesus hints at the fact that he is a man of David's line, but also God, David's Lord.

Saturday   **Tb 12:1.5-15.20 Mk 12:38-44**

Now they wanted to pay Raphael for his help. He told them that it was he who presented their prayers to God when their faith was being tested. Then he told them he was Raphael, the angel. 'Bless the Lord and give thanks to God.'

Now Jesus attacks the hypocritical attitudes of the Pharisees – proud and overbearing. He contrasts this with the attitude of the poor widow. She was total in her commitment, while the others were conditional.

Tenth Week in Ordinary Time – 1

Monday   **II Co 1:1-7 Mt 5:1-12**

Corinth was a leading city in Greece – often described as the gateway between the east and the west. In Paul's time it was a Roman colony and had people of many races living and working there. Paul had gone there during his second missionary journey, and developed a deep and lasting relationship with the Christians. They tended to be over-enthusiastic at times. They had strange ideas on the characteristics of an apostle, and some believed that Paul did not live up to their criteria. So he had great difficulty in trying to restrain them and keep them on a steady track. He wrote many letters to them and only two have survived. The one we begin today may be a compilation of a number. But he begins as usual with a greeting from himself and Timothy. He then praises God for giving us his consolation in the midst of all our sorrows.

Today we switch to the gospel of St Matthew and take it up at the beginning of the Sermon on the Mount. Here we have the real commandments of Jesus – these are the ideals that he expects us to strive to achieve. These are the marks of the true follower – poor in spirit, gentle, hungry and thirsty for justice, merciful, pure in heart, peacemaking, suffering for Christ.

Tuesday   **II Co 1:18-22 Mt 5:13-16**

In this letter we get a very good idea of Paul's passionate nature. We can look inside him and see both his vulnerability and his strong feelings for others. We get a good knowledge of his great depth and affection. He is most anxious to sort out the many crises that the Church in Corinth is experiencing. Here we have Paul being angry – his detractors in Corinth said he did not visit them again because he had lost interest in them. He reminds them of how Jesus taught that a 'yes' always meant 'yes'. So when he said 'yes' he meant it, and they must trust in him. God had anointed him with the Spirit and he was their apostle

The followers of Jesus are expected to be noticed – like salt, which adds zest to food, or a city on a hilltop, or a lamp on a stand. Only if people can see our good works will they give praise to God.

Wednesday   **II Co 3:4-11 Mt 5:17-19**

Paul strongly defends the title of apostle given to him by the Lord. The Corinthians had strange notions of how their various teachers had obtained their qualifications and titles. Paul claimed that all his qualifications came from God. He was one of those given the responsibility of administering the New Covenant, the covenant of the Spirit, the covenant of life. The old covenant was not able to bring life, even though it had its great and powerful moments. But the new is so much superior and will last forever.

The law of the old covenant was good – all parts will be completed by Jesus. They must be interpreted in the proper spirit by the teachers and promoted by them in full.

Thursday   II Co 3:15-4:1.3-6 Mt 5:20-26

Paul continues to emphasise how the New Covenant gives true freedom to those who are on the way to salvation, who are in the Spirit of the Lord. They are like mirrors and reflect the brightness of the Lord. Those who are blinded by the gods of this world do not see the light shed by the Good News of the glory of Christ. So when Paul preaches, he is not preaching himself, but Christ Jesus – he is a true apostle of Jesus.

Continuing his advice about Old Testament law which we heard yesterday, Jesus condemns some of the Pharisees because they interpreted the law to suit themselves. 'You have heard it said... but I say to you.' For the next few days we hear this over and over again. Sincerity of heart and genuine concern are most important in dealing with others. So be reconciled with your brother before honouring God.

Friday   II Co 4:7-15 Mt 5:27-32

Paul continues to defend his position as apostle, in spite of what his detractors say. They believed that he did not have certain signs of apostleship that were necessary in their eyes. Paul strongly states that his ministry is based on the experience of God's grace. We are only earthenware jars that hold this great treasure. No matter what problems arise, the power of God will overcome all. Through his sufferings and death, Jesus brought life. Life comes for the Christians when they join their sufferings with those of Christ. The power of the resurrection is taking place among the believers.

Jesus reiterates his teaching on obeying the laws of their religion from their hearts. Mere ritual observance is not enough. Adultery, for instance – a sin that the Jews regarded as very serious – can be committed by giving in to serious lustful thoughts. 'You have heard it said... but I say to you.'

Saturday   II Co 5:14-21 Mt 5:33-37

The Corinthians judged people by human standards and Paul is trying to steer them away from that kind of thinking. Christ died for all and was raised to life for them. So now there is a new creation. We are ambassadors for that news – all of us, through reconciliation achieved by Christ, would become the goodness of God.

Jesus gives another positive interpretation of the law. 'You have heard it said... but I say to you.' There is no need to swear to the truth if one is sincere – a 'yes' means 'yes' and a 'no' means 'no'.

Eleventh Week in Ordinary Time – 1

Monday   **II Co 6:1-10 Mt 5:38-42**

Paul reminds the people that this is the favourable time spoken of by
Isaiah. So they must not neglect the grace that God gave them. They show
to others that they are God's servants by the way they live – by having
fortitude in times of suffering, by their purity and knowledge, patience
and kindness, by their holiness and sincere love.

Jesus continues his radical teachings. Not any more is it to be an eye
for an eye. The follower of Christ goes even to the opposite extreme to try
to bring about the wicked person's conversion.

Tuesday   **II Co 8:1-9 Mt 5:43-48**

Paul tells of the Macedonians with whom he was staying. Out of their
poverty they were extremely generous and cheerful. Now it is the
Corinthians' turn to show their generosity towards the Christians in
Jerusalem, who were being persecuted. Titus was to take up the collection
for them. Paul hoped that they would remember how generous Jesus
Christ was – he made his followers rich out of his poverty.

Jesus gives his sixth radical teaching. 'You have heard it said... but I
say to you.' They must now love their enemy. God makes no distinctions,
but awaits the conversion of the sinner. You must aim to be perfect as
your heavenly Father is perfect.

Wednesday   **II Co 9:6-11 Mt 6:1-6, 16-18**

Paul continues his appeal for the Jerusalem collection. He gives a
theological and scriptural basis for this. Generosity is its own reward –
anyone who gives liberally will benefit from the same gift. The Lord
loves the cheerful giver, for the Lord is full of richness and generosity. He
will make the almsgiver richer in every way.

Three religious practices had a very high priority for the Jews –
almsgiving, prayer and fasting. Here Jesus warns against any form of
'showiness' in carrying out these three excellent practices. 'Your Father,
who sees all that is done in secret, will reward you.'

Thursday   **II Co 11:1-11 Mt 6:7-15**

Paul comes back to the earlier theme of opposing his detractors who
believed he was good with the written word, but weak in preaching –

hence a poor apostle. The Corinthians are a very superficial people, and Paul suggests that they would accept any new doctrine presented with enthusiasm. He reminds them that while he was with them, he was not a burden to anyone. He has great love for them and would like to present them as a spotless bride to Christ.

Yesterday Jesus spoke of the way to say prayers. He now gives an example, which has become the 'Our Father'. There are three 'You-petitions' – may your name be held holy, may your kingdom come, may your will be done . These are followed by three 'we-petitions' – give us our daily bread, forgive us our debts, do not put us to the test but save us. He finishes by pointing out that our willingness to forgive others is the necessary condition for getting God's forgiveness.

Friday   II Co 11:18. 21-30 Mt 6:19-23

Paul continues to oppose his detractors. For the Corinthians wisdom by worldly standards was very important – especially for one who claimed to be an apostle. Paul shows that such 'wisdom' is foolishness in God's eyes. His apparent weakness is really his strength before God. He boasts of all these indicators of his weakness. He is a descendant of Abraham and a servant of Christ. He worked hard, experienced prison, beatings, shipwrecks, brigands, and many other dangers.

The final section of the sermon gives us some practical advice concerning the pursuit of Christian holiness. Earthly treasures are fragile and we mustn't depend on them. Store up heavenly treasure instead. Aim to have a sound spiritual vision.

Saturday   II Co 12:1-10 Mt 6:24-34

We have the last extract from St Paul's letter – he continues to refute his detractors and talks about the ecstasy that he had. That was given to him by God. To bring him back to reality after his vision he got this 'thorn in the flesh', and asked three times to be rid of it – three times, like Jesus in Gethsemane. He was told that God's grace would be sufficient for him. It is in weakness and frailty that God's power is shown forth. So it is for us. When we are weak, then we are really strong in Christ.

Some more practical advice for Christian living. We must not worry about material things, but believe that the Lord is looking after us. We are worth more than the birds in the sky, the flowers and grass in the fields.

Twelfth Week in Ordinary Time – 1

Monday   **Gn 12:1-9 Mt 7:1-5**

This week we begin the history of God's dealings with the Chosen People. They were descended from Abraham. Today we hear of the call of Abram, as he was called then. Even though he was on in years he was promised that he would be the father of a great nation.

Jesus tells us that it is very important not to judge one another – very often we are the ones who need to be judged and corrected.

Tuesday   **Gn 13:2.5-18 Mt 7:6.12-14**

Abram is again promised many descendants who will take up their abode in this land of the Canaanites. We also see that he was a peaceful man, not wanting to have a row with his travelling companion, Lot.

Jesus tells us to treat others as we would like to be treated ourselves. He also reminds us that this is not easy.

Wednesday   **Gn 15:1-12. 17-18 Mt 7:15-20**

Abram's faith is being tested. He had no heir, yet he was told his descendants would be as numerous as the stars. God made a covenant, or sacred pact, with Abram; his descendants would have all the land from Egypt to the Euphrates.

A good person will produce good results. Beware of the false prophets – you will know them by their fruits.

Thursday   **Gn 16:1-12. 15-16 Mt 7:21-29**

Abram wondered how he was going to have any children. He believed his wife was too old, so he had a child by his servant girl, Hagar. She too would have many descendants.

The person who listens to the words of Jesus and takes them seriously is like one who builds his house on a rock. That house perseveres.

Friday   **Gn 17:1. 9-10.15-22 Mt 8:1-4**

As a sign of the covenant or sacred pact given by God to Abram, his name was changed to Abraham and his wife's name to Sarah. She would eventually bear him a son, who would be circumcised as a further sign of God's covenant – as would all the male children descended from Abraham.

Jesus cures the leper who has faith in him. He also tells him to obey the laws of his religion and show himself to the priests to have his cure confirmed.

Saturday   **Gn 18:1-15 Mt 8:5-17**

Both Abraham and Sarah laughed when a stranger (an angel) said she would have a child within a year. But with God, nothing was impossible.

We have a great example of faith – Jesus cures the centurion's servant and goes on to demonstrate his healing ministry. 'He took our sicknesses away and carried our diseases for us.'

Thirteenth Week in Ordinary Time – 1

Monday   **Gn 18:16-33 Mt 8:18-22**

Abraham would be blessed in his descendants because he was a just man.
Evil men would be punished, but here we see Abraham pleading with the
Lord to spare the people if at least fifty, forty, thirty, twenty, ten virtuous
people remain in the city of Sodom.

Full commitment is necessary if we are to follow Jesus. We pray for
that commitment.

Tuesday   **Gn 19:15-29 Mt 8:23-27**

Lot and the other virtuous people are allowed to leave the wicked cities of
Sodom and Gomorrah before they are destroyed.

Faith is also necessary if we are to follow Jesus. We pray for an
increase in faith.

Wednesday   **Gn 21:5.8-20 Mt 8:28-34**

Isaac was born to Abraham and Sarah. Sarah was jealous of the slave
girl's son. Because Isaac was also Abraham's son he would be the father
of a great nation.

We have the strange story of the demoniacs being cured and the devils
ending up in the pigs – animals whose meat the Jews were forbidden to
eat. We pray that evil may be uprooted from our hearts.

Thursday   **Gn 22:1-19 Mt 9:1-8**

Abraham is given his greatest test of faith – would he offer up his only
son as a sacrifice to God? His faith is sure, so God gives him another
victim.

Behind many of the miracles of Jesus was a spiritual message. Today it
is more explicit – he can forgive sins just as he can cure the paralytic. We
pray for trust in the mercy of God.

Friday   Gn 23:1-4.19.24:1-8.62-67 Mt 9:9-13

After his mother died, Isaac was warned by Abraham not to marry one of the Canaanites but one of his own kin. He eventually met Rebekah and married her.

Jesus reminds his followers that he has come not to call the virtuous, but sinners. Mercy was vital in his dealings with others. We pray that we can be merciful.

Saturday   Gn 27:1-5. 15-29 Mt 9:14-17

We have skipped over the death of Abraham, the birth of Isaac's twins, Jacob and Esau, and the details of the life of Isaac. He is now blind and at the end of his life and wants to give a blessing to his first-born, Esau. He had sold his birthright so it was Jacob who received the important blessing through the actions of his mother. 'Cursed be he who curses you; blessed be he who blesses you!'

While Jesus is with his disciples they will not fast. The time will come when they will. Everything in its own time.

Fourteenth Week in Ordinary Time – 1

Monday   **Gn 28:10-22 Mt 9:18-26**

The story of the Chosen People continues with Jacob, the son of Isaac and grandson of Abraham. Again he is promised in a vision that his descendants will be very numerous.

We have further examples of the healing power of Jesus. Let us trust in that power that can come to us through the Blessed Sacrament.

Tuesday   **Gn 32:23-33 Mt 9:32-38**

We are moving along quickly through the early history of the Jews. Today we have the incident when Jacob had a meeting with an angel of God and showed how strong he was. His name was changed to Israel. We also have mention of his eleven sons.

Jesus continues to carry out his work of healing and casting out devils – though the Pharisees remained sceptical. Jesus is sad because the people are without good leaders.

Wednesday   **Gn 41:55-57.42:5-7.17-24 Mt 10:1-7**

We skip over the details of Jacob's youngest son, Joseph. He was special to his father, who made him a coloured coat. He had dreams of how he would rule over his brothers. Naturally the brothers were very jealous and intended to kill him, but sold him instead and he ended up in Egypt. Later, through his powers of interpreting dreams he was made Pharaoh's right-hand man. Because there was a famine in Canaan Israel sent his sons to Egypt for grain and they met with Joseph, but didn't recognise him. Joseph played with them, demanding that they send their youngest brother.

The apostles are named and sent to the lost sheep of the house of Israel. Later they would travel to Samaria and to the rest of the known world.

Thursday   **Gn 44:18-21. 23-29. 45:1-5 Mt 10:7-15**

Joseph's brothers are sent back to him a second time to get more grain. They are very much afraid of him and tell the story of their father's loss. This time Joseph breaks down and tells them who he is.

Jesus gives his instructions to the apostles. Above all they must bring peace to the homes and towns they visit.

Joseph invites all his family to come to Egypt. His father Israel, or Jacob, also comes with them with all they had in the land of Canaan. The meeting between Joseph and his father is very moving. They settle in Egypt.

Jesus gives more instructions to his apostles. They must not be afraid of what to say – the Spirit of his Father will be with them. He hints that they may run into trouble for the sake of the kingdom of heaven.

Jacob was buried back in his own country. Joseph promised his brothers he would look after them. So they all settled there and the numbers of the clan grew over the years. Just before he died, Joseph reminded his descendants that God would bring his people back to the country that he had promised to Abraham.

Jesus gives more instructions to his apostles. The disciple should grow to be like his teacher; what I say in the dark, tell in the light; fear those who can kill both the body and soul; anyone who declares himself for me I will declare before my Father.

Fifteenth Week in Ordinary Time – 1

Monday   **Ex 1:8-14.22 Mt 10:34-11:1**

The scene changes and the good of Joseph is forgotten. The descendants of Abraham are now a downtrodden people in Egypt as we begin the book of Exodus – the outward journey. Their numbers were getting too big for Pharaoh and he ordered that all newborn males be thrown in the river.

Being a follower of Christ involves much hardship as many will not accept his teachings. This may cause division, even among families. The true follower would see Christ in all.

Tuesday   **Ex 2:1-5 Mt 11:20-24**

The people of God were being oppressed and suppressed, but through a little ruse Moses was brought up in Pharaoh's house. When he grew up he turned out to be a man of great integrity, promoting justice both among the Egyptians and his own people. But he was afraid of the consequences of his actions and disappeared.

In spite of his miracles, the people did not listen to Jesus. He showed his sorrow in his remarks – these towns would suffer more than Tyre, Sidon and Sodom.

Wednesday   **Ex 3:1-6.9-12 Mt 11:25-27**

Moses was out in the wilderness looking after his father-in-law's flocks when he had the vision that transformed his life. In the burning bush that did not burn he was called by the God of his fathers, the one, true God, to bring his people out of Egypt. They were then to worship God on that mountain.

No one knows the Father except the Son and those to whom he revealed him. We thank God for choosing us and pray that we live up to his calling.

Thursday   **Ex 3:13-20 Mt 11:28-30**

In the great vision at the burning bush Moses was sent to free his people. 'I Am who I Am,' he was told. He was to tell the leaders of his people 'I Am sent me to you.' Then he foretold that it would take many wonders before Pharaoh would let them go.

Jesus is the source of consolation for all those who are burdened with life's problems.

Friday   **Ex 11:10-12:14 Mt 12:1-8**

We skip all the strange happenings that eventually persuaded Pharaoh to let the Israelites go. Their last act in the land was to eat the first Passover meal – the meal that all good Jews partake of each year to commemorate what the Lord had done for them. Moses gives them the details of this ritual meal.

We have an example of how the Pharisees put the details of the law before the person. They made the laws of the sabbath very strict indeed. Instead of it being a day of rest to honour God, it was a day filled with restrictions.

Saturday   **Ex 12:37-42 Mt 12:14-21**

The Israelites begin their march out of Egypt after so many hundreds of years there. Everything had to be done in a hurry, but they were being guided by their God.

The same Pharisees began to plot against Jesus, but he was only fulfiling the prophecy of Isaiah – 'Here is my servant whom I have sent.'

Sixteenth Week in Ordinary Time – 1

Monday   **Ex 14:5-18 Mt 12:38-42**

Pharaoh relented when he saw the Israelites leaving Egypt – it was a massive loss of his work-force. The faith of the Israelites in their God was not strong and they were terrified when they saw the huge army coming after them. They grumbled at Moses. But God was with them and would defend them.

The message of Jesus is similar – this people is looking for a sign that he is from God – they won't accept his words or his miracles. So he gave them the sign of Jonah – he would be three days in the earth and rise up again. We pray for a deeper faith and greater sincerity in dealing with one another.

Tuesday   **Ex 14:21-15:1 Mt 12:46-50**

We have the very famous incident of the crossing of the sea and the drowning of the pursuing Egyptians. As with our Baptism, they were saved by passing through water. Now they sang the Lord's praises.

We are reminded in the gospel that Jesus regards anyone who does the will of his Father as part of his family. We pray for a better realisation of that closeness.

Wednesday   **Ex 16:1-5.9-15 Mt 13:1-9**

The Israelites had short memories. Once in the wilderness they began to grumble against Moses again. 'We had plenty of food in Egypt, why come out here to die in the wilderness?' The Lord did not desert them, but sent them the quail and the manna.

In the gospel we have the well-known parable of the sower and the seed. We pray that the word of God which has been sown in us will produce good fruit.

Thursday   **Ex 19:1-2.9-11.16-20 Mt 13:10-17**

At the foot of Mount Sinai in the wilderness, Moses was given a public seal of approval from God. This should have been enough for them to trust in this one, true God, and not in the gods of the Egyptians.

Jesus speaks to the people in parables. It was the method of the time. The stories always bring a spiritual message. Only those who close their ears will miss the message – 'You will listen and listen again, but not understand.' We pray that our hearts will be open to the word of God.

Friday   **Ex 20:1-7 Mt 13:18-23**

The God of the Israelites gives his rules for living to Moses. These are
still our Commandments – how well do we remember them?

Jesus explains the parable he taught in Wednesday's gospel, about the
sower and the seed. We pray that our hearts may be rich soil to accept the
seed of the Lord and bear fruit a hundredfold.

Saturday   **Ex 24:3-8 Mt 13:24-30**

Having received the Commandments, Moses gathered the people together
and they made a covenant with God that they would obey all those rules.

Another parable from Jesus reminds us that the evil and the good will
live side-by-side until the day of judgment.

Seventeenth Week in Ordinary Time – 1

Monday   Ex 32:15-24.30-34 Mt 13:31-35

Last week we heard about Moses trying to form the people into the People of God. God gave him the Commandments. Now Moses comes down from the mountain and finds that they have gone back to their old ways – they are honouring the false gods of their neighbours. They are embarrassed and, like a child who is tackled about a broken window and says, 'it broke', they excuse themselves by saying that the calf came out of the furnace. Moses pleads with God for their forgiveness.

Jesus continues with his parables. The kingdom of God may begin as something small and insignificant, but it will eventually have a huge influence.

Tuesday   Ex 33:7-11.34:5-9.28 Mt 13:36-43

Moses was trying to form this people into the People of God. He was trying to give them a new identity. The Tent represented the presence of the one true God. They saw Moses communicating with that God. He pleads again with the Lord for the headstrong people – forgive them their faults.

Jesus explains a parable he had told earlier: just as the weeds are to be left until the harvest, so will the evildoers be left with the virtuous until the final judgment. This will give those who are sinning the chance to reform.

Wednesday   Ex 34:29-35 Mt 13:44-46

After praying for so long in the presence of God, the face of Moses was radiant and showed forth the glory of God. The people realised that God was really with them and so they began at last to listen to Moses as he passed on the instructions he got from God.

Jesus gives two more parables which remind us that our faith is like a pearl of great price and we should value it as such.

Thursday   Ex 40:16-21. 34-38 Mt 13:47-53

The tablets on which the details of the law were written were now put into a special tent or tabernacle and brought with them wherever they went. The Lord guided them on their journey.

Jesus gives another parable that tells of the separation of the good and the evil people at the end of time.

Friday   **Lv 23:1.4-11. 15-16. 27. 34-37 Mt 13:54-58**

Moses tried to prepare the people for their new life in the Promised Land. It was important that they would remember the providence of God, so they were to have a number of feasts to commemorate the various events that had occurred to them – much like our holy days.

Jesus goes to his home place and meets with a lot of scepticism. As a result he did not perform many miracles there.

Saturday   **Lv 25:1.8-17 Mt 14:1-12**

As yesterday, we have the reading from the Book of Leviticus, the rules for the priests. One big festival was the jubilee celebration – every fifty years after they had come to the Promised Land. Especially during this festival, they must ensure that no wrong was done to any neighbour.

Today we have the account of the martyrdom of John the Baptist. He stood by his principles and lost his head to a selfish woman and a weak man.

Eighteenth Week in Ordinary Time – 1

Monday   **Nb 11:4-15. Mt 14:13-21 or Mt 14:22-36**

This week we move on to the Book of Numbers as we follow the plight of the Israelites in the desert. Earlier they complained of having no food. Now they were getting dissatisfied with the manna. Moses finds this a bit hard to take as they are blaming him, and he in turn complains to God.

Jesus feeds the multitude by multiplying the five loaves and two fish. This was to prepare them for the Eucharist.

[Jesus walks on the lake and disciplines Peter and the other disciples for their lack of faith and trust in him. All the time he was demonstrating to them the need for faith.]

Tuesday   **Nb 12:1-13 Mt 14:22-36 or Mt 15:1-2.10-14**

We have another account of the misfortunes of Moses and his band. This time his closest associates showed how jealous they were. So in a vision they were reminded very forcibly that a prophet had to be given a vision or a dream. But Moses was special – he was at home in his house and God spoke to him face to face.

Jesus walks on the lake and disciplines Peter and the other disciples for their lack of faith and trust in him. All the time he is demonstrating to them the need for faith.

[Jesus was a little annoyed at the blindness and the unbending attitude of the Pharisees. They put the law before the good of people. They insisted on carrying out all the legal purifications to ensure that people were clean. But true purification was found in the heart.]

Wednesday   **Nb 13:1-2. 25-14:1. 26-29. 34-35 Mt 15:21-28**

Moses has to put up with more wailing. Those who were sent in to the Promised Land to reconnoitre came back with fearful tales. They complained again against Moses. So for every day they spent reconnoitreing the land they would spent a year in the desert. In this way their faith and loyalty would be built up.

We see a great example of faith in today's reading. The Samaritan woman persuaded Jesus to heal her daughter, even though she was not of the House of Israel.

Thursday   **Nb 20:1-13 Mt 16:13-23**

More wailing and tests of faith. The people had to stay in the desert without water. Moses' prayer was answered, but his faith was a little weak and he had to strike the rock twice.

Today we have the very important and well-known account of the confession of Peter. 'You are the Christ, the Son of the living God', he said. He was given a new name, Peter, coming from the word 'rock'. However, Peter needed a little humility – he did not know all the answers. When he tried to tell Jesus that the things he spoke about would not happen, Jesus rebuked him: 'Get behind me, Satan! You are an obstacle in my path, because the way you think is not God's way but man's.'

Friday   **Dt 4:32-40 Mt 16:24-28**

We move on to the Book of Deuteronomy, which contains many of the discourses of Moses. It is the fifth and final book of the Pentateuch. The Israelites had been influenced by the gods of the Egyptians, and Moses was trying to get them to break away from those traditions and believe in the one, true God. He reminded them of the wonders the Lord had worked and of the Commandments that they had been given. The first requires them to love God.

To be a follower of Jesus involves hardship – 'anyone who loses his life for my sake will find it.'

Saturday   **Dt 6:4-13 Mt 17:14-20**

Moses reminds his people that their first duty in life is to honour and love God. 'You shall love the Lord your God with all your heart, with all your soul, with all your strength.' These words must be written in their hearts and repeated over and over again. Perhaps we need reminders like that too.

To be a follower of Jesus you must have a strong faith. If you have faith, nothing will be impossible to you.

Nineteenth Week in Ordinary Time – 1

Monday   **Dt 10:12-22 Mt 17:22-27**

We continue with the Book of Deuteronomy. Moses reminds the Israelites that the second Commandment requires them to take care of their neighbour – the orphan, the widow, the stranger.

Jesus knows he is going to be handed over to the Jews and be condemned. Yet he follows the law of the land and gives his tax.

Tuesday   **Dt 31:1-8 Mt 18:1-5.10.12-14**

The Israelites have spent almost forty years in the wilderness. Moses is coming to the end of his days. He reminds them that the Lord will be with them when they cross the Jordan into the Promised Land, and Joshua will be their leader.

We get two important messages today – we must be like little children and have the same openness as a young child; we can trust in the mercy of God who will go after the sheep that strays.

Wednesday   **Dt 34:1-12 Mt 18:15-20**

From a nearby mountain, Moses was shown the Promised Land just before he died. For thirty days the Israelites mourned the loss of the greatest prophet they ever had. Joshua then took over.

Jesus tells his followers that everyone must be given every possible chance to undo a wrong. Only as a last resort should a person be thrown out of the community. He also gives us the important message – 'wherever two or three meet in my name, I shall be there with them.'

Thursday   **Jos 3:7-11.13-17 Mt 18:21-19:1**

We move away from the Pentateuch into the Book of Joshua, who took over from Moses. The Israelites move into the Promised Land at last, bringing the symbol of God with them, the ark of the covenant, containing the Commandments. God would also be with them when they made their way into the great city of Jericho.

We are back to another parable which Jesus tells to show the type of forgiveness his followers must have – 'not seven, I tell you, but seventy-seven times.'

Friday   **Jos 24:1-13 Mt 19:3-12**

Unfortunately, we skip the dramatic account of the taking of Jericho as
well as the early history of the Israelites in the Promised Land. Today and
tomorrow we have the last discourse of Joshua, where he reminds the
people again of God's place in their history and encourages them to
remain faithful to him.

Jesus tells his followers that they must respect the dignity of marriage –
from now on the exceptions that Moses allowed would no longer be
acceptable.

Saturday   **Jos 24:14-29 Mt 19:13-15**

Joshua continues his last discourse before his death. The Israelites must
always honour the one, true God and stay away from the idolatrous
practices of their neighbours. 'Your God is a jealous God.' The people
made a very solemn covenant and set up a memorial to remind the people
who would come after them.

Again, Jesus reminds his followers that they should be like little
children – to such the kingdom of heaven belongs.

Twentieth Week in Ordinary Time – 1

Monday   **Jg 2:11-19 Mt 19:16-22**

In our history of the early Israelites, we move on to the book of Judges – the next in sequence. For their early years in the Promised Land, they were directed by leaders called judges. These tried to keep the people on the road set down by Moses and Joshua. But the people went over to the gods of their neighbours – they had a great selection of fertility gods with doubtful sexual practices.

We are reminded again in the gospel how easy it is for material possessions to keep God out of our lives. Let's pray for the proper attitude in using God's gifts to us.

Tuesday   **Jg 6:11-24 Mt 19:23-30**

Gideon was chosen to save the people from their enemies – this had been allowed because they had strayed away from the way of the Lord. He was convinced that he had spoken to a messenger from the one true God.

Jesus continues his teaching on treating material possessions carefully. The 'needle' in this case is believed to be the little door in a gate – the wicker door. Blessed are those who renounce the things of the world for the sake of God.

Wednesday   **Jg 9:6-15 Mt 20:1-16**

For their early years in the Promised Land, their only king would be their God. The leaders were judges and no one would claim kingship for himself. Jotham told them in no uncertain terms what a king would be to them by using the parable of the trees. The thorn bush would be the king!

We have the famous parable of the landowner and the vineyard workers. He was generous and gave to the last the same as he gave to the first. The first were upset. 'Why are you envious because I am generous?' Pray for trust in our generous God.

Thursday   **Jg 11:29-39 Mt 22:1-14**

We take a brief look at another judge, Jephthah, who made a rash vow. He believed he had to keep it as the vow was made to his God.

We have another well-known parable – the invitation to the wedding feast. We are all invited, but the least we do is prepare ourselves for entry in God's kingdom.

Friday   **Rt 1:1.3-6.14-16.22 Mt 22:34-40**

We finish the history of the early Israelites for the moment with two pieces from the Book of Ruth. She was from the tribe of Moab. When she married one of the sons of Naomi she became a firm believer in the God of her husband's people. After his death she would not go back to the worship of the gods of her pagan people.

On the prompting of the Pharisees, Jesus reaffirms the basic Commandments – love God, love your neighbour. All Jews were expected to follow these. Jesus wasn't making any changes here.

Saturday   **Rt 2:1-3.8-11.4:13-17 Mt 23:1-12**

The very sad Naomi, after the death of her husband and two sons, went back to her own country with her daughter-in-law, Ruth. Out in the fields Ruth met Boaz who eventually became her husband. Her son was the grandfather of the greatest of Israel's kings, King David. Next year we take up the history of the Israelites, beginning with David.

The Pharisees have let the people down. They interpreted the law and made it more important than the people. We must avoid this sort of hypocrisy.

Twenty-First Week in Ordinary Time – 1

Monday   **I Th 1:2-5.8-10 Mt 23:13-22**

We move on to the first letter of St Paul to the Thessalonians. He came to Thessalonica, which is modern Salonika, during his second missionary journey. It was one of the most important cities in the Roman province of Macedonia – we hear that name quite frequently now. It had a sizeable Jewish community. St Paul spoke in its synagogue on three occasions, explaining that Jesus was the true Messiah. Some Jews and many Greeks accepted his teaching and became Christians. He was persecuted and had to leave. The letters were written later to console the Christians and to clarify some points of doctrine. Paul begins this letter by thanking God for their faith and complimenting them for their faith and constancy.

There was one thing Jesus could not take and that was hypocrisy, especially from the leaders. They made it very difficult for the people. Let us keep watch over ourselves in this matter

Tuesday   **I Th 2:1-8 Mt 23:23-26**

Paul is stating his reasons for the work he had done with the Thessalonians. It involved much hardship and persecution, but he did it for love of them. It wasn't for his own self-gratification, but for God that he preached the Good News. He was eager not only to hand over the Good News to them, but his whole life as well.

Jesus continues today with his tirade against the hypocrisy of the spiritual leaders of the people. Pray for us priests that we may give the message of Jesus in its purity.

Wednesday   **I Th 2:2-13 Mt 23:27-32**

Paul continues his account of the hard work he did for the Thessalonians and his efforts to get the Good News across to them. He treated everyone like a good father, appealing to them to live a life worthy of God. He thanks God for the way they immediately accepted his message and for the fact that it is still a living power among them.

Again we have Jesus lashing out at the hypocrisy of the scribes and Pharisees – they are like whitewashed tombs. Again, let's watch ourselves.

Thursday   **I Th 3:7-13 Mt 24:42-51**

Paul again thanks God for the faith of the Thessalonians. He would like to get back to see them again. In the meantime, he prays that they increase their love for one another and for the whole human race. May they be blameless in the sight of God, the Father.

Today we are reminded to try to be ready at all times for the call of the Lord. Let us pray that we will be working hard at being faithful followers when the Lord comes for us.

Friday   **I Th 4:1-8 Mt 25:1-13**

Paul now tells the Thessalonians to be holy and live the life that God wants. They must keep away from all sexual immorality – no sex outside marriage, no selfish lust, no taking advantage of others. Such sins will be punished. We have been called to be holy and not immoral.

Jesus uses a nice parable to stress the fact that we must always be ready for the call of the Lord – we do not know the day or the hour.

Saturday   **I Th 4:9-12 Mt 25:14-30**

Paul has two messages here for the Thessalonians. They must keep on loving one another. They must also quietly continue earning their living and living out their lives quietly. Some had the idea that as the second coming of Christ was around the corner, they had nothing to do in this world but wait. Paul scotches this idea again and again.

Today we have another famous parable – the last extract for the moment from St Matthew. We are reminded that each of us is given various talents in life. They are to be used for the greater glory and honour of God. Let's do our best so that we can have the reward of the good and faithful servant and avoid the calamity of the good-for-nothing servant.

Twenty-Second Week in Ordinary Time – 1

Monday   **I Th 4:13-18. Lk 4:16-30**

Many of the Thessalonians believed that the second coming of Christ was imminent and that those who had died before it may lose out. Paul assured them that all who died in Jesus will rise like Jesus and will be with God. At the end of the world all people will rise and be with the Lord for ever.

For the rest of the year we read from St Luke's gospel. We take it up towards the beginning of Jesus' public mission. Jesus is sad because the people of his own city don't believe in him – a prophet is not without honour, except in his own country.

Tuesday   **I Th 5:1-6.9-11 Lk 4:31-37**

The Thessalonians expected Paul to tell them when the second coming of Christ would be. In this last segment from his letter he makes it clear that no one knew when this event was to happen. They are children of the light and so would never be caught off guard. Eventually, whether people were alive or dead when Christ came, all would live united to him forever.

Away from his home town, Jesus finds more faith. The people listened to him and were amazed at the great things he did.

Wednesday   **Col 1:1-8 Lk 4:38-44**

We move on to the letter of Paul to the Colossians for the next week or so. Colossae was a town near modern Denizli in Turkey. In Paul's time it was a town on the trade route from Ephesus to the interior. Its main industry was in dyed woollen goods. The Christians here seem to have been converted by a representative of Paul. He is writing this letter to combat some heresies that were being preached in the town. Paul opens his letter by thanking God for the faith of the people. They have two great characteristics – faith in Christ and love of their neighbour.

Jesus makes a great impact in the Capernaum area. He reminds his disciples that he must proclaim the Good News in other towns too.

Thursday   Col 1:9-14 Lk 5:1-11

Paul is making a powerful prayer for the Colossians – he asks that they may be filled with an ever-growing knowledge of the will of God; that they may have wisdom and understanding so that they may have a fuller knowledge of the great truths of Christianity and apply them to the tasks and decisions which meet them in everyday life. This wisdom will lead to right conduct. He asks that they be strengthened by the power of God, now that they have been rescued from the powers of darkness.

Jesus uses the miracle of the great catch of fish as a sort of living parable. Just as you caught these fish, trusting in me, so you will bring many people to my kingdom, trusting in me.

Friday   Col 1:15-20 Lk 5:33-39

Today we have Paul's most developed ideas on the nature of Jesus Christ set out in a powerful hymn. Christ is the image of the unseen God, who created all things in heaven and on earth. The Church is now his body and he is the head, the beginning, the first to be born from the dead. All things were reconciled when he made peace by his death on the cross.

Again, we have the Pharisees and scribes trying to catch Jesus out. You must use the old with the old and the new with the new. You rejoice when the bridegroom is present; you are sad when he is gone.

Saturday   Col 1:21-23 Lk 6:1-5

Paul reminds his readers that they used to think and do evil things. Now they have been reconciled by Christ and must persevere and stand firm on a solid base. They must never let themselves drift away from the hope promised them by the Good News.

A continuation of yesterday's ideas – the sabbath was made for people, not people for the sabbath – and you live according to this.

Twenty-Third Week in Ordinary Time – 1

Monday   **Col 1:24-2:3. Lk 6:6-11**

Paul begins this passage with a daring thought. By working to extend the Church, he is doing the work of Christ and any suffering or sacrifice involved is filling up and sharing the very suffering of Christ! This task has been given to him by God. He is to bring a new secret of God's salvation of humankind to the Gentiles. Christ is not just for the Jews but for all. Other gifts of life are not open to everyone – not everyone has the gift of music, for instance – but Christ is for all.

The gospel gives us another example of how the Pharisees twisted the law of Moses on the sabbath. Jesus gets the point across by showing that he was doing good and saving life by restoring the man's hand.

Tuesday   **Col 2:6-15. Lk 6:12-19**

Today Paul gives us rich food for thoughtful meditation. He appeals to the Colossians – and to us – to live our whole life according to the Christ we have received – be rooted in him, built on him, held firm by faith, full of thanksgiving. He warns them, and us, to be wary of worldly philosophy, which does not understand. He reminds us that, through baptism, we have died to sin and been raised by the power of God.

Today we see the importance of prayer. It was only after a full night of prayer that Jesus chose the apostles. Then he brought them with him as he set out to heal, forgive sins and, above all, preach the Good News. For the next few days we will have extracts from the Sermon on the Mount.

Wednesday   **Col 3:1-11. Lk 6:20-26**

Today Paul gives some very practical advice. Since we have been brought back to true life with Christ, our thoughts must be on heavenly things. Eventually, the hidden life of Christ in us will be shown forth in all its glory. In the meantime, we must stay away from the evil practices of those around us – sexual immorality, greed, evil desires, spitefulness, lies. We have put on a new self which is renewed in the image of our creator.

Jesus gives the basic recommendations for being his followers – happy are the poor in spirit, who know the harshness of hunger and weep over their misfortune. Blessed are those who are able to take hatred, abuse, being denounced as criminals for the sake of God – their reward will be great in heaven.

Thursday   **Col 3:12-17 Lk 6:27-38**

Yesterday we had Paul giving us practical don'ts. Today, in the last extract from his letter to the Colossians, he tells us that because we are God's chosen race and that he loves us, we must have compassion, kindness, humility, gentleness and patience. We must bear with one another and forgive each other. Above all we must have love. Then the peace of Christ will always be with us. Never say or do anything except in the name of the Lord Jesus, giving thanks to God the Father through him.

Jesus expects high standards – love, do good, bless your enemies – something that was unheard of among the people of his time, and perhaps today too. Treat others well without expecting anything in return. You will be rewarded in heaven.

Friday   **I Tm 1:1-2. 12-14 Lk 6:39-42**

For the next week and a half we listen to the first letter of St Paul to Timothy. He was a convert from Lystra who accompanied Paul on his second missionary journey. He left him in Ephesus to continue his work there. This letter was written to give him the details of how the community was to be organised, and also to give him advice on his personal conduct. After his greeting to Timothy, he begins by referring to the fact that he was once a blasphemer and did things to injure the faith. But through the grace of God he was shown mercy and is now filled with the love that is in Jesus Christ.

Jesus advises his listeners – and us – to be careful about judging others. We might miss the evil in ourselves. Look at yourselves first.

Saturday   **I Tm 1:15-17 Lk 6:43-49**

In his introduction to his letter to the faithful Timothy, Paul restates his main message – that Christ Jesus came into the world to save sinners, and he was one of the greatest. Mercy was shown to Timothy and now he is to be the greatest evidence of Christ's great patience. Through this others would trust in Christ and come to eternal life.

Jesus stresses sincerity. Judge yourselves by the fruit you produce. If you haven't good in you, you cannot produce good. Ensure that you have a solid base in life – like the man who built his house on rock.

Twenty-Fourth Week in Ordinary Time – 1

Monday   **I Tm 2:1-8 Lk 7:1-10**

St Paul's message in the continuation of his letter to Timothy is very clear. We must pray at all times for one another, and especially for those in positions of authority. Our prayers should be prayers of petition and prayers of thanksgiving.

After the Sermon on the Mount Jesus goes to Capernaum in the north. He meets a centurion with tremendous faith and heals his servant. Pray for a deeper faith.

Tuesday   **I Tm 3:1-13 Lk 7:11-17**

Today Paul is giving details to Timothy of the type of people he should look for to help run the Church. Celibacy hadn't come in at this time. Paul insists that priests and deacons, and also the women who worked in the Church, should be temperate, discreet, and able to manage their own families.

Jesus goes on to Nain and meets a distraught mother. He brought the young man back to life and gave him back to his mother. Jesus can restore our spiritual life to its fullness.

Wednesday   **I Tm 3:14-16 Lk 7:31-35**

Paul gives the reason for writing – he wanted Timothy to know how the Church was to be organised. He goes on to restate the central theme of his message – the mystery of our religion is very deep indeed – Christ was made visible in the flesh, attested by the Spirit, proclaimed to the pagans, believed in by the world, taken up in glory.

Having performed two great miracles (curing the centurion's servant and giving life back to the man from Nain), Jesus criticises his listeners for their lack of faith. No matter what good people do, they will find fault – they believed that John was possessed, and that Jesus was a glutton.

Thursday   **I Tm 4:12-16 Lk 7:36-50**

Paul goes on to give more personal details of how Timothy should carry
out his work. He reminds him that he has within him a spiritual gift that
came through his ordination. He should use this in his preaching, so that
he can save himself as well as those who listen to him.

Jesus continues to condemn those who are quick to make moral
judgements. The prostitute had been pardoned by Jesus and was thanking
him by her actions. Yet the ordinary customary ablutions were not carried
out by the host, who was a 'good' man. Let us trust in the mercy of God.

Friday   **I Tm 6:2-12 Lk 8:1-3**

Paul emphasises to Timothy the need to preach the sound teaching of
Jesus and not to be influenced by those looking for profit to modify that
teaching. Money is the root of all evil, but he must avoid all that, be
dedicated to God and fight the good fight.

Jesus continues his journey through the towns and villages preaching
and proclaiming the Good News. As well as the twelve apostles there
were a number of women in his party, including Mary of Magdala.

Saturday   **I Tm 6:13-16 Lk 8:4-15**

We finish St Paul's letter to Timothy today. Before God and his Son,
Jesus Christ, he puts to him the duty to do all that he has been told to do.
He finishes with a prayer of praise – 'to Christ Jesus be honour and
everlasting power. Amen.'

On his way through the towns and villages, Jesus stops to tell the story
of the seed falling in different places. Only that which fell on good
ground produced any fruit. What sort of soil are we?

Twenty-Fifth Week in Ordinary Time – 1

Monday   **Ezr 1:1-6 Lk 8:16-18**

Over the next three weeks we look at various books of the Old Testament which were written after the end of the Babylonian Exile. The final phase of this exile began in 587 BC. One of the first things that King Cyrus did when he came to power was to allow captives in Babylon to go home. The first group went back to Judea in 537. This is recounted today in the first of three extracts from Ezra. The first thing they did was bring back the sacred vessels so that they could be used in the Temple which they intended to rebuild.

Jesus continues with his parables. We are reminded that what we are given we must show to the world and not keep to ourselves. My faith and religion is for all and not for myself alone.

Tuesday   **Ezr 6:7-8.12.14-20 Lk 8:19-21**

The rebuilding of the Temple took many years. Eventually, King Darius allowed money from the state coffers to be used, and this helped them finish it. They were inspired in their work by two prophets, Haggai and Zechariah – we will be hearing from these later this week. They all had a great celebration when the Temple was being dedicated.

The relatives of Jesus come looking for him. He uses the occasion to demonstrate that all of us who follow him are his brothers and sisters.

Wednesday   **Ezr 9:5-9 Lk 9:1-6**

Ezra's prayer is a genuine confession of sin, but it is also meant to impress on the community the gravity of the situation. God had spared the exiles – they were the remnant through whom Israel lives on – they were the Chosen People. In the past they had abandoned their mission, but now they were given a second chance.

Jesus now moves to the stage that he can safely send out his apostles on a trial run. He gave them power and authority over all devils and to cure diseases. They went out proclaiming the Good News and healing everywhere.

Thursday   **Hg 1:1-8 Lk 9:7-9**

On Tuesday we saw that the rebuilding of the Temple took many years. It was very slow to begin. Haggai was the prophet at the time and exhorted them to get down to work and not to make excuses.

Jesus was now making too many waves in the area. Even Herod, who had beheaded John, was getting worried. Many believed he might be Elijah.

Friday   **Hg 1:15-2:9 Lk 9:18-22**

After the initial labours of a few weeks of rebuilding the Temple, the builders lose heart at the magnitude of the task. They despair of restoring the Temple to its former splendour. Haggai encourages them and tells them that God is with them, so they cannot fail.

The apostles are now given their chance to say who Jesus is. He is not Elijah or John the Baptist, but, as Peter says, the Christ of God. Let us pray for the same faith.

Saturday   **Zc 2:5-9.14-15 Lk 9:43-45**

Zechariah was the second prophet for the Israelites after their exile in Babylon. He used accounts of his visions to get his message across. In today's vision he told them not to build walls around Jerusalem yet as its population was going to increase. Many more would become part of the Lord's people.

Yesterday we saw the Apostles, through Peter, make their act of faith in Jesus, the Christ. They find it difficult to accept that their hero should suffer.

Twenty-Sixth Week in Ordinary Time – 1

Monday   **Zc 8:1-8 Lk 9:46-50**

Zechariah gives a series of oracles – 'the Lord of the hosts says this.' They were to encourage the small group – the remnant – who had come back from exile. The day would come when Jerusalem would be a very fine city indeed. The people will be God's people.

The all-powerful question – 'who is the greatest, who is going to be in charge?' Jesus replies, 'anyone who welcomes this little child welcomes me, welcomes the one who sent me.'

Tuesday   **Zc 8:20-23 Lk 9:51-56**

Today we have two more oracles. Jerusalem will eventually be the city that all people will come to who are seeking favours of the Lord. Many will be encouraged to come, because they will see that God is with them.

The disciples had a lot to learn. They had to be prepared for rejection when they went out on their own to continue the work of Jesus.

Wednesday   **Ne 2:1-8 Lk 9:57-62**

Nehemiah was a cupbearer of the Persian king – he had to taste the wine to make sure it wasn't poisoned. He used his position to appeal to the king to let him go back to Jerusalem and help rebuild it. He took a risk in this, as no courtier could appear sad. But the king allowed him to go.

A variety of people wished to join Jesus' band, but he looked for commitment. 'If you place your hand on the plough and look back, you are not fit for the kingdom of heaven.'

Thursday   **Ne 8:1-12 Lk 10:1-12**

Nehemiah became governor of Jerusalem and set about rebuilding the walls. When this was finished he tried to set up a religious reform as there were many abuses. Ezra appears on the scene again to read out the Law of God on the Feast of the Trumpets. Afterwards the people made great rejoicing in a community meal.

The group following Jesus has got quite big. Earlier he had sent out his apostles. Now he gives the rest of the disciples their test.

We shift back a little in time to the beginning of the exile in Babylon. Baruch seems to have been a contemporary of the prophet Jeremiah. Here we have his prayer which reminds the Israelites that their situation is due to their disobedience and disloyalty. They served alien gods and did what was displeasing to their God.

Yesterday we saw Jesus telling his disciples what to do if they were rejected in a town. Now he condemns the towns that have closed their ears to his message. 'Anyone who listens to you listens to me, anyone who rejects you, rejects me and the one who sent me.'

We have another prayer from Baruch. He reminds the Israelites again that they provoked God by offering sacrifices to demons. As a result they were sold to the nations. But they were to take courage. Their God would not neglect them. But they must turn back and search for God, so that he will rescue them.

The disciples come back after their first test. 'Rejoice that your names are written in heaven – happy the eyes that see what you see.'

Twenty-Seventh Week in Ordinary Time – 1

Monday   **Jn 1:1-2:1.11 Lk 10:25-37**

Today we move on to another book connected with the Babylonian exile. The book of Jonah is regarded as a sermon in the form of a story. It teaches that the mercy of God extends to all nations and is not restricted to the Chosen People. Jonah was afraid to carry out his mission of preaching repentance to the citizens of Niniveh and tried to travel in the opposite direction. The Lord had other plans and eventually caused Jonah to be brought back, having spent three days and three nights in a great fish.

The lawyers have always had trick questions. This was true in Jesus' time. They believed that one should take care of one's own kind – only Jews. That is what was meant by 'love your neighbour'. This beautiful story of the good Samaritan teaches otherwise.

Tuesday   **Jn 3:1-10 Lk 10:38-42**

When Jonah eventually got to the great city of Nineveh, he was successful in preaching repentance. From the king down they fasted and did penance. The result was that God relented and did not allow disaster to fall on them.

A reminder to us all. Take time off from the everyday rat race to be in the presence of Christ. Stop in your tracks, find a place with silence, and pray.

Wednesday   **Jn 4:1-11 Lk 11:1-4**

Jonah felt that God's mercy should only be shown to the Chosen People, but the reaction in Nineveh demonstrated otherwise. The little parable of the plant first giving shade to Jonah and then being taken away – both actions due to God's providence, gets the message across to Jonah. Many of those in Nineveh did not realise the evil they were doing. People are more important than plants.

Yesterday we were told to take time off and pray. Today Jesus gives us his special prayer. Say it at different times during the day.

Thursday

Malachi was a prophet who lived some years after the end of the exile period. He taught through the use of dialogue. In this single extract the people who were doing their best were annoyed that the evil-doers were prospering – God did not seem to be interested in punishing them. Malachi assures them that the good deeds are to be recorded and that the time will come when the evil-doers will be burnt up like stubble.

Jesus is continuing his lesson on prayer. Have complete trust in the goodness of the Father and don't hesitate to ask. The heavenly Father will give the Holy Spirit to those who ask him.

Friday

Joel is the last of the books which deal with the period after the Babylonian exile. In this extract we get a real sense of doom and gloom. The Israelites have brought this on themselves because they turned away from their God. This day of darkness and gloom, of cloud and blackness, will cause terror among the people. The day of the Lord is coming.

From prayer you will get the strength to fight the evil that is all around you. The power of God will cast this evil away from you.

Saturday

At the end of this book Joel is calling on all the nations, especially those who have oppressed Israel, to come to the great valley for judgment. The day of the Lord is near in the Valley of Decision, when the sun and moon will grow dark. Afterwards there will be great harmony in Israel, but desolation in the land of their enemies.

Jesus gives us another special lesson. We can't be his mother, but we are really blessed if we hear the word of God and keep it.

Twenty-Eighth Week in Ordinary Time – 1

Monday   **Rm 1:1-7 Lk 11:29-32**

We begin reading one of the greatest of St Paul's letters today, that to the Romans, and we continue for three weeks. It seems that he wrote this to the new community in Rome, to prepare for his arrival in the city (while in Corinth at the end of his stay there on his third missionary journey). He speaks of the need for the salvation of the gospel, the way to this salvation and the effects of it. In the introduction Paul states that he is specially chosen as an apostle to bring the Good News about Jesus, the Son of God, who died and rose for our sins.

This is a wicked generation asking for a sign. The only sign will be that of Jonah. The Ninevites repented when Jonah preached. The Queen of the South came from a great distance to hear the wisdom of Solomon. They will judge this generation. There is something greater than both Jonah and the Queen of the South.

Tuesday   **Rm 1:16-25 Lk 11:37-41**

Paul gets into the detail quickly. In the Christian gospel God really offers us salvation; this salvation is to be obtained through faith; it is offered to all; it is in full agreement with the Old Testament. All people need this salvation, both Jews and Gentiles. The Gentiles, especially the Greeks, are capable of knowing God from nature, nevertheless they have degraded themselves through false philosophies and immoral practices.

The Pharisees were at their legalism again. Jesus attacks this – they are clean outside, but inside are full of wickedness. Make the inside clean too.

Wednesday   **Rm 2:1-11 Lk 11:42-46**

All are under the power of sin, so all need salvation. It is important that you do not judge others – when you judge those who behave like you, you are condemning yourself. God will give eternal life to those who are always doing good. Jews and Greeks will be treated alike – he has no favourites. 'There is no partiality with God.'

Jesus continues his tirade against the hypocrisy of the Pharisees and the lawyers. You are like unmarked tombs that people walk on without knowing it!

Thursday   **Rm 3:21-30 Lk 11:47-54**

Paul now sets out to describe the means by which the salvation of the Gospel is obtained – God's answer to our need. This salvation is a justification that does not come by way of any law, but through faith in Jesus Christ. This is open to all and comes through the death of Christ. There is no room for boasting, because we are justified not by what we do, but by our faith. Faith is a fully human and personal act in which a person acknowledges his insufficiency by assenting to truths about the authority of God. So God himself justifies or renders upright each person on the basis of faith.

Jesus continues speaking against all forms of hypocrisy. This generation will have to answer for all the sins of the past.

Friday   **Rm 4:1-8 Lk 12:1-7**

Paul continues with his thesis that we are justified through faith and not as a reward for our labours. Abraham pre-existed the Law. Faith must come first. This was how Abraham was justified. The Jews tended to think that they would be justified by following the letter of the law, without any real faith in God. Obeying the law would be the way to continue in the justified state begun by the gift of faith in Christ.

Be on your guard against the yeast of the Pharisees. Do not be afraid of those who may be able to kill the body, but cannot kill the soul. Every hair on your head is numbered, so there is no need to be afraid.

Saturday   **Rm 4:13.16-18 Lk 12:8-12**

Even though Abraham was an old man with a wife who was barren he still believed in the promise made to him, that he would be the father of many nations. Paul emphasises that the fulfilment of this great promise made to him was due to his faith and not any law. So his uprightness was not due to any law, but to his faith.

Jesus makes his solemn promise – anyone who declares himself openly for me, I will declare that person in the presence of God. If you need my guidance in the meantime, don't worry; I will send you the Holy Spirit to teach you what you must say.

Twenty-Ninth Week in Ordinary Time – 1

Monday   **Rm 4:20-25 Lk 12:13-21**

Abraham refused either to deny or to doubt God's promise. He drew strength from his faith and this faith justified him. Our faith too will be considered as justifying us if we believe in him who raised Jesus from the dead. He was put to death for our sins and raised to life to justify us.

As we live, so shall we die. We must be ever prepared. If we store up treasures in heaven, we will be prepared.

Tuesday   **Rm 5:12.15.17-21 Lk 12:35-38**

Sin entered the world through one man, and through sin came death. But life and grace come through Jesus Christ, in greater abundance. If through one so many died; if it brought condemnation on everyone; if that disobedience created many sinners; how much more abundant will grace and life be, will justification be, will obedience making many righteous be. Yes, sin and death once reigned, but now grace will bring eternal life thanks to Jesus Christ.

Be ready for the call of the Lord – dressed for action with your lamps lit.

Wednesday   **Rm 6:12-18 Lk 12:39-48**

For St Paul sin is a force which not only destroys the human body, but also causes a separation from God. By Christ's death the Christian has been liberated from this hostile force. Now the believer has a real share in the new relationship with the Father. So you must not let sin reign in your bodies, but consider every part of your bodies as weapons fighting on the side of God. Then sin will no longer dominate your lives. Now you are the slave of Christ through baptism.

Again, we are reminded that we must be ready for the call of the Lord – he will come on a day you do not expect and at an hour you do not know.

Thursday   **Rm 6:19-23 Lk 12:49-53**

Paul continues to emphasise that we are now slaves of Jesus Christ. We must never again put our bodies at the service of vice and immorality and do things that would make us blush. Rather, now you have been set free from sin and you will get the reward leading to your sanctification and ending in eternal life.

My message is tough, so tough that it may divide families.

Friday   **Rm 7:18-25 Lk 12:54-59**

Even though we have been justified by faith in Jesus Christ, we are still under the influence of the force or power of sin. That is why we are tempted to do what is evil and find it difficult to do what we know to be right. He cries out – 'Who will rescue me from this power of sin?' The answer is given over the next few days.

Try to read the signs and interpret the times. Be careful how you judge others.

Saturday   **Rm 8:1-11 Lk 13:1-9**

The liberator is the Spirit, which is nothing else but the power or force of the risen Jesus present on earth. The believer comes into contact with this force by living in union with Jesus Christ – a union begun at baptism. God sent his own Son in a body as physical as any sinful body, and in that body condemned sin. If the Spirit who raised Jesus from the dead is living in you, then your own mortal bodies will be given life.

A common message from Jesus. Repent and produce good fruit – the parable of the fig tree. It was given just one more chance.

Thirtieth Week in Ordinary Time – 1

Monday   **Rm 8:12-17 Lk 13:10-17**

This Spirit that we have received is not one that makes us afraid of God. It makes us dear to God, it makes us God's very own children. It gives us the power to recognise God as our Father – it enables us to say 'Abba, Father'. So we are co-heirs with Christ, sharing both in his sufferings and in his glory.

We see the healing power of Jesus – both a physical and spiritual healing – we see the hypocrisy of the synagogue official. We are not made for the sabbath, the sabbath is made for us. Isn't it good to heal on the sabbath?

Tuesday   **Rm 8:18-25 Lk 13:18-21**

Paul continues about the suffering we share with Christ. It is nothing compared to the glory that is waiting for us. In fact the whole of creation is groaning and waiting to be set free from its slavery to decadence to enjoy the first fruits of the Spirit. So we are full of real hope.

The kingdom of God begins in a very small way, but grows to have a great influence.

Wednesday   **Rm 8:26-30 Lk 13:22-30**

This Spirit that Paul has been speaking about is one which can help us in our weaknesses, which can help us to pray. For it is his will that we be conformed to the image of Christ by a gradual share in the risen life of Christ himself. The ultimate goal is that we become like the God who revealed himself in Jesus Christ. Those he called he justified, with those he justified he shared his glory. These are great consoling words. ['Prayer is the divine in us appealing to the Divine above us' – Dodd].

Many will try to come into the kingdom, but will find it very difficult. Just knowing the Lord is not sufficient, we have to do his works.

Thursday   **Rm 8:31-39 Lk 13:31-35**

St Paul finishes this section with a sort of hymn to the victory of Christ, to the reality of being in the Spirit. We must remember that God is for us, and that Jesus, who died for us, is standing at God's right hand pleading for us. So, no matter what happens to us, nothing in heaven or on earth can come between us and the love of Christ. And this is the answer to the question we had from Paul last week — 'Who will rescue me from this power of sin?'

We see the great sadness of Jesus about Jerusalem, the city he is so proud of, keeping its ears closed to his teaching.

Friday   **Rm 9:1-5 Lk 14:1-6**

In this next section Paul is dealing more directly with the Jews. He has insisted that the Jewish Torah no longer binds as law, it is only valid now as a sacred story to tell of God's dealings with people through history. How is it that the old Jewish law is no longer? Why have the Jews been rejected, after so many promises were made to them? Paul is deeply sensitive about this – he wants to help his Jewish brothers and sisters, who have received so many privileges from God.

For the second time this week we have the account of Jesus healing someone on the sabbath – an example of the people never learning. No wonder he was sad about the future of Jerusalem.

Saturday   **Rm 11:1-2.11-12.25-29 Lk 14:1.7-11**

Paul declares very definitely that God has not rejected the Jews. But they have fallen, they have defected. But through their defection the pagan world has benefited. They are now asleep, but they too will awaken and will be saved. They are still loved by God.

Jesus reminds his listeners that they must know their true selves. Don't put yourself in a higher place. Go where you belong. Then the Lord may call you to a higher place.

Thirty-First Week in Ordinary Time – 1

Monday   **Rm 11:29-36 Lk 14:12-14**

Paul finishes off this special section for the Jews in Rome. Because many have sinned, there is need for mercy, and this mercy is shown by God. He concludes with a marvellous prayer of praise to the all-merciful God. How rich are the depths of God, how deep his wisdom and knowledge. Who could ever know the mind of God? To him be glory for ever. Amen!

Jesus continues in the vein of Saturday's reading. Don't invite those to a party who can return the invitation. Ask those who have no way of repaying you.

Tuesday   **Rm 12:5-16 Lk 14:15-24**

As in his other letters, Paul turns his attention in the remaining part of his letter to practical exhortations. The new demands for the believer are based on love and not on the old law. We all form one body with different parts, but must work together. Each person will have different gifts. They must all be used to promote unity, and must all be based on love. Let your love be sincere, both for one another and for your enemies.

Jesus gives the parable of the unjust guests, who made many excuses not to come to the party. Instead people from the rough areas of life were invited. So the non-Jews were invited to hear the Good News as well.

Wednesday   **Rm 13:8-10 Lk 14:25-33**

Paul emphasises the need to see all the Commandments of the old law being included in the law of the new dispensation – 'love your neighbour as yourself.' Here the neighbour means more than it does for the Jews. It means everyone, and not just fellow-Jews.

Be realistic if you want to be a follower of mine, because it is not easy. But once committed you must not turn back, but keep your hand to the plough.

Thursday   **Rm 14:7-12 Lk 15:1-10**

If we live, we live for the Lord. So we do not look down on others with contempt, we should never pass judgment on our brother. Ultimately, we shall all have to stand before the Lord's judgment seat and be totally exposed. Then we shall have to give an account of ourselves to God himself.

Jesus goes on to tell the parable of the lost sheep and the lost silver pieces. There is rejoicing in heaven over one repentant sinner. That should help us keep up the effort.

Friday   Rm 15:14-21 Lk 16:1-8

Today and tomorrow we take parts out of the conclusion of St Paul's letter. He praises the Romans for their good intentions and sound judgment. Again, he gives his reason for writing his letter – he has been appointed by God to carry out the priestly duty of preaching the Good News to the pagans. He is proud of the work he has done so far in the east in union with Christ Jesus. Whether the work was begun by himself or others, his task was to fulfil the text – those who have never been told about him will see him, and those who have never heard about him will understand.

Be as energetic and as resourceful in looking after spiritual things as the unjust steward was about his position.

Saturday   Rm 16:3-9.16.22-27 Lk 16:9-15

Paul concludes his letter with some personal greetings to the few people he knew in Rome. Prisca and Aquila were leading missionaries, who had moved to Corinth and later Ephesus. Epaenetus was the first convert in western Asia. Andronicus and Junia were early Jewish-Christian converts. The others were probably slaves. Finally, the scribe or actual writer of the letter, Tertius, adds his greetings. The letter ends with another great hymn of praise to God.

Use the goods of this world properly – don't let them lead you away from the spiritual. If money becomes your master, then the Lord can mean nothing to you.

Thirty-Second Week in Ordinary Time – 1

Monday   **Ws 1:1-7 Lk 17:1-6**

This week we move on to the Book of Wisdom, one that is full of poetry. It is one of the latest books of the Old Testament – it was written in Greek by a pious Jew, perhaps in Egypt, during the first century BC. The first section of the book is often called the Book of Eschatology – it has to do with the last and final things. Today we begin with an exhortation to justice. Love justice, the writer says, because this is the key to wisdom. Seek God in simple piety, and God will come to you. Wisdom will never make its way into a crafty soul, nor stay in a person who is in sin.

Have faith and you won't cause scandal to the little ones. Learn how to forgive – forgive whenever and as often as the other says sorry.

Tuesday   **Ws 2:23-3:9 Lk 17:7-10**

The Jews at this time did not have a clear idea about life after death. The author here believes that the just would have life with God forever, because his mercy endures forever. The just have been tested like gold in a furnace. This passage is often used in Masses for the dead, as it is full of consolation. They who trust in him will understand the truth and will live with him in love.

Without question we must do our duty. 'We are merely servants; we have done no more than our duty.'

Wednesday   **Ws 6:1-11 Lk 17:11-19**

This is the end of the first section of the Book. Here the author is speaking to those with power on earth. God is the source of all their power. So their works are subject to God's scrutiny, and they will be called to answer for the way they used their power. Learn wisdom by learning how to live justly, and without sin.

Always include a prayer of thanks when we are praying.

Thursday   **Ws 7:22-8:1 Lk 17:20-25**

The second section of this book acclaims the glories of wisdom. Here wisdom is personified. Today we have a long list of her great attributes. The language is very poetic – 'She is a breath of the power of God, pure emanation of the glory of the Almighty. She is a reflection of the eternal light, untarnished mirror of God's active power, the image of his goodness.' What marvellous ideas to meditate on!

The Son of Man must suffer grievously and be rejected by his generation.

Friday   Ws 13:1-9 Lk 17:26-37

We move on to the third section of the book. Today the author reminds people that they can see the beauty and glory of God in the wonderful things of nature. Yet, many got lost in these great things and believed that they were gods. The Lord excels all these creatures, since the very author of beauty has created them. So by contemplating the beauty of the creatures they should contemplate their author, God. We too can stop and observe nature and see the powerful hand of God in it.

We have a reference to the last day. Always be ready.

Saturday   Ws 18:14-16. 19:6-9 Lk 18:1-8

The author made many references to God's powerful actions in redeeming the Israelites from the Egyptians. Their captors suffered very greatly, yet they ignored the clear lesson of God's protection for Israel. So we have this very vivid description of the all-powerful Lord coming to the earth and filling the universe with death. The Israelites, on the other hand, were protected by the great cloud and eventually sang the praises of God. God chooses his people – he rewards the good and punishes the unrepentant sinners.

We try to have persistence in our prayer – like the old lady with the judge.

Thirty-Third Week in Ordinary Time – 1

Monday   **I M 1:10-15.41-43.54-57.62-64 Lk 18:35-43**

The two Books of Maccabees were probably written around a hundred years before Christ, telling of events which had taken place some years before. They depict the confrontation between the traditional Jewish religion and the Greek and Near Eastern culture. It is a story of a particular family, nicknamed the Maccabees, after 'hammer', who decided to rebel against the forces, including the country's leaders, who were trying to promote this foreign religious culture. This revolt was led first by the father, Mattathias, and later by his three sons in turn, Judas, Jonathan and Simon. In today's account we hear of the king supporting the move to push out the traditional religion of the Jews, by burning the books and setting up practices that were against the religion. But some people stood firm and would not contaminate themselves.

We have the beautiful story of the blind man being cured near Jericho, the very ancient city. 'Your faith has saved you.'

Tuesday   **II M 6:18-31 Lk 19:1-10**

The ruler, Antiochus, outlawed all Jewish customs and there were many persecutions. Many refused to comply. Today, we see the old man, Eleazar, refusing to break the Jewish law, in spite of the persuasion of his friends. He became a great martyr.

Zacchaeus becomes the special host for Jesus. He overcame his physical size to look for Christ, an example of faith. Faith saved him from his sins.

Wednesday   **II M 7:1.20-31 Lk 19:11-28**

Today we have more martyrs. Here was the 'perfect' family with seven sons. Each son gave a different theological reason for his martyrdom. The mother encouraged her sons to remain faithful and later she too was martyred. As a result of their example the traditional Jews eventually won the day and were able to restore their Temple.

We are all given some talents in life. The reward we get will depend on the effort we put into using them positively.

Thursday   **I M 2:15-29 Lk 19:41-44**

We jump back a bit to the beginning of the Maccabean revolt – the attempt to get Mattathias, the father of the Maccabees, to turn his back on the traditional religion. He reacts violently to this and then stirs up the people to revolt. All who intend to remain faithful to the covenant are invite to join them. They go out to the desert to protect themselves and prepare their defences.

Jerusalem did not take the opportunity offered to it – it will be destroyed.

Friday   **I M 4:36-37. 52-59 Lk 19:45-48**

There was a lull in the war under Judas, so they decided to restore and eventually rededicate the Temple. This great celebration went on for eight days, a full octave. Every year the event was to be commemorated for the eight days.

We must have respect for the Temple of the Lord.

Saturday   **I M 6:1-13 Lk 20:27-40**

Antiochus, the king of the region, is suffering because of the evil he did, particularly in Jerusalem. Here he had desecrated the Temple, which was now restored. So he was to die in distress, with all his plans gone astray and very far away from home. This was the punishment inflicted on him because of the evil he had done. The Jews, on the other hand, could sing the responsorial psalm – 'I will rejoice in your saving help, O Lord.'

Jesus confounds the Sadducees who said there was no resurrection. We are all going to rise on the last day.

Thirty-Fourth Week in Ordinary Time – 1

Monday   **Dn 1:1-6. 8-20 Lk 21:1-4**

During the last week of the Church's year we use the book of Daniel. Part of this contains the fictional tales of heroes during the Babylonian exile which were used to encourage the people during the Maccabean revolt. There are also accounts of various visions – often called apocalyptical material or the revelations, and generally referring to the Last Judgment. Today's tale tells of the fidelity of Daniel and his three companions in refusing to take food that was foreign to their religion.

The woman is praised because she gave a large proportion of what she had to help the poor.

Tuesday   **Dn 2:31-45 Lk 21:5-11**

The second tale from Daniel is about the King's dream. The king, Nebuchadnezzar, had already condemned his own enchanters and magicians, because none of them were able to describe the dream or interpret it. Daniel was able to do both, after he had prayed to God. All the four empires from Babylon to the regime at the Maccabean revolt are included. Eventually all will be swept away and a new kingdom will be set up by God.

Jesus reminds his listeners that even the things that seem to be most permanent will disappear. The end of the world will come with much chaos.

Wednesday   **Dn 5:1-6.13-14. 16-17.23-28 Lk 21:12-19**

The next tale is that of the writing on the wall. It is a simple one-scene mystery story about how a sacrilege was swiftly punished by God. At the banquet the sacred vessels taken from the Temple in Jerusalem were used for the guests. Then the disembodied hand appeared and wrote the strange message. Only Daniel was able to interpret it – God has measured your sovereignty and put an end to it; you have been weighed in the balance and found wanting; your kingdom is to be taken away from you.

As the years go by, those who are loyal to Christ must suffer much persecution at the hands of wicked men.

Thursday   **Dn 6:12-28 Lk 21:20-28**

We have the tale of Daniel in the lions' den. The king had made a decree forbidding anyone to pray for a month. Daniel was caught praying so the king reluctantly had him put into the lion pit. He had a sleepless night and was glad to find that the God of Daniel had saved him. Then the king proclaimed publicly that this was the God to be worshipped.

More desolation will occur as the world comes to an end. Eventually the Son of Man, Christ, will come in his power and glory. Stand with your heads high, because your liberation is near at hand.

Friday   **Dn 7:2-14 Lk 21:29-33**

For the last two days of the Church's year we have one of the apocalyptic visions from Daniel. These are all very symbolic. Today we have the first part of the vision of the four beasts. These were fearful things and brought great misery to people. But then the one of great age came upon the scene and with great power and majesty the four beasts were destroyed. Evil was destroyed by good.

Use nature, for example the changes in the life history of the fig tree, to help you see that the kingdom of heaven is at hand.

Saturday   **Dn 7:15-27 Lk 21:34-36**

We continue the great vision begun yesterday. The interpretation shows that the beasts represented the various evil kingdoms. They would ultimately be judged and destroyed. 'God's sovereignty is an eternal sovereignty and every empire will serve and obey him.' Evil can often erupt from time to time in human affairs, but always the power of God will prevail. The message of the vision is one of hope. That is why we can say, with the psalmist, 'Give glory and eternal praise to him!'

For the past week we have been looking at the teachings Jesus gave just before his arrest and crucifixion. Watch and pray. Stay awake, praying at all times for the strength to survive all that is going to happen, and to stand with confidence before the Son of Man.

First Week in Ordinary Time – 2

Monday   **I S 1:1-8 Mk 1:14-20**

Last year we listened to the history of the Chosen People from the time of Abraham until shortly after they arrived in the Promised Land. We take it up from there in the first book of Samuel, which concerns the establishment of a monarchy in Israel. The books of Samuel are not history in the modern sense but theological history – narrative accounts of God's dealings with the Chosen People. The principal message to the Israelites over the years was that if they were faithful to the laws given by Moses, faithful to the covenant, they would have prosperity and peace; if they were to disobey, they could expect punishment through natural disaster, invasion, and even exile. The three main characters in these books are Samuel, Saul and David. We begin today with the background to the birth of Samuel. Elkanah favoured his second wife Hannah very much, but she was barren. The couple were very devout and made their annual pilgrimage to Jerusalem.

For the first nine weeks of ordinary time we use the gospel of Mark and today we see the beginning of Jesus' public mission. He calls the first of his disciples – 'he called them once'.

Tuesday   **I S 1:9-20 Mk 1:21-28**

Barrenness was a terrible cross for a woman. Hannah makes a vow that if she has a son she will dedicate him to God. At first, Eli, the priest thought she was drunk, but then blessed her. He little realised that his priesthood would be replaced by that of Hannah's son. Hannah goes home a happy woman and eventually Samuel is born.

It wasn't long after the beginning of his public ministry that Jesus began to make an impression. This was due to his style of teaching – he taught with authority, and he also had authority over the demons.

Wednesday   **I S 3:1-10. 19-20 Mk 1:29-39**

We have the lovely account of the call of Samuel to become the Lord's prophet and take over from his master priest, Eli. Samuel was open to the promptings of the Lord – 'Speak, Lord, your servant is listening.'

Jesus heals Simon Peter's mother-in-law and then goes on to cure many others. But afterwards, he goes off to a quiet place to pray.

Thursday   **I S 4:1-11 Mk 1:40-45**

Ever since their journey through the desert, the Israelites were
accompanied by the ark of the covenant. It was a gold-plated box
containing the tablets of the law. They brought it with them to a big battle
against the neighbouring Philistines, who were very dangerous enemies.
Unfortunately, they lost the battle, the precious ark, and even their priests,
all of which gave rise to a total loss of morale.

Today we see Jesus healing the leper – it was almost unheard of that a
leper could be cured. Jesus tried to keep a low profile, but his listeners
would not let him.

Friday   **I S 8:4-7. 10-22 Mk 2:1-12**

The Philistines found that the ark brought them many problems, so
eventually they sent it back to Israel. Under Samuel's leadership the
Israelites repented their idolatry and returned to follow their God. When
he was coming to the end of his days, Samuel appointed his sons as
judges. They did not follow his ways so the people looked for a king who
might lead them. Up to this they had judges, as God was regarded as their
king. He warned them about the difficulties of having a king, but they
insisted. The voice of the Lord told him to agree to their requests.

Jesus was not interested in merely healing the sick. There was always a
spiritual message to be learned. We see the value of faith and also the fact
that Jesus had power to forgive sin. No ordinary person could have that
power. These were the little references to the fact he was man and God –
much of it went unnoticed at the time.

Saturday   **I S 9:1-4. 17-19.10:1 Mk 2:13-17**

Saul was from the north of the kingdom. One day this handsome man
went in search of his father's asses. He sought the help of the 'seer', who
turned out to be Samuel. He told him to go up to the high place in the city
and eat a special religious meal with him. There he was anointed and told
that he was to rule over the Lord's people and save them from their
enemies. Thus Saul became their first king.

The passage is a very consoling one for us. Jesus did not come to help
those who believed that they were spiritually healthy. He came to help
those who were striving to overcome sin in their lives, those who were
genuine.

Second Week in Ordinary Time – 2

Monday   **I S 15:16-23 Mk 2:18-22**

Saul had a number of battles against the Philistines and the other enemies. But he wasn't a good king – he often 'interpreted' Samuel's words from God to suit himself. Today we see Samuel tackling him because he did not follow his orders to the full. Saul thought that a good sacrifice was the answer. Samuel insisted that obedience was much more important. His reign was to come to an end.

While the bridegroom is still at the party there will be no fasting. But when he goes they must fast. It is important to recognise the signs of the times.

Tuesday   **I S 16:1-13 Mk 2:23-28**

Samuel was disappointed that Saul had allowed himself to be rejected by God as king. Eventually he sets out to look for a new king. He goes to the southern kingdom, to Bethlehem and the family of Jesse. He anoints the youngest of the family, David.

We see again Jesus' horror of hypocrisy. He pointed out that the laws were made for people, and not people for the laws.

Wednesday   **I S 17:32-33. 37.40-51 Mk 3:1-6**

Saul did not know that David had been anointed, but took him on as one of his soldiers. He offered to fight the huge Philistine, Goliath and won. He went to fight him in the name of the Lord of hosts, the God of Israel.

Jesus again shows his power: the Pharisees needed to know that Jesus promoted the Commandments. Faith is the essential characteristic.

Thursday   **I S 18:6-9. 19:1-7 Mk 3:7-12**

As David's popularity increased, so did Saul's jealousy of him. Eventually, he set out to kill him. However, David found a good ally in Saul's son, Jonathan. He persuaded his father not to kill David.

Jesus is overwhelmed with the approach of all those looking for a cure. Faith was the essential requirement.

Saul did not keep his oath and made several attempts to get rid of David. He believed that David was trying to kill him. David had his chance when Saul went into the cave, but David merely cut off the end of his cloak. Thus he demonstrated that he had no evil intentions towards Saul. This speech so moved Saul that he admitted that David would be king.

At this stage in his mission, Jesus picks his apostles for his chosen disciples. They were then sent out to complete the mission.

Saturday   **II S 1:1-4. 11-12.17.19.23-27 Mk 3:20-21**

When David heard the news about the death of Saul and his son Jonathan, he was very upset. He tore his garments and composed a beautiful elegy about the two men, especially Jonathan, who had always remained faithful to him. This showed the depth of his sorrow.

Jesus is under great pressure. Even his relatives misunderstood what he was about.

Third Week in Ordinary Time – 2

Monday   II S 5:1-7.10 Mk 3:22-30

David first became the king of Judah, the southern kingdom. There was a civil war between Judah and Israel, the northern kingdom, which was ruled by one of Saul's sons. Eventually David became the king of Israel as well. One of his first acts was to take Jerusalem from the Jebusites. The two states were now united in one and became very powerful under David.

The scribes are already trying to discredit Jesus – he works through the devil, they say. Jesus turned this back on them. He also reminds them that all sins will be forgiven, if they go to the throne of grace and repent.

Tuesday   II S 6:12-15.17-19 Mk 3:31-35

The Philistines, from the coastal region, were finally defeated and then David set out to bring the ark of the covenant back to Jerusalem, from Abinadab's house, where it had been since the Philistines returned it. He brought it back with great celebrations.

Jesus reminds his listeners that anyone who does the will of God can become his brother, sister and mother.

Wednesday   II S 7:4-17 Mk 4:1-20

David wished to build a Temple, but the prophet Nathan told him it was to be left to his son. However, David was promised that his dynasty would last, and from it would come the messiah. This section is theologically very important as the promise of the dynasty to David occupies a central place in the history of Israel. The king is the Lord's representative in bringing Israel victory and blessings.

Today's parable and explanation needs no further elaboration. Just ask yourselves where you stand.

Thursday   II S 7:18-19.24-29 Mk 4:21-25

In grateful response to the Lord's promise, David, in his prayer, contrasted his own littleness with the Lord's greatness. 'The Lord is the only God and Israel is his specially favoured people.' He reaffirmed Israel as the Lord's people and the Lord as their God. He finished up by asking for the Lord's blessing.

Whatever talents we are given in life, we are expected to use them to the best of our ability. We should be the beacons of virtue in the community.

Friday   **II S 11:1-10.13-17 Mk 4:26-34**

We skip over the accounts of the various wars of David and the Israelites and we come to his grave personal sin. He was very human and weak and fell for a beautiful woman. He was able to use his power to cause the death of her husband, and so cover up his crime.

Some further parables on a difficult question – how is it that the evil exist side-by-side with the good? The harvest will give the answer.

Saturday   **II S 12:1-7.10-17 Mk 4:35-41**

The prophet Nathan tells David a parable and he becomes emotional about it. The prophet uses this to convey to David the gravity of his own sin. David acknowledges his sin and does penance for it. He is pardoned, but accepts the punishment of the death of his son and some other serious disasters.

Jesus calms the waters – the disciples were trying to get away for some quiet reflection and prayer. Having faith is essential. With faith Jesus can calm our fears.

Fourth Week in Ordinary Time – 2

Monday   **II S 15:13-14. 30.16:5-13 Mk 5:1-20**

David had two sons, Solomon and Absalom. The latter eventually took arms against him and tried to destroy him. This is part of the prophecy of Nathan. David fled from Jerusalem, stopping at different parts of the Mount of Olives. None of the cursing of this follower of Saul compared with the humiliation of his son's rebellion.

The strange story of the demons and the pigs – forbidden meat to the Jews. The power of Jesus is without limit.

Tuesday   **II S 18:9-10.14.24-25.30-19:3 Mk 5:21-43**

Eventually the rebellion of David's son, Absalom, is put down. David gave orders that the soldiers should deal gently with his son, but they disobeyed and killed him. We have a very moving picture of David grieving over this death. As a result the soldiers were unable to celebrate their victory and went back to the town quietly.

Two great stories of the results of faith in the healing power of Jesus. Remember how close we are to Jesus in the Mass.

Wednesday   **II S 24:2. 9-17 Mk 6:1-6**

This is the last account of the acts of David. He took a census of the people. This was wrong because it implied a lack of trust in God and showed that he depended on the numbers he could muster for his army. This was David's public sin and the people were punished for it by experiencing a pestilence.

We go from great faith to great doubt – Jesus was not accepted in his own community, who found it hard to have faith in him.

Thursday   **I K 2:1-4.10-12 Mk 6:7-13**

The books of Samuel dealt with Samuel, Saul and David. The book of Kings deals with David's dynasty. This was initiated with David's son, Solomon succeeding him. The first book deals with Solomon's reign, the building of the Temple, and the eventual unfaithfulness of Solomon. The second book deals with the later kings. Again, their infidelity led to various evils and eventually the destruction of the Temple and the deportation to Babylon. Today we see David at the end of his life, encouraging his son, Solomon, to be faithful to the ways of God. After this he died and Solomon inherited his throne.

Jesus sends his disciples out on their first mission – this was to be their test of faith. They brought the healing power of Jesus.

Friday   **Si 47:2-11 Mk 6:14-29**

Before we go on to hear the exploits of Solomon, we have the great hymn of praise for David, the greatest of the kings of Israel. By his work he caused the name of the Lord to be praised. His sins were forgiven and he was given a lasting royal covenant.

We switch to the story of the beheading of John the Baptist. The power of women is greater than they realise!

Saturday   **I K 3:4-13 Mk 6:30-34**

When Solomon became king the country was at peace. He was very faithful to God at first, offering sacrifice at the best places until he built the Temple. In a dream he was offered anything he wanted from the Lord. He looked for a discerning heart so that he could distinguish good from evil. He was given a wise and shrewd heart, and also plenty of riches and a long life. At the time they did not believe in life after death, so the best reward for doing good was a long life with riches.

They tried to get away to a quiet place to reflect after the death of John, but the crowds followed them. Jesus took pity on them for they were like sheep without a shepherd – they were hungry for knowledge.

Fifth Week in Ordinary Time – 2

Monday   **I K 8:1-7. 9-13 Mk 6:53-56**

We skip the details of the building and furnishing of the Temple. When everything was finished it was dedicated by bringing in the ark of the covenant (with its two stone tablets of the law) and placing it there. The cloud that fills the Temple is a clear indication of the Lord's approval. Thus the prophecy that David's son would sit on the throne and build the Temple were both fulfiled.

Jesus continues his healing mission. Spiritual healing was always a very important part of this work.

Tuesday   **I K 8:22-23. 27-30 Mk 7:1-13**

We have part of Solomon's great prayer at the dedication of the Temple. He praises the good God, who cannot be contained even in the heavens, not to speak of the Temple. But here the Lord is to be honoured. Here he is to watch over his chosen people, forgive their sins and listen to their needs.

The Pharisees and some of the scribes were critical that Jesus did not observe the various purification rites. He reminds them that sincerity and internal purification are what is really important.

Wednesday   **I K 10:1-10 Mk 7:14-23**

Knowledge of Solomon's wisdom went far and wide. The Queen of Sheba heard about it and came to see it for herself. She was duly impressed by his grand style and by his fidelity to God. They exchanged various gifts.

Jesus continues his discourse on inner purity. What comes from the heart is either good or bad. If bad we have fornication, theft, murder, adultery, avarice, malice, deceit, indecency, slander, pride, folly.

Thursday   **I K 11:4-13 Mk 7:24-30**

Solomon had married many foreign women. When he grew old he also began to worship their gods. He did not follow the ways of David any more. God spoke to him and told him his kingdom would be divided after his time and part would be given to his servant. He died some time afterwards, having reigned for forty years.

We have a great example of the faith of a non-believing pagan. Faith was not confined to the Jews.

Friday   **I K 11:29-32.12:19 Mk 7:31-37**

The kingdom was now divided in two. Solomon's line continued in the south – Judah – through his son Rehoboam, while Jeroboam became king of Israel in the north. This division is indicated by the actions of the prophet, Ahijah.

This time Jesus uses a sign to carry out his healing – Ephphatha, be opened. It was like a forerunner of the sacraments.

Saturday   **I K 12:26-32.13:33-34 Mk 8:1-10**

Jeroboam, the king of Israel (also called Samaria) in the north wanted to keep the people from travelling to Jerusalem to worship God. So he set up his own false shrines for his people to worship. He even ordained non-levitical priests and established a feast. He was punished and his kingdom eventually passed on to another family. We now leave aside the history of God's people for a few weeks.

We have an account of the multiplication of the loaves and fishes. This ultimately led to the establishment of the Eucharist – if Jesus was able to feed this number, he could give his flesh and blood as spiritual food.

Sixth Week in Ordinary Time – 2

Monday   **Jm 1:1-11 Mk 8:11-13**

We leave aside the Old Testament story for a few weeks. The letter of St James, which may have been written by some of his followers, is a collection of popular moral teachings, in the style of the Sermon on the Mount. The main concerns of the document are perseverance in conversion to God and growth in the living of gospel morality. The author stresses the close relationship between faith in God and love of neighbour. He also stresses that we cannot pick and choose among God's laws. At all times people must try to control the various roots of disorder in their lives. In this first extract we are told of the need for perseverance which will lead to spiritual maturity. Prayer said with a strong faith in God will bring about this maturity more quickly. But we must not be 'pray-ers' with doubts – then we will be like the surf tossed by the wind.

The Pharisees are getting touchy with Jesus – they are not able for his wisdom and insights. They wanted things too 'cut and dried'. Now they were looking for a sign.

Tuesday   **Jm 1:12-18 Mk 8:14-21**

James encourages his readers to have endurance in the face of temptation, for it leads to the crown of glory. Temptation itself does not come from God, but giving in to it leads to death. All good things come from God. He has given us a special place, for we are the first fruits of all that he has created.

Jesus is getting a little annoyed with his disciples. They are looking on the material side all the time. Jesus tests their faith.

Wednesday   **Jm 1:19-27 Mk 8:22-26**

James encourages us to control our desires and actions. Be quick to listen and slow to speak – control your anger. Listen to the word and obey – otherwise you are like someone who looks in the mirror, but forgets the image immediately. Be religious by controlling your tongue, helping the orphans and widows, and remaining uncontaminated by the world.

We have the miracle of giving sight to the blind man. This time the miracle occurred over a period of time.

Thursday   **Jm 2: 1-9 Mk 8:27-33**

James gives us more practical advice. If we have the proper faith in Jesus Christ we will not give in to making distinctions between people. We will treat the rich and poor alike. Remember that God chose those who were poor according to the world to be rich in faith and to be heirs to the kingdom he promised.

We have Peter's proclamation of faith, followed by his criticism of what Jesus had to say about his future. At this stage he did not fully understand the spiritual message that Jesus was delivering.

Friday   **Jm 2:14-24.26 Mk 8:34-9:1**

James contrasts a live faith with a dead faith, an active faith with a verbal faith. A live or active faith involves actions and not just words. True religion is real faith in God along with a consistent love of one's neighbour. The live faith is demonstrated by its good deeds.

Today Jesus give the conditions of following him – they must renounce themselves and take up their cross daily.

Saturday   **Jm 3:1-10 Mk 9:2-13**

James gives very sound advice. The person who controls the tongue is a perfect person. The tongue is like the bit in the horse's mouth, or the helmsman on a ship. Both are used to control. So guarding the tongue can control the whole person. It is wrong if the tongue is used both to bless God and also to curse humankind, made in God's image.

The disciples were given a very unique experience – to strengthen their faith that was still so weak. He was transfigured before them and they got a glimpse of how he was in his glory.

Seventh Week in Ordinary Time – 2

Monday   **Jm 3:13-18 Mk 2:1-11**

James strongly contrasts the harmony that comes from wisdom and the disharmony that comes from bitterness and jealousy. Heavenly wisdom leads to peace, compassion and good works. Earthly wisdom promotes self. Peacemakers sow the seeds which will bear fruit in holiness.

Jesus casts out the difficult devil – this kind needs prayer.

Tuesday   **Jm 4:1-10 Mk 9:30-37**

Christians are not perfect and must strive to let God's grace rule in their hearts. The wickedness of 'desire' leads to murder, quarrelling and self-indulgence, even in prayers. Christians who are still under the dominance of this 'desire' or envy are friends of the world and so are enemies of God. God is a jealous God and wants us for himself. So we must wage war on sin, run away from the devil and give in to God. The nearer you go to God, the nearer he comes to you. Clean your hands and clear your minds and God will lift you up.

Jesus speaks about his future sufferings and yet he finds his disciples talking about who was the greatest. 'You must be simple like a little child – that is the way to welcome me.'

Wednesday   **Jm 4:13-17 Mk 9:38-40**

James reminds us that we are not fully in control. We are no more than a mist that is here for a little while and then disappears. So we plan everything in accordance with God's will. God is Lord, not we. So we make a complete conversion to God – a conversion of our whole heart, mind and strength.

A timely reminder by Jesus to his disciples that anyone who is not against him must be for him.

Thursday   **Jm 5:1-6 Mk 9:41-50**

James gives a strong warning to those who got their riches by exploiting others. Their wealth is all rotting and their clothes are all eaten up by moths, because they condemned the innocent and mistreated them.

Two serious points – give a cup of cold water to a fellow human and it is given to Christ. Scandalise a young one and you are worse than useless – like insipid salt.

James encourages us to avoid grumbling about others and to leave all judging in the hands of God. Take as models of perfection the prophets – their endurance showed that they were blessed. Also, we are to avoid swearing – proper speech is blessing and praise – this builds up the community.

Jesus gives his disciples a strong warning that marriage must be protected, and that a proper marriage can never end in divorce.

Saturday   **Jm 5:13-20 Mk 10:13-16**

In this final extract James encourages us to pray always, to pray with the faith of Elijah, to pray for those who are ill. Indeed, those who are ill should be anointed with oil in the name of the Lord – a reference to the sacrament of the anointing of the sick. They will be healed and their sins will be forgiven. Finally, he reminds us of the importance of bringing back anyone who has strayed from the right path. When we do this we will find favour with God.

Jesus gives a good practical example of how we are to be – like little children. Otherwise we shall not enter the kingdom of heaven.

Eighth Week in Ordinary Time – 2

Monday I P 1:3-9 Mk 10:17-27

Peter's first letter is very pastoral and was written to Christians scattered throughout the provinces of Asia Minor. It aims at encouraging these new converts in the face of the real problems and crises that they meet in their daily lives. It reminds them of their election by God, and the noble and rich life they have in Christ after their conversion. The Christian God cares for them and exalts them, and is far superior to their former pagan gods. It opens with a beautiful prayer, which sums up the Christian teaching. We have been given new birth through the death of Jesus Christ and with it the hope of an everlasting inheritance. In the meantime we are filled with a great joy because we love him.

Jesus shows that the Commandments are only the basic rules of good living. He presents great ideals for us to follow as well. The rich man found these too hard – if we become too attached to riches we will never live up to the ideals of Jesus Christ.

Tuesday I P 1:10-16 Mk 10:28-31

Peter tells his readers to realise that they are specially privileged. The prophets of old foretold that grace would come to them – it wasn't for the prophets themselves. So be filled with joy and be holy in all you do.

Those who do try to follow the ideals of Jesus Christ and leave all to follow him, will definitely receive their reward. This reward will be greater than they can ever expect in this life – it will be eternal life.

Wednesday I P 1:18-25 Mk 10:32-45

Peter asks the Christians to be faithful to their conversion, to remember the price of their ransom. It wasn't flesh and blood, it wasn't anything corruptible like gold or silver, but the blood of Christ. The response to this act of redemption should be the effort to have love for each other that is real and from the heart. The new birth has come from the everlasting word of God, the Good News.

Suffering is to be the lot of Christians, just as it was the lot of Jesus. So too is service with generosity. The Son of Man did not come to be served, but to serve, and to give his life as a ransom for many.

Thursday   **I P 2:2-5. 9-12 Mk 10:46-52**

Peter uses very rich images. Christ is the living stone, rejected by people,
but precious to God. We too must become living stones making a temple
for the Lord. We are a chosen race, a royal priesthood, a consecrated
nation, a people set apart. Now we are the people of God. So be
honourable among the people.

We have a great example of the power of faith. The blind man at the
roadside would not give up in spite of those trying to quieten him. As a
result of his commitment he was cured.

Friday   **I P 4:7-13 Mk 11:11-26**

We skip to near the end of the letter, where Peter lists off various
household duties and the attitudes the new Christians should have.
Because they have God's grace, Christians are expected to show
distinctive virtues – constant sincere love, hospitality and generosity.
They must use the special grace given to each.

Two lessons are given today. Respect the house of God. Have faith in
God and your prayer will be heard. In your prayer always include one
asking for forgiveness just as you forgive others.

Saturday   **Jude 20-25 Mk 11:27-33**

Before we hear St Peter's second letter, we pause to listen to St Jude. This
short letter seems to have been written to combat some heresies. It does
not mention the heretics, so that they will not get any free publicity. He
reminds the readers that they must build on the foundation of their holy
faith. Pray to the Holy Spirit and keep within the love of God, wait for the
mercy of Jesus Christ. He finishes with a poetic prayer of praise to God.

Jesus is too shrewd to be caught out by the chief priests, who were
jealous of his influence. If they couldn't tell whether John's baptism came
from heaven or man, then he wouldn't tell them where his authority came
from. Open your eyes and you will know the answer.

Ninth Week in Ordinary Time – 2

Monday   **II P 1:2-7 Mk 12:1-12**

This was probably not written by Peter, but by a devoted churchman many years after Peter's time. But it reflects Peter's teachings and deals with some topics of great relevance today. The main debate is between living faith and practical atheism. Christians have been given a guarantee of something great and wonderful to come, by which they will be able to share the divine nature. To achieve this they have to work at goodness, self-control, patience and kindness.

The parable of the vineyard and the unjust stewards – like the Jewish leaders. The crowds loved Jesus for this story. The leaders were very angry, but could do nothing.

Tuesday   **II P 3:11-15.17-18 Mk 12:13-17**

The writer encourages the people to live holy and saintly lives as they wait for the Day of the Lord – they should do their best to live lives without spot or stain and not be influenced by those around them who have no principles. Go on growing in grace and knowledge of Jesus Christ.

The leaders now tried to catch Jesus out. 'Should we have to pay tax?' If his answer was no, the Romans would object; if yes, the Jews would object. He got out of the trap.

Wednesday   **II Tm 1:1-3.6-12 Mk 12:18-27**

Timothy was a convert from Lystra who accompanied Paul on his second missionary journey. He left him in Ephesus to continue his work there. This letter, along with the first letter to Timothy and the letter to Titus are called the pastoral letters, since they deal with issues regarding the ongoing care of the communities founded by Paul. This is a more personal letter to Timothy than the first. Paul is warning against false teachings. In this first part Paul is reminding Timothy to fan into flame the gift given to him, when he laid his hands on him – there must be no timidity, but only the Spirit of power, love and self-control. Bear the hardships that this fidelity will bring.

The Sadducees, who had no belief in life after death, tried to set another trap. Jesus got out of that too – marriage was to ensure life; it is not necessary in eternity.

Thursday   II Tm 2:8-15 Mk 12:28-34

Paul is speaking from the heart. Timothy must not be afraid of the hardships that preaching the Good News will bring. Teach the people the message given to him and never be ashamed of it. If we have died with Christ, we shall live with him; if we hold firm, then we shall reign with him.

They still questioned him: Which are the greatest Commandments? He gave the answer that every good Jew should know.

Friday   II Tm 3:10-17 Mk 12:35-37

Timothy had difficulties in looking after his church. There were many who tried to propose false doctrines. Paul encourages him by referring to the many sufferings he endured for the sake of the Good News. He suggests that he use scripture to help him in his work, because it is inspired by God.

Jesus hints at the fact that he is a man of David's line, but also God, David's Lord.

Saturday   II Tm 4:1-8 Mk 12:38-44

Paul gives Timothy a solemn commission – before God and before Christ Jesus I put this duty to you. He must carry out his job of teacher and guardian of the faith; he must rebuke and give correction and do it all with patience. If left to themselves, people will go after every novel idea that is presented to them. Paul finishes by referring to his own death. He has fought the good fight, he has run the race, he has kept the faith. Soon he is to receive the crown of righteousness.

Now Jesus attacks the hypocritical attitudes of the Pharisees – proud and overbearing. He contrasts this with the attitude of the poor widow. She was total in her commitment, while the others were conditional.

Tenth Week in Ordinary Time – 2

Monday   **I K 17:1-6 Mt 5:1-12**

We move back to the history of the Israelites again and take up where we left off some weeks ago. The old kingdom of David and Solomon has been divided in two, Israel in the north and Judah in the south. For the next few weeks we hear from the prophets in the reign of Ahab, king of Israel between 869 and 850 BC, about sixty years after Solomon. He was condemned because he married Jezebel, a foreign princess, and was led to worship false gods. The prophet Elijah suddenly appears to condemn Ahab and foretells the drought. Elijah is looked after by the Lord.

Today we switch to the gospel of St Matthew and take it up at the beginning of the Sermon on the Mount. Here we have the real commandments of Jesus – these are the ideals that he expects us to strive to achieve. These are the marks of the true follower – poor in spirit, gentle, hungry and thirsty for justice, merciful, pure in heart, peacemaking, suffering for Christ.

Tuesday   **I K 17:7-16 Mt 5:13-16**

Today we have another account of the acts of the Lord's power through the prophet Elijah. The drought foretold by him was now taking place. It was Ahab's sin that brought suffering on the people of Israel. Elijah's fidelity brings nourishment. The woman who looked after him had faith and so Elijah was able to bring her nourishment too. For the duration of the drought, she would always have food – 'jar of meal shall not be spent, jug of oil shall not be emptied.'

The followers of Jesus are expected to be noticed – like salt, which adds zest to food, or a city on a hilltop, or a lamp on a stand. Only if people can see our good works will they give praise to God.

Wednesday   **I K 18:20-39 Mt 5:17-19**

Today we have the dramatic story of Elijah and the prophets of Baal. Baal was the fertility god worshipped by Jezebel and Ahab. At issue was the question of which god controls the fertility of the land. While the Israelites were in the desert, their God was seen as a Warrior God. Now they were settled and needed fertility in their land and among their animals. Many worshipped both to be on the safe side. Ahab met Elijah at Mount Carmel and we see the calm behaviour of Elijah contrasted with the activity of the ecstatic prophets of Baal. As a result they see that there is only one, true God, and that God must be worshipped by all.

The law of the old covenant was good – all parts will be completed by Jesus. They must be interpreted in the proper spirit by the teachers and promoted by them in full.

Thursday   I K 18:41-46 Mt 5:20-26

Only when the Lord's supremacy has been established and accepted by all, does the drought cease and the rains fall. Now Elijah has clearly shown to Ahab that he is the prophet of the one, true Lord, who must be worshipped by all.

Continuing his advice about Old Testament law which we heard yesterday, Jesus condemns some of the Pharisees because they interpreted the law to suit themselves. 'You have heard it said... but I say to you.' For the next few days we hear this over and over again. Sincerity of heart and genuine concern are most important in dealing with others. So be reconciled with your brother before honouring God.

Friday   I K 19:9. 11-16 Mt 5:27-32

In spite of all his work, Elijah finds that many of the people of Israel continue to desert the Lord and he is very despondent. He travels for forty days and nights and reaches Mount Horeb or Sinai to find the Lord. God was not found in the expected elements – wind, earthquake or fire, but in the still voice – the 'whispering sound'. The Lord lifts Elijah's depression and assures him that he has not deserted his Chosen People.

Jesus reiterates his teaching on obeying the laws of their religion from their hearts. Mere ritual observance is not enough. Adultery, for instance – a sin which the Jews regarded as very serious – can be committed by giving in to serious lustful thoughts. 'You have heard it said... but I say to you.'

Saturday   I K 19:19-21 Mt 5:33-37

The prophet Elijah picks Elisha as his successor. He consecrates him by throwing his mantle over him. Elisha then turns his back on his past and follows him. Later, after a long period of training, he is to take over from Elijah.

Jesus gives another positive interpretation of the law. 'You have heard it said... but I say to you.' There is no need to swear to the truth if one is sincere – a 'yes' means 'yes' and a 'no' means 'no'.

Eleventh Week in Ordinary Time – 2

Monday   **I K 21:1-16 Mt 5:38-42**

Today and tomorrow we have the story of how Ahab got Naboth's vineyard, through the deviousness of Jezebel, his wife, and the consequences for the king when confronted by the prophet Elijah. Naboth would not sell his property because of the laws of his religion. The king reluctantly accepts, but Jezebel, who had killed prophets and threatened Elijah, got it for him, getting Naboth killed in the process.

Jesus continues his radical teachings. Not any more is it to be an eye for an eye. The follower of Christ goes even to the opposite extreme to try and bring about the wicked person's conversion.

Tuesday   **I K 21:17-29 Mt 5:43-48**

Elijah now confronts the wicked king Ahab for his double dealing. He foretells terrible doom for him and his wife – the dogs will lick your blood and eat your wife. But Ahab does penance and the Lord relents – the disaster will strike his house in the days of his son.

Jesus gives his sixth radical teaching. 'You have heard it said... but I say to you.' They must now love their enemy. God makes no distinctions, but awaits the conversion of the sinner. You must aim to be perfect as your heavenly Father is perfect.

Wednesday   **II K 2:1. 6-14 Mt 6:1-6. 16-18**

We move to the second book of Kings and the end of Elijah's ministry. His true successor is Elisha, who had followed him very closely. Now, when Elijah uses his cloak to divide the waters of the Jordan, he is the only one of the group who goes across with him. He sees the vision of Elijah being taken up to heaven in a whirlwind. He destroyed his own cloak, took that left behind by Elijah the symbol of his power. He uses it to recross the river to join the rest of the company of prophets.

Three religious practices had a very high priority for the Jews – almsgiving, prayer and fasting. Here Jesus warns against any form of 'showiness' in carrying out these three excellent practices. 'Your Father, who sees all that is done in secret, will reward you.'

Thursday
Si 48:1-14 Mt 6:7-15

We jump to the book of Sirach to hear the great canticle of praise for the prophet, Elijah. All his great works are summed up in this poem – the drought and how he ended it, the various miracles he performed, his speaking with the Lord at Horeb, and finally his disappearance in the great whirlwind. Elisha was filled with his spirit and continued his work.

Yesterday Jesus spoke of the way to say prayers. He now gives an example, which has become the 'Our Father'. There are three 'You-petitions': may your name be held holy, may your kingdom come, may your will be done. These are followed by three 'we-petitions': give us our daily bread, forgive us our debts, do not put us to the test but save us. He finishes by pointing out that our willingness to forgive others is the necessary condition for getting God's forgiveness.

Friday
II K 11:1-4. 9-18. 20 Mt 6:19-23

We move south into the kingdom of Judah some years after Ahab in the north. It was still ruled by the descendants of David. His dynasty was to remain, yet when King Ahaziah died his mother took over and tried to get rid of all the descendants of David. But the sister of the dead king saved Ahaziah's child, Joash. When he was seven years old he was anointed by the priest of the Temple, with the support of the military. They killed the queen and knocked down the temple of Baal.

The final section of the sermon gives us some practical advice concerning the pursuit of Christian holiness. Earthly treasures are fragile and we mustn't depend on them. Store up heavenly treasure instead. Aim to have a sound spiritual vision.

Saturday
II Ch 24:17-25 Mt 6:24-34

The second book of Chronicles gives us the account of how Joash behaved himself as King of Judah. Jehoiada was the priest who looked after him when he was hidden in the Temple. While he was alive the king carried out the Lord's work and got rid of the Baal temple. However, when the priest died he was influenced by others. Jehoiada's son tried to prophesy against him, so Joash dispatched him. But the Lord would not allow such evil to go unpunished, and eventually Joash was overcome and killed.

Some more practical advice for Christian living. We must not worry about material things, but believe that the Lord is looking after us. We are worth more than the birds in the sky, the flowers and grass in the fields.

Twelfth Week in Ordinary Time – 2

Monday   **II K 17:5-8. 13-15. 18 Mt 7:1-5**

We skip some years to around 720 BC to the reign of Hosea in the northern kingdom, Israel. Assyria destroyed the kingdom once and for all about 721 BC. All the leading citizens were exiled and the country planted with foreigners. This was a warning to Judah in the south – Israel was destroyed because of the evil committed against the Lord. They refused to listen to the warnings of the prophets. If Judah did not reform, the same fate would befall it.

Jesus tells us that it is very important not to judge one another – very often we are the ones who need to be judged and corrected.

Tuesday   **II K 19:9-11. 14-21.31-36 Mt 7:6, 12-14**

At the time of the destruction of Israel, Hezekiah was king of Judah. He was regarded as a good king because he carried out the work of the Lord. He was threatened by the Assyrians and consulted the prophet Isaiah. He gave the prophecy that eventually a remnant would go out from Jerusalem; their God was a jealous God and would look after them. The city of Jerusalem would be spared for now. And this is what happened.

Jesus tells us to treat others as we would like to be treated ourselves. He also reminds us that this is not easy.

Wednesday   **II K 22:8-13. 23:1-3 Mt 7:15-20**

About forty years later we come to the reign of another good king, Josiah. While the Temple was being repaired the book of the law was found and this gave the king the impetus to bring about a great reform. He purged all the pagan elements that could be found in Judah, where many of the rural people worshipped fertility gods.

A good person will produce good results. Beware of the false prophets – you will know them by their fruits.

Thursday   **II K 24:8-17 Mt 7:21-29**

When Josiah died the leaders went back to their evil ways again. Now the

Babylonians were in power, under their great leader Nebuchadnezzar. Jerusalem was besieged and captured and the chief citizens brought into exile. The Temple was also desecrated. Only the poor were left behind, and Zedekiah was put on the throne.

Those who listen to the words of Jesus and take them seriously are like the person who builds a house on a rock. It perseveres.

Friday   **II K 25:1-12 Mt 8:1-4**

Disaster finally struck and Judah was destroyed. The people of Judah continually disregarded the warnings of the prophets. The king, set up by Nebuchadnezzar, started a rebellion which was put down savagely. Now the city and the Temple were totally destroyed and the rest of the citizens brought off to Babylon. Thus began, in 586 BC, the seventy-year Babylonian exile. It was from these exiles that the remnant would come back to continue the dynasty of David and the Chosen People of God.

Jesus cures the leper who has faith in him. He also tells him to obey the laws of his religion and show himself to the priests to get his cure confirmed.

Saturday   **Lm 2:2. 10-14.18-19 Mt 8:5-17**

We finish our history of the Chosen People as they go off into exile with a very sad reading from the book of Lamentations. This is a large prayer book, written to help people cope with grief. Even meaningless suffering can have a good purpose, for God, who is compassionate enough to bear our human outrage, walks us through the dark valleys and onto the plateaux of peace. We see great sadness in this extract and an intense cry to God for deliverance. Everything that they held dear was gone. All they could hold onto was the prophecy that eventually a remnant of the people of David would continue as God's Chosen People. In their misery, their Lord would look after them in his own way.

We have a great example of faith – Jesus cures the centurion's servant and goes on to demonstrate his healing ministry. 'He took our sicknesses away and carried our diseases for us.'

Thirteenth Week in Ordinary Time – 2

Monday   **Am 2:6-10. 13-16 Mt 8:18-22**

Amos came from the southern kingdom, but preached mainly in the northern kingdom about forty years or so before its destruction. He was not a member of a guild of prophets, but was a shepherd and a dresser of the fruits of sycamores. Unlike other prophets he did not depend on the king for support and so could speak independently. He used very strong oracles to condemn different types of social injustice – each one beginning 'It is the Lord who speaks.' Today's section comes after he uses oracles to condemn Israel's neighbours – his listeners would have reacted very favourably. Then suddenly he issues an oracle against Israel. Now they have to listen as he lists the crimes they have committed against their fellow human beings. They did this in spite of the care and attention that God had given them. They broke the covenant that God made with them and for this they would be punished.

Full commitment is necessary if we are to follow Jesus. We pray for that commitment.

Tuesday   **Am 3:1-8.4:11-12 Mt 8:23-27**

Amos gives another strong oracle against Israel and we have a part of it here. These people have been specially favoured by God – he took them out of Egypt – and yet they commit serious crimes against one another. They are acting like the animals. 'Now be prepared to meet your Lord.'

Faith is also necessary if we are to follow Jesus. We pray for an increase of faith.

Wednesday   **Am 5:14-15. 21-24 Mt 8:28-34**

'Woe to those who do evil.' Rather, Amos preaches, seek good and not evil, so that you may live, so that the Lord will be truly with you. Only then will your sacrifices and external prayers be of value. Let your justice surge like water and your integrity like an unfailing stream. How relevant this is to our day!

We have the strange story of the demoniacs being cured and the devils ending up in the pigs – animals whose meat the Jews were forbidden to eat. We pray that evil may be uprooted from our hearts.

Thursday   Am 7:10-17 Mt 9:1-8

We have a short biographical account of the work of Amos. The priests of
the pagan gods at Bethel in the northern kingdom tried to get him out and
back to Judah, because they did not like what he was saying. He did not
depend on the king, as the other prophets did; he believed that the Lord
had called him, so he was not afraid to make his prophecy, which told the
Israelites that they would be sent into exile.

Behind many of the miracles of Jesus was a spiritual message. Today it
is more explicit – he can forgive sins just as he can cure the paralytic. We
pray for trust in the mercy of God.

Friday   Am 8:4-6.9-12 Mt 9:9-13

We have further denunciations of the social injustices that the rich were
inflicting on the poor. They were being swindled, trampled on and
reduced almost to slavery. But the day of the Lord is coming, a day when
the sun will really be eclipsed, a day of mourning, a day when you will
look for God and will not find him.

Jesus reminds his followers that he has come not to call the virtuous,
but sinners. Mercy was vital in his dealings with others. We pray that we
can be merciful.

Saturday   Am 9:11-15 Mt 9:14-17

In this last extract we have two oracles, which were probably written after
the exile. These give the returned exiles some hope. In the first oracle the
nation will be rebuilt – 'I will re-erect the tottering hut of David, it is the
Lord who speaks'. In the second the cities and vineyards will be restored
– 'I will plant them in their own country, never to be rooted out again; it
is the Lord who speaks.'

While Jesus is with his disciples they will not fast. The time will come
when they will. Everything in its own time.

Fourteenth Week in Ordinary Time – 2

Monday   **Ho 2:16-18. 21-22 Mt 9:18-26**

We come to the second of the twelve minor prophets. Hosea lived around the same time as Amos, some years before the destruction of the northern kingdom. It was a time of great instability and crisis for Israel. His oracles are in the form of very beautiful poetry, and he mainly attacks the idolatry of the people. They had turned their backs on the God who saved them and made a covenant with them. In the first part Hosea uses his marriage in a metaphorical way. He married one who was a prostitute, who had taken part in pagan fertility rites. She had three unhappy children. Israel had behaved in a similar way and had done evil things . But there is hope. The day will come when his wife – and Israel – will return to the master, away from the despicable pagan rites and back to integrity, justice, love and tenderness.

We have further examples of the healing power of Jesus. Let us trust in that power that can come to us through the Blessed Sacrament.

Tuesday   **Ho 8:4-7. 11-13 Mt 9:32-38**

Hosea gives a powerful denunciation of the idolatrous practices of the Israelites. Politically, they have ignored God. Religiously they have blasphemed God. Because they sow the wind, they will reap the whirlwind. The Lord will remember their iniquity and punish their sins and they will be back to their pre-Exodus days.

Jesus continues to carry out his work of healing and casting out devils – though the Pharisees remained sceptical. Jesus is sad because the people are without good leaders.

Wednesday   **Ho 10:1-3. 7-8.12 Mt 10:1-7**

More doom and gloom is forecast for the Israelites by Hosea. They were once gifted by God. But they rejected him and turned to worship of fertility gods instead. Their kingdom will be destroyed and the people will be so afraid that they will want the mountains to cover them. However, there is hope if they return to their former ways of integrity, justice, and actively seeking the Lord for his salvation.

The apostles are named and sent to the lost sheep of the house of Israel. Later they would travel to Samaria and to the rest of the known world.

Thursday   **Ho 11:1. 3-4. 8-9 Mt 10:7-15**

Today we have one of the most striking feminine images of God in the

Hebrew scriptures. God has treated the people as a mother treats her child, even when it is wayward. 'When Israel was a child I loved him, I called him out of Egypt, I took him in my arms and looked after him.' Now, the child has done evil and should be destroyed, but the merciful love of God wins the day – 'I have no wish to destroy.'

Jesus gives his instructions to the apostles. Above all they must bring peace to the homes and towns they visit.

Friday   Ho 14:2-10 Mt 10:16-23

At the end of the book we have a very optimistic section. The Lord says to Israel: 'Come back to the Lord your God, take all iniquity away, offer words of praise. Then I will love them with all my heart. I will give them my divine gift of life – symbolised by the dew, Israel will bloom like the lily, will have the beauty of the olive, will come back to live in my shade.' The final sentence is important for us too. Understand and know all of these words. The paths of the Lord are straight: the just can walk in them, but sinners stumble.

Jesus gives more instructions to his apostles. They must not be afraid of what to say – the Spirit of his Father will be with them. He hints that they may run into trouble for the sake of the kingdom of heaven.

Saturday   Is 6:1-8 Mt 10:24-33

Isaiah was one of the major prophets. After the Psalms, this book is the longest in the Old Testament, and may have been written by a number of people. These are often referred to as the First, Second and Third Isaiah. It spans several centuries, from before the destruction of Israel and Judah, through the exile and return of the remnant, to the efforts to revive the old kingdom (742-500 BC). There are three main themes – the Temple at Jerusalem becomes a symbol of Messianic hopes, there is a gradual change in emphasis to include the Gentiles within Israel's salvation, and there is a great sense of justice. God is the Holy One of Israel and his holiness shows up the sinfulness of humanity. We must have faith and trust in God and not in our own resources. It was a very popular book both among the Jews and early Christians. Now it is read mainly during Advent and for some of Lent. We look at it here for the next week. Today we have the account of the call of Isaiah. He had a vision – he saw God and was terrified. But God was calling him to be his spokesman or prophet. This Isaiah freely accepted.

Jesus gives more instructions to his apostles. The disciple should grow to be like his teacher; what I say in the dark, tell in the light; fear those who can kill both the body and soul; anyone who declares himself for me I will declare before my Father.

Fifteenth Week in Ordinary Time – 2

Monday   **Is 1:11-17 Mt 10:34-11:1**

Again and again we hear the prophets condemn the sacrifices, the rituals, and the external prayers of people who do not practice justice or take care of the orphan and widow. Here Isaiah calls the local leaders, princes of Sodom, the city that was destroyed because of its corruption. The same fate awaits them. If their hands are full of blood they cannot offer true worship to God. Ritual is only as good as the intentions its expresses.

Being a follower of Christ involves much hardship as many will not accept his teachings. This may cause division, even among families. The true follower would see Christ in all.

Tuesday   **Is 7:1-9 Mt 11:20-24**

About ten years before its destruction, Israel, also called Ephraim, was allied to Syria. They tried to get Judah to join with them against the common enemy, Assyria. Ahaz was the king of Judah at this time and he did not want to join, but was very afraid. Isaiah told him that the other countries would soon be no more and that the kingdom of David would last provided that they believed in the Lord.

In spite of his miracles, the people did not listen to Jesus. He showed his sorrow in his remarks – these towns would suffer more than Tyre, Sidon and Sodom.

Wednesday   **Is 10:5-7. 13-16 Mt 11:25-27**

Pagan Assyria was the rod with which the Lord chastised Israel. However, Assyria went too far and destroyed the country. The king believed that everything was done through his power. But the axe cannot claim more credit than the man who yields it. For their disobedience and pride this kingdom too would be destroyed. All this took place after the destruction of Israel, when those in Jerusalem were afraid that the same fate would befall them.

No one knows the Father except the Son and those to whom he revealed him. We thank God for choosing us and pray that we live up to his calling.

Thursday   **Is 26:7-9. 12. 16-18 Mt 11:28-30**

Isaiah gives us a beautiful psalm of trust in the goodness of God. This affirms the life of the righteous poor. The lords who ruled over the people are soon to be no more and cannot rise. But out of the remnant will arise a new people of God. There will be a resurrection of the Israelite people. Here too we seem to have the beginning of the idea of the doctrine of the resurrection of the dead.

Jesus is the source of consolation for all those who are burdened with life's problems.

Friday   **Is 38:1-6.21-22. 7-8 Mt 12:1-8**

In this, the last extract from Isaiah, we have the account of the last king before the exile. He is afraid and ill, but because of his personal faithfulness, he is healed through the prayer of Isaiah. He was given a supernatural sign to help him believe. This story was to inspire the people and give them a sense of awe before their God, in whom they must trust. Those who remain faithful will form the remnant after the exile.

We have an example of how the Pharisees put the details of the law before the person. They made the laws of the sabbath very strict indeed. Instead of it being a day of rest to honour God, it was a day filled with restrictions.

Saturday   **Mi 2:1-5 Mt 12:14-21**

After a few short snippets from Isaiah we now listen to the next of the prophets, Micah. He lived around the same time as Isaiah, Amos, and Hosea. He was a prophet in the southern kingdom. He is preoccupied with issues of social justice and the coming of the Assyrian invasion. Here he condemns those who plan evil against others in the community, especially by taking the fertile land between the mountains and the sea. Just as they plot, so will the Lord plot against them and they will be stripped of everything.

The same Pharisees began to plot against Jesus, but he was only fulfiling the prophecy of Isaiah – 'Here is my servant whom I have sent.'

Sixteenth Week in Ordinary Time – 2

Monday   **Mi 6:1-4.6-8 Mt 12:38-42**

The people, who were brought out of the land of Egypt have turned their backs on him by the way they treat others. Today Micah is telling those who think they can placate God by ritual offerings, that what God really wants is sincerity of heart. They have been reminded of this many times, to no avail. What is needed is 'to act justly, to love tenderly and to walk humbly with your God'.

The people are looking for a sign that Jesus is from God – they won't accept his words or his miracles. So he gave them the sign of Jonah – he would be three days in the earth and rise up again. We pray for a deeper faith and greater sincerity in dealing with one another.

Tuesday   **Mi 7:14-15. 18-20 Mt 12:46-50**

We have the last extract from Micah today. In this prayer of confidence he gives the people in exile a message of hope. He sees God as a gentle shepherd leading his flock to really good pastures. God does not let his people down if they try to follow him. They will be a model.

We are reminded in the gospel that Jesus regards anyone who does the will of his Father as part of his family. We pray for a better realisation of that closeness.

Wednesday   **Jr 1:1.4-10 Mt 13:1-9**

Jeremiah was the second major prophet after Isaiah. He lived about a hundred years later in very eventful times. During his lifetime there were five kings in Judah and he was there to see the destruction of Jerusalem and the kingdom of Judah. He was a rather shy and extremely sensitive person. He was called to be a prophet during his adolescence – as we saw today. 'Before I formed you in the womb I knew you... I have appointed you as prophet to the nations.' 'Do not say "I am a child." Go now to those I send you.' The Lord touched his mouth and said 'There! I am putting my words into your mouth.'

In the gospel we have the well-known parable of the sower and the seed. We pray that the word of God which has been sown in us will produce good fruit.

Thursday   **Jr 2:1-3.7-8.12-13 Mt 13:10-17**

Jeremiah is in a very sad mood today, and very anxious about his people. He speaks for God – I remember the affection of your youth, you followed me through the wilderness. Israel was sacred to the Lord. I brought you to a fertile country to enjoy its produce and good things; but no sooner had you entered than you defiled my land. My people have abandoned me, the fountain of living water. But, worse, they have made for themselves cisterns, leaky ones that can hold no water.

Jesus speaks to the people in parables. It was the method of the time. The stories always bring a spiritual message. Only those who close their ears will miss the message – 'you will listen and listen again, but not understand.' We pray that our hearts be open to the word of God.

Friday   **Jr 3:14-17 Mt 13:18-23**

The gentle and shy Jeremiah is still anxious for his people. Come back, disloyal children, for I alone am your master. I will look after you and give you the best. This message is summed up in our responsorial psalm, 'The Lord will guard us as a shepherd guards his flock.'

Jesus explains the parable he taught in Wednesday's gospel, about the sower and the seed. We pray that our hearts may be rich soil to accept the seed of the Lord and bear fruit a hundredfold.

Saturday   **Jr 7:1-11 Mt 13:24-30**

Today we see the gentle Jeremiah opening his heart to the people at the gate of the Temple. You come with words, you believe that it is enough to say that this is the sanctuary of the Lord. You think that you are safe – safe to go on committing all the wrongdoings – you steal, you murder, you commit adultery, you perjure yourselves, you offer worship to false gods. No, you must turn from these things, and then you can come to the sanctuary of the Lord.

Another parable from Jesus reminds us that the evil and the good will live side-by-side until the Day of Judgment.

Seventeenth Week in Ordinary Time – 2

Monday   **Jr 13:1-11 Mt 13:31-35**

As we have seen, Jeremiah was a rather shy and extremely sensitive person. Today we see him teaching a sort of parable. 'Just as a loincloth clings to a man's waist, so I intended you to cling to me, for you to be my people.' But 'this evil people who refused to listen to my words and followed alien gods will become like the loincloth [which Jeremiah buried], good for nothing.'

The gospel continues with more parables – stories with a spiritual message. Today we are reminded that the word of God starts out very small, but grows and grows. We pray that we can allow the word to grow in us.

Tuesday   **Jr 14:17-22 Mt 13:36-43**

Jeremiah did not relish the public life he had. But he had made a commitment to his God. Today he is making a very heartfelt prayer so that this God would come and rescue his people. 'O our God, you are our hope.'

Jesus explains the parable of the good seed and the weeds. Just as the good farmer lets both grow together, so will God allow good and evil to co-exist side by side. But there will be a day of judgment when the good will be separated from the evil.

Wednesday   **Jr 15:10. 16-21 Mt 13:44-46**

The shy, quiet Jeremiah is very anxious because he is getting a lot of opposition from the people. They don't like his message. Often he feels that even the Lord has abandoned him. But the Lord told him that in spite of the sufferings he had to undergo, 'I mean to deliver you from the hands of the wicked and redeem you from the clutches of the violent.'

We hear some more parables today. If we really appreciated the word of God, we would pay a big price, make a huge sacrifice, to ensure that it is being nurtured.

Thursday   **Jr 18:1-6 Mt 13:47-53**

Jeremiah loved his people and wanted to bring them back to the Lord.
Today we see him using one of his many life stories and messages from
God. Just as the potter moulds the clay, so will God do for us. 'As the
clay is in the potter's hand, so you are in mine, House of Israel.'

Today we have the parable of the fisherman's net. All sorts of fish are
caught, good and bad. Later these will be separated. The wicked shall be
cast out. We pray for a stronger determination to stay on the road with
Jesus Christ.

Friday   **Jr 26:1-9 Mt 13:54-58**

The quiet, inoffensive Jeremiah runs into serious difficulties today. The
'official' prophets – the paid ones – did not like to hear what Jeremiah
said. 'If you will not listen to me ..... I will make this city a curse for all
the nations of the earth.' So they threw him out.

Jesus also meets difficulties. Back at home they couldn't understand
how he got all his knowledge. Their scepticism kept him from doing any
work there. 'A prophet is despised in his own country.' Let us pray that
we will open our hearts fully to the Lord.

Saturday   **Jr 26:11-16. 24 Mt 14:1-12**

Today Jeremiah had a lucky escape. He continued to preach a message
that was unpopular because he was convinced that the Lord had spoken to
him. He was a great man of prayer.

In the gospel we move away from the parables. Today we read about
the fate of St John the Baptist, who remained loyal to his mission. Let us
pray for that commitment.

Eighteenth Week in Ordinary Time – 2

Monday   **Jr 28:1-17 Mt 14:13-21**

Jeremiah was living in dangerous times – at this stage many had been
exiled to Babylon. The false prophet Hananiah gave the people false
hope. Jeremiah had been going around showing the subjection of God's
people by wearing a yoke like the farm animals. This subjection wasn't
going to be as easy as breaking a wooden yoke, but as difficult as
destroying an iron one. The remnant of the people would have to wait for
their time of purification.

Jesus, saddened by the death of John the Baptist, tries to get away to a
quiet place. The crowds follow him, so he puts his own grief aside and
ministers to them, even making sure they had enough to eat. This miracle
is the forerunner of the miracle of the Eucharist, where he gives us his
Body and Blood as spiritual food. Let us ever grow in our love for that
sacrament.

Tuesday   **Jr 30:1-2.12-15.18-22 Mt 14:22-36**

The people are in exile. They are in the depths of despair. They feel there
is no hope. But the remnant are to be saved. From them will spring a new
community with one of their own to lead them. 'You shall be my people
and I will be your God.' This is Jeremiah's message of hope.

After the feeding of the multitudes he lets his disciples go back across
the lake, while he goes to pray – something he had set out to do before the
miracle. In spite of this miracle, the disciples lack faith in him, when he
comes to them walking on the water. Let us say with St Peter, 'Truly, you
are the Son of God.'

Wednesday   **Jr 31:1-7 Mt 15:21-28**

Jeremiah continues his message of hope for the remnant of the people
who are exiled in Babylon. The Lord will restore them, because they have
undergone their purification and have found pardon. I will be the God of
all the clans of Israel, they shall be my people. Shout with joy: the Lord
has saved his people, the remnant of Israel.

In the gospel we have another example of faith. This time it comes from
another alien, the Caananite woman. The disciples were embarrassed by
her and wanted to get rid of her. Jesus tested her faith and granted her
wish.

Thursday   **Jr 31:31-34 Mt 16:13-23**

This is the last reading we have from Jeremiah, that shy, gentle, suffering prophet. It is a message of hope. After their exile in Babylon, the Lord will make a new covenant with his people, one that must not be broken like the last, The Lord says, 'I will forgive their iniquity and never call their sin to mind. I will plant my law in their hearts.'

Today we have a further test of faith – this time for the disciples. It is Simon who speaks up. 'You are the Christ, the Son of the living God.' Simon is given a new name, Peter, which comes from the word for rock. He is to be the foundation of the Church. He will have the keys of God's kingdom. Let us pray that we think God's way and not our way.

Friday   **Na 2:1. 3; 3:1-3. 6-7 Mt 16:24-28**

Nahum lived around the latter years of Jeremiah. He speaks to the people of Nineveh, the capital of Judah's warring neighbour which committed so many atrocities. Nineveh has now fallen and Jeremiah tries to persuade the people to repent. He stresses the justice and mercy of God, who always comes to the defence of those who love him and keep his Commandments.

The test for being a follower of Jesus is to take up the cross daily and follow him. It is difficult to be his follower – it requires much work and hardship. But the Lord will eventually reward each one according to his or her behaviour.

Saturday   **Hab 1:12-2:4 Mt 17:14-20**

Today we move on to the prophet Habakkuk, the next prophet in chronological order. He lived towards the end of Jeremiah's lifetime. Why is God allowing so much evil and hardship to come on his people? Why do evil people go unpunished? God speaks through Habakkuk – there is hope for the just and upright; the others will get their just desserts eventually. The just must live in faithfulness and hope.

We have another reference to the necessity of faith in today's gospel. Our faith can only grow if we keep in touch with Christ through daily personal prayer. Let us try to make the effort to stay in touch.

Nineteenth Week in Ordinary Time – 2

Monday   **Ezk 1:2-5. 24-28 Mt 17:22-27**

Ezekiel was the third of the major prophets and today we begin reading his works and continue for the next two weeks. He lived at the time of the destruction of Jerusalem and was among the Israelites who went into exile in Babylon. Today we have the beginning of the great vision he had when he was first called to be a prophet of the Lord.

God has come in solidarity with all humankind in the person of Jesus. He shares in all our sufferings, including the paying of taxes.

Tuesday   **Ezk 2:8-3:4 Mt 18:1-5. 10. 12-14**

Today we have the second part of Ezekiel's great vocation vision. In the vision he was offered a scroll with prophetic writings to eat. When he had done so he was told to go to the House of Israel and tell them what the Lord had said.

You must be like the little children who have no guile. Your Father in heaven seeks out the lost sheep and tries to get them to come back.

Wednesday   **Ezk 9:1-7. 10. 18-22 Mt 18:15-20**

Ezekiel had rather strange visions. Today we see him telling the people that the remnant of those who go into exile will be purified and eventually come back to form the people of God.

Try to sort out all your problems with others on a one-to-one level. It should not be necessary to go before the higher courts.

Thursday   **Ezk 12:1-12 Mt 18:21-19:1**

Again Ezekiel is giving a sort of living parable. Just as he sneaked out through a hole in the wall into exile, so will those remaining in Jerusalem. The last of them will go to Babylon.

The parable of the unjust steward touches all our hearts. Let's learn to forgive one another.

Friday   Ezk 16:1-15. 60. 63 [16:59-63] Mt 19:3-12

Ezekiel gives a grim reminder of how the chosen people have fallen. He uses the vivid parable of the child born unloved, taken eventually and given everything, who became too fond of herself. That's what the Israelites had done.

[Even though you broke the covenant I made with you when you were a little girl, even though you will be covered with shame, I will pardon you and renew the covenant with you.]

Jesus redefines the law of marriage – what God has joined together, no-one must divide. We pray for all married couples.

Saturday   Ezk 18:1-10. 13. 30-32 Mt 19:13-15

Ezekiel reminds the people that the Lord will judge those who turn their backs on him and practice evil against others. He asks them to repent. Repent and live!

Again, be as little children – it is to such as these that the kingdom of heaven belongs.

Twentieth Week in Ordinary Time – 2

Monday   **Ezk 24:15-24 Mt 19:16-22**

Again Ezekiel uses a life parable. He tells of what happened when the wife he loved very much died. That is to be an example to the Israelites: all that mattered to the good Jew was to be taken away and the last of them deported. It was a just punishment for their sins.

We are reminded again in the gospel how easy it is for material possessions to keep God out of our lives. Let's pray for the proper attitude in using God's gifts to us.

Tuesday   **Ezk 28:1-10 Mt 19:23-30**

In the second part of Ezekiel, the prophet is now in Babylon with the deported Jews. Many of his teachings bring hope to this deported people. Some others refer to some of the neighbouring countries. Today he castigates Tyre for neglecting God and becoming greedy.

Jesus continues his teaching on treating material possessions carefully. The 'needle' in this case is believed to be the little door in a gate – the wicker door. Blessed are those who renounce the things of the world for the sake of God.

Wednesday   **Ezk 34:1-11 Mt 20:1-16**

Today Ezekiel speaks against all the false prophets that led the people away from God. They are to be called to account. The flock will be taken away from them and God will look after the remnant himself. 'The Lord is my shepherd, there is nothing that I shall want.'

We have the famous parable of the landowner and the vineyard workers. He was generous and gave to the last the same as he gave to the first. The first were upset. 'Why are you envious because I am generous?' Pray for trust in our generous God.

Thursday   **Ezk 36:23-28 Mt 22:1-14**

Ezekiel gives the displaced Israelites great hope. God will take out their hearts of stone and give them new hearts of flesh – he will give them his spirit, and through his actions his name will be glorified. He will restore them to their own land.

We have another well-known parable – the invitation to the wedding feast. We are all invited, but the least we do is prepare ourselves for entry into God's kingdom.

Friday   **Ezk 37:1-14 Mt 22:34-40**

Today we have the famous vision of the dry bones – featured in the old spiritual 'Dem dry bones'. The house of Israel is desolate at the moment, but is going to be given a new life. Their purification will soon be over and they will return to their old land and be God's people again.

On the prompting of the Pharisees, Jesus re-affirms the basic Commandments – love God, love your neighbour. All Jews were expected to follow these. Jesus wasn't making any changes here.

Saturday   **Ezk 43:1-7 Mt 23:1-12**

Today we have the last extract from the Prophet Ezekiel. The remnant of the people would return to Israel and would rebuild the Temple, where the glory of their God would remain. Can we sense that glory here in our own Church?

The Pharisees have let the people down. They interpreted the law and made it more important than the people. We must avoid this sort of hypocrisy.

Twenty-First Week in Ordinary Time – 2

Monday   **II Th 1:1-5. 11-12 Mt 23:12-22**

Today we begin reading from St Paul's second letter to the Thessalonians. He came to Thessalonica, which is modern Salonika, during his second missionary journey. It was one of the most important cities in the Roman province of Macedonia and had a sizeable Jewish community. St Paul spoke in its synagogue on three occasions, explaining that Jesus was the true Messiah. Some Jews and many Greeks accepted his teaching and became Christians. He was persecuted and had to leave. The letters were written later to console the Christians and to clarify some points of doctrine. The Thessalonians were very happy with his first letter, but as a result there were other questions to be answered. A number of the people in this city, where there were many idle, began to speculate about the Lord's second coming – why work when you are waiting for him? There was much gossip and confusion as a result. In today's extract Paul encourages his faithful followers, because their faith is continually growing. Continue what you have been doing – in this way the name of our Lord Jesus Christ will be glorified, and you will be glorified because of his grace.

There was one thing Jesus could not take and that was hypocrisy, especially from the leaders. They made things very difficult for the people. Let us keep watch over ourselves in this matter.

Tuesday   **II Th 2:1-3.14-17 Mt 23:23-26**

St Paul continues to encourage the faithful followers of Christ in Thessalonica. Don't believe the gossip that the day of the Lord's second coming has arrived or is just around the corner. Stand firm and keep the traditions that we taught you. May the Lord Jesus Christ comfort you and strengthen you.

Jesus continues today with his tirade against the hypocrisy of the spiritual leaders of the people. Pray for us priests that we may give the message of Jesus in its purity.

Wednesday   **II Th 3:6-10. 16-18 Mt 23:27-32**

In Thessalonica there were many who would not work – why work when the Lord's coming is just around the corner? Keep away from these people. Take my example – I worked very hard when I was with you. May the Lord of peace give you peace at all times.

Again we have Jesus lashing out at the hypocrisy of the scribes and Pharisees – they are like whitewashed tombs. Again, let's watch ourselves.

Thursday   **I Co 1:1-9 Mt 24:42-51**

Today we go on to St Paul's first letter to the Corinthians. Corinth was the capital of one of the great Roman provinces at the time, with two ports. It was a loose-living city, where there was a religious cult to the goddess Venus. St Paul had established his Christian community while on his second missionary journey. Some two years later a number of Christian Jews came with rather unsound doctrine – false apostles, St Paul called them. Paul's letter was in response to a letter from some influential Christians asking for guidance. He began this letter, as we saw today, with praise for those who were faithful and a prayer of thanks to God. He reminds them of the gift of the Holy Spirit who will keep them steady.

Today we are reminded to try and be ready at all times for the call of the Lord. Let us pray that we will be working hard at being faithful followers when the Lord comes for us.

Friday   **I Co 1:17-25 Mt 25:1-13**

Today Paul reminds the faithful in Corinth that they must not depend on the language of philosophy. God has shown up the foolishness of human wisdom. The Jews demand miracles and the Greeks look for wisdom, but we preach a crucified Christ – to many it is totally illogical. To the Jews this is an obstacle, to the Greeks it is madness. But to those who have been called it is a Christ who is the power and the wisdom of God.

Jesus uses a nice parable to stress the fact that we must always be ready for the call of the Lord – we do not know the day or the hour.

Saturday   **I Co 1:26-31 Mt 25:14-30**

St Paul continues his argument against depending on human reason. God shamed the wise by choosing what is foolish by human reckoning and shamed the strong by choosing what is weak by human reckoning. God has become our wisdom, virtue, holiness and freedom. If anyone wants to boast, let him boast about the Lord.

Today we have another famous parable. We are reminded that each of us is given various talents in life. They are to be used for the greater glory and honour of God. Let's do our best so that we can get the reward of the good and faithful servant and avoid the calamity of the good-for-nothing-servant.

Twenty-Second Week in Ordinary Time – 2

Monday   I Co 2:1-5 Lk 4:16-30

St Paul continues his treatise on faith. I didn't come with great philosophical and rational arguments. In fact, I came in 'fear and trembling', because I knew the people expected such philosophy. My sermons demonstrated the power of the Spirit. So your faith must depend on the power of God and not human philosophy.

For the rest of the year we read from St Luke's gospel. We take it up towards the beginning of Jesus' public mission. Jesus is sad because the people of his own city don't believe in him – a prophet is not without honour, except in his own country.

Tuesday   I Co 2:10-16 Lk 4:31-37

St Paul continues his great work on faith. He reminds the Corinthians that they can never know God if they depend on human philosophy. We teach in the way that the Spirit teaches us. We teach things spiritually. A spiritual person is able to judge the value of everything – such a person has the mind of Christ.

Away from his home town, Jesus finds more faith. The people listened to him and were amazed at the great things he did.

Wednesday   I Co 3:1-9 Lk 4:38-44

Having stated his position on knowing things through the spirit, Paul chastises the Corinthians for behaving in an unspiritual way, like ordinary people. They were letting their human values distort the true message. Their slogans demonstrated this – 'I'm for Paul', 'I'm for Apollos'. We are just servants of God – the one who plants or the one who waters. It is God who makes things grow. He makes our faith grow.

Jesus makes a great impact in the Capernaum area. He reminds his disciples that he must proclaim the Good News in other towns too.

Thursday   I Co 3:18-23 Lk 5:1-11

Paul reminds the Corinthians that to God the wisdom of this world is foolishness. God is not convinced by the arguments of the wise. You belong to Christ and Christ belongs to God.

Jesus uses the miracle of the great catch of fish as a sort of living parable. Just as you caught these fish, trusting in me, so you will bring many people to my kingdom, trusting in me.

We are all servants of Christ, stewards entrusted with the mysteries of God. Each one should be found worthy of his trust. Let God be our judge in this matter.

Again, we have the Pharisees and scribes trying to catch Jesus out. You must use the old with the old and the new with the new. You rejoice when the bridegroom is present; you are sad when he is gone.

Saturday   **I Co 4:6-15 Lk 6:1-5**

Paul upbraids the Corinthians for moving away from the teachings he gave them. 'Keep to what is written', he tells them. Don't be confident in worldly riches or influence – we are fools for the sake of Christ. Don't shirk the hardship this brings.

A continuation of yesterday's ideas – the sabbath was made for people, not people for the sabbath – and we live according to this.

Twenty-Third Week in Ordinary Time – 2

Monday   I Co 5:1-8 Lk 6:6-11

St Paul turns to another failing of the Corinthians. They are tolerating a serious ongoing case of incest in the community. Such a person must be expelled, when he continues sinning publicly. You must make sure you are not associating with people of low moral standards, because they can influence the rest – the case of the one rotten apple.

The gospel gives us another example of how the Pharisees twisted the law of Moses on the sabbath. Jesus gets the point across by showing that he was doing good and saving life by restoring the man's hand.

Tuesday   I Co 6:1-11 Lk 6:12-19

Paul takes up another matter where the Corinthians are at fault. They are bringing their own petty legal cases against one another to the pagan judge – washing their laundry in public. Paul reminds them of the type of people who will definitely not get to heaven – idolaters, adulterers, sodomites, thieves, usurers, slanderers and swindlers.

Today we see the importance of prayer. It was only after a full night of prayer that Jesus chose the apostles. Then he brought them with him as he set out to heal, forgive sins and, above all, preach the Good News. For the next few days we will have extracts from the Sermon on the Mount.

Wednesday   I Co 7:25-31 Lk 6:20-26

Paul is answering one of the questions asked by the Christians at Corinth about sex and marriage. At this stage the early Christians believed that the end of the world was near. That is why Paul suggested celibacy to those who were not already married. Those who were married must remain faithful to their commitment.

Jesus gives the basic recommendations to those who would be his followers – happy are the poor in spirit, who know the harshness of hunger and weep over their misfortune. Blessed are those who are able to take hatred, abuse, denunciation as criminals for the sake of God – their reward will be great in heaven.

Thursday   I Co 8:1-7. 11-13 Lk 6:27-38

Paul deals with another problem. Many attended functions where food that had been sacrificed to idols was available. The stronger Christians knew that there were no such thing as idols and were not worried about what they ate. But others who saw them might have thought that they were honouring the idols. For the sake of the weaker brethren, don't give any misleading messages.

Jesus expects high standards – love, do good, bless your enemies (something that was unheard of among the people of his time, and perhaps today too). Treat others well without expecting anything in return. You will be rewarded in heaven.

Friday   I Co 9:16-19. 22-27 Lk 6:39-42

Paul stresses that he preaches the gospel, because it is a duty that was given to him. He has made himself the slave of everyone to win over as many as possible. He is like the athletes striving for a trophy – but the trophy or wreath he is working for is one that does not wither.

Jesus advises his listeners – and us – to be careful about judging others. We might miss the evil in ourselves. Look at yourselves first.

Saturday   I Co 10:14-22 Lk 6:43-49

Paul comes back to the problem of those who sacrifice to idols – they are dealing with demons. You, on the other hand, have the one bread, which is a communion with the body of Christ. We share the same loaf, showing that we are one with Christ.

Jesus stresses sincerity. Judge yourselves by the fruit you produce. If you haven't good in you, you cannot produce good. Ensure that you have a solid base in life – like the man who built his house on rock.

Twenty-Fourth Week in Ordinary Time – 2

Monday   **I Co 11:17-26.33 Lk 7:1-10**

It was the custom in the early Church to have a communal meal or *agape* in the church-homes, followed by the celebration of the Lord's Supper. Unfortunately, many people created divisions, upsets and brawls during the first part, with the result that the Lord's Supper, or the Eucharist, was not respected. Paul calls for a deep respect for the Lord's Supper. 'Until the Lord comes, therefore, every time you eat this bread and drink this cup, you are proclaiming his death.'

After the Sermon on the Mount Jesus goes to Capernaum in the north. He meets a centurion with tremendous faith and heals his servant. Pray for a deeper faith.

Tuesday   **I Co 12:12-14. 27-31 Lk 7:11-17**

The human body is made up of many parts, each working for the good of the whole person. So each of us is a member of Christ's body, and we should be working together for the good of the whole. Each person has different gifts, but we all share the one Spirit.

Jesus goes on to Nain and meets a distraught mother. He brought her son back to life and restored him to his mother. Jesus can restore our spiritual life to its fullness.

Wednesday   **I Co 12:31-13:13 Lk 7:31-35**

Paul reminds the Corinthians (and us) to be ambitious for the higher gifts. If we have great eloquence, the gift of prophecy and knowledge, faith in all its fullness, give away everything, but have no love, then we are nothing. Love is patient, kind, always ready to excuse, to trust, to hope, and to endure.

Having performed two great miracles (curing the centurion's servant and giving life back to the man from Nain), Jesus criticises his listeners for their lack of faith. No matter what good people do, they will find fault – they believed John was possessed, and Jesus a glutton.

Thursday   **I Co 15:1-11 Lk 7:36-50**

We come to the last part of this letter, where Paul speaks of the resurrection of the dead. This is possible because Christ died for our sins, was buried and was raised to life. He gives the background to this, finishing off with his own special visions. 'I am the least of the apostles – by God's grace I am what I am.'

Jesus continues to condemn those who are quick to make moral judgments. This prostitute had been pardoned by Jesus and was thanking him by her actions. Yet the ordinary customary ablutions were not carried out by the host, who was a 'good' man. Let us trust in the mercy of God.

Friday   **I Co 15:12-20 Lk 8:1-3**

Some of the Corinthians are questioning the doctrine of the resurrection of the dead. If there is no resurrection then Christ did not rise. If he did not rise, then our preaching is useless, and you would still be in your sins. But Christ in fact did rise from the dead, as he can testify.

Jesus continues his journey through the towns and villages preaching and proclaiming the Good News. As well as the twelve apostles there was a number of women in his party, including Mary of Magdala.

Saturday   **I Co 15:35-37.42-49 Lk 8:4-15**

We finish the New Testament readings for the moment after today. Many of the doubters among the Corinthians were asking, if the dead arise, what sort of body are they going to have. Paul uses a simple parable to demonstrate that we will be new types of being. The grain of wheat dies, but produces a new and stronger form of life. For us, what is sown is perishable, but what is raised is powerful. That is our prayer – to be with the Lord, to be like him, for we shall see him face to face.

On his way through the towns and villages, Jesus stops to tell the story of the seed falling in different places. Only that which fell on good ground produced any fruit. What sort of soil are we?

Twenty-Fifth Week in Ordinary Time – 2

Monday   **Pr 3:27-34 Lk 8:16-18**

We leave the New Testament for two weeks and listen to some of the
Wisdom and Poetic books. We begin today with the Book of Proverbs.
Some of these were from the sayings of Solomon – the wise son of David.
Today we are reminded never to refuse kindness, never to plot harm,
never to pick a quarrel. The Lord's curse lies on the house of the wicked,
but he blesses the home of the virtuous.

Jesus continues with his parables. We are reminded that what we are
given we must show to the world and not keep it to ourselves. My faith
and religion is for all and not for myself alone.

Tuesday   **Pr 21:1-6.10-13 Lk 8:19-21**

Today we have a collection of sayings from the Book of Proverbs. One of
the most important is that which tells us that 'to act virtuously and with
justice is more pleasing to the Lord than sacrifice'.

Jesus' relatives come looking for him. He uses the occasion to
demonstrate that all of us who follow him are his brothers and sisters.

Wednesday   **Pr 30:5-9 Lk 9:1-6**

We have the third and final extract from the Book of Proverbs. God can
be known only through faith and not reason alone. Our prayer is to use
our faith and reason to stay on the straight and narrow.

Jesus now moves to the stage that he can safely send out his apostles
on a trial run. He gave them power and authority over all devils and to
cure diseases. They went out proclaiming the Good News and healing
everywhere.

Thursday   **Qo 1:2-11 Lk 9:7-9**

We move on to another Book of Wisdom, the book of Ecclesiastes or,
more correctly, Qoheleth, the Hebrew word for preacher. Our extract
begins: 'Vanity of vanities, and all is vanity'. This refers to the uselessness
of human things. In Hebrew the word means wind, puff or vapour; as
used here it means barrenness, impermanence and the illusory nature of
things. They deceive anyone who puts their trust in them.

Jesus was now making too many waves in the area. Even Herod, who
had beheaded John, was getting worried. Many believed that Jesus might
be Elijah.

Friday   Qo 3:1-11 Lk 9:18-22

We continue with the book of Ecclesiastes, with an extract that has been made into a beautiful song. 'A time for giving birth, a time for dying..... a time for war, a time for peace.' As human beings we are within time, so we can't comprehend the work of God from the beginning to the end. God is a great mystery.

The apostles are now given their chance to say who Jesus is. He is not Elijah or John the Baptist, but, as Peter says, the Christ of God. Let us pray for the same faith.

Saturday   Qo 11:9-12:8 Lk 9:43-45

Time marches on for us all. We are young for a while, but all is vanity. The day will come when all will be silenced and we will go to our everlasting home. God gave breath, God takes it away. Make good use of it while we still have it.

Yesterday we saw the Apostles, through Peter, make their act of faith in Jesus, the Christ. They find it difficult to accept that their hero should suffer.

Twenty-Sixth Week in Ordinary Time – 2

Monday   **Jb 1:6-22 Lk 9:46-50**

All this week we listen to a summary of the Book of Job. It is a very famous poem and tries to deal with the huge problem of human suffering. Why does God allow a good person to suffer? What part has suffering to play in the life of a person? Today we have a piece from the prologue, which tells us that Job was a pious and blameless man, who was perfectly happy and contented. Satan insinuates himself among the angels of God's court and argues that Job's virtue is not genuine. So God allows Satan to test his virtue – but not to touch Job himself. As a result Job lost everything. 'The Lord gave, the Lord has taken back. Blessed be the name of the Lord.'

The all-powerful question is: 'Who is the greatest, who is going to be in charge?' Jesus replies: 'Anyone who welcomes this little child welcomes me, welcomes the one who sent me.'

Tuesday   **Jb 3:1-3. 11-17. 2-23 Lk 9:51-56**

We are in the second part of the Book of Job, the dialogue. He is in the depths of his misery. He curses the day of his birth and longs for death. 'Why is a man allowed to be in the world, if God baulks him on every side?' 'Why give light to a man of grief?' We hear the cries of someone in deep depression.

The disciples had a lot to learn. When they were to get out on their own to continue the work of Jesus, they must be prepared for rejection.

Wednesday   **Jb 9:1-12. 14-16 Lk 9:57-62**

Three of Job's friends come to try to sort out his problems – to fix them for him. They consider suffering to be a punishment for sin, so they tell him to 'humbly recognise the faults and beg God's forgiveness'. Job knows he is not completely sinless, but he also realises that the suffering is far greater than his faults deserve. He is looking for someone who would plead his cause.

A variety of people wished to join his band, but Jesus looked for commitment. 'If you place your hand on the plough and look back, you are not fit for the kingdom of heaven.'

Thursday **Jb 19:21-27 Lk 10:1-12**

Job is still in despair and has got little consolation from his three well-meaning friends. 'Pity me, pity me, you, my friends.' But there is a sign of hope. 'I know that my redeemer lives and he will take his stand on earth. And after my awakening into new life I shall look on God.'

Now the group following Jesus has grown quite big. Earlier he had sent out his apostles. Now he gives the rest of the disciples their test.

Friday **Jb 38:1. 12-21. 40:3-5 Lk 10:13-16**

After over thirty chapters of dialogue between Job and his three friends, we have God speaking to Job in this great poem. If you were able to understand how God looks after the world, know the extent of the world, experience both life before and after death, then you would be like God. And Job admits his pride – 'I have been frivolous.'

Yesterday we saw Jesus telling his disciples what to do if they were rejected in a town. Now he condemns the towns that have closed their ears to his message. 'Anyone who listens to you listens to me, anyone who rejects you, rejects me and the one who sent me.'

Saturday **Jb 42:1-3. 5-6. 12-17 Lk 10:17-24**

We come to the end of our flying visit to the book of Job. God rebukes Job's friends and restores Job. Job realises that the Lord is all-powerful. 'I am the man who obscured your designs with my empty-headed words. I have been holding forth on matter I cannot understand, on marvels beyond me and my knowledge.'

The disciples come back after their first test. 'Rejoice that your names are written in heaven – happy the eyes that see what you see.'

Twenty-Seventh Week in Ordinary Time – 2

Monday   **Ga 1:6-12 Lk 10:25-37**

Today we begin to listen to St Paul's letter to the Galatians. He had visited this Christian community around 53 AD during his third missionary journey. He was surprised to find that they had been led astray by 'false brethren', Judaizers, who made out that Christians should conform to the Mosaic law of the Jews. He wrote this letter, mainly to refute these errors. If anyone preaches a version of the gospel different from the one you have already heard, he is to be condemned.

The lawyers have always had trick questions, even in Jesus' time. They believed that one should take care of one's own kind – only Jews. That is what was meant by 'love your neighbour'. This beautiful story of the good Samaritan teaches otherwise.

Tuesday   **Ga 1:13-24 Lk 10:38-42**

Paul is preaching against the Judaizers who believed that Christians must accept all of the Mosaic law. He speaks of his own credentials, especially how he was so zealous initially in being a good Jew. He gives details of his training and time of preparation to be one of the apostles.

A reminder to us all. Take time off from the everyday rat race to be in the presence of Christ. Stop in your tracks, find a place with silence, and pray.

Wednesday   **Ga 2:1-2. 7-14 Lk 11:1-4**

When Paul's apprenticeship was over he went to Jerusalem. Many tried to persuade him to get one of his Greek companions to become a Jew. He was under great pressure, but did not give in. He was well-received in Jerusalem and even opposed some of Peter's practices. He used to eat with the Gentiles but had given in to the pressure of the Judaizers and changed his practice. 'You have no right to make the pagans copy Jewish ways.'

Yesterday we were told to take time off and pray. Today Jesus gives us his special prayer. Say it at different times during the day.

Thursday   **Ga 3:1-5 Lk 11:5-13**

Paul is angry with the Galatians. 'Has someone put a spell on you? You want the Law; but did God give you the Spirit so freely and work miracles among you because of the Mosaic law, or because you believed what was preached to you?'

Jesus is continuing his lesson on prayer. Have complete trust in the goodness of the Father and don't hesitate to ask. The heavenly Father will give the Holy Spirit to those who ask him.

Friday   **Ga 3:7-14 Lk 11:15-26**

Paul is still refuting the Judaizers. He reminds them that Abraham became the Father of the Chosen People through faith and not through the law, which didn't exist then. It was through Christ that the pagans received the blessing of Abraham. Through faith we have received the promised Spirit.

From prayer you will get the strength to fight the evil that is all around you. The power of God will cast this evil away from you.

Saturday   **Ga 3:22-29 Lk 11:27-28**

The law simply made people realise that they were sinful. It was impossible to keep the law, so they would always be in sin. That is, until grace through faith in Jesus came along. Now, all of you are sons of God through faith in Christ Jesus. There is no more distinction between gentile and Jew. We are all part of the posterity of Abraham. Through Baptism you have put on Christ.

Jesus gives us another special lesson. We can't be his mother. But we are really blessed if we hear the word of God and keep it.

Twenty-Eighth Week in Ordinary Time – 2

Monday   **Ga 4:22-24. 26-27. 31-5:1 Lk 11:29-32**

Paul has developed his teaching against the Judaizers. He uses an allegory or parallel with the biblical story of Abraham and his two sons. The first was born of his slave-girl, Hagar, and the second from God's promise to his wife Sarah. The first tried to punish the second and was eventually dispossessed. No longer are we slaves to the law, but are free due to the promise of God. Christ freed us, so we remain free – we will not submit to the yoke of slavery again.

This is a wicked generation asking for a sign. The only sign will be that of Jonah. The Ninevites repented when Jonah preached. The Queen of the South came from a great distance to hear the wisdom of Solomon. The Ninevites will judge this generation. There is something greater than both Jonah and the Queen of the South.

Tuesday   **Ga 5:1-6 Lk 11:37-41**

Christ freed us and meant us to remain free. If the Judaizers insist on circumcision then they have to obey the full law and become slaves of the law. They become separated from Christ and have fallen from grace. We are free due to Christ and faith makes its power felt through love.

The Pharisees were at their legalism again. Jesus attacks this – they are clean outside, but inside are full of wickedness. Make the inside clean too.

Wednesday   **Ga 5:18-25 Lk 11:42-46**

We come to the last extract from the letter to the Galatians. We are free because of Christ. But this does not mean we are free to indulge in the lower side of human nature. Those who indulge in fornication, indecency, idolatry, feuds, envy, etc., cannot inherit the kingdom of God. The Spirit brings love, joy, peace, patience, kindness, goodness, trustfulness, gentleness and self-control. So we must crucify all self-indulgent passions.

Jesus continues his tirade against the hypocrisy of the Pharisees and the lawyers. You are like unmarked tombs that men walk on without knowing it!

Thursday   **Ep 1:3-10 Lk 11:47-54**

Today we begin our study of St Paul's letter to the Ephesians. This is regarded as the greatest of his writings and is often called the queen of his epistles. It is believed that he wrote it while in prison, when he had more leisure than at the times he was writing for the other churches. Paul waxes strongly and poetically about God's dealing with men and women. It is so full of material, that a few moments here and there just cannot do it justice. God chose us to be his most perfect adopted children. 'Such is the richness of grace which he showered on us in all wisdom and insight.'

Jesus continues speaking against all forms of hypocrisy. This generation will have to answer for all the sins of the past.

Friday   **Ep 1:11-14 Lk 12:1-7**

Paul continues his poetic description of what God has done for us. 'It is in Christ that we were claimed as God's own, chosen from the beginning under the predetermined plan, to be the people who would put their hopes in Christ.' You have heard that news; you have believed it, now you are stamped with the seal of the Holy Spirit, which is the pledge of our inheritance. For those whom God has chosen as his own, there is freedom. Through this we give praise to God.

Be on your guard against the yeast [the hypocrisy] of the Pharisees. Do not be afraid of those who may be able to kill the body, but cannot kill the soul. Every hair on your head is numbered, so there is no need to be afraid.

Saturday   **Ep 1:15-23 Lk 12:8-12**

Today's extract is a tremendous one, full of power and inspiration and promise. May God give you a spirit of wisdom and good common sense; may he enlighten your mind so that you can see what hope his call holds for you. You can see that he raised Christ from the dead to sit on his right hand in heaven: he has made him the head of the Church, which is the body of Christ. We are inspired to shout out the words of the psalmist: 'How great is your name, O Lord our God, through all the earth!'

Jesus makes his solemn promise – anyone who declares himself openly for me, I will declare him in the presence of God. If you need my guidance in the meantime, don't worry; I will send you the Holy Spirit to teach you what you must say.

Twenty-Ninth Week in Ordinary Time – 2

Monday   **Ep 2:1-10 Lk 12:13-21**

It is really difficult to do justice to the text of St Paul's letter to the Ephesians in such a short time. We can put ourselves in the place of the Ephesians. We were dead when we followed the way of the world, and gave way to sensual and sinful lives. We were living in sin – we always missed the target of good living. The sin in us killed our innocence, our ideals and our will-power. But God was generous in his mercy to us – he brought us to life in Christ Jesus. It is not due to any work on our part, but to his goodness. So now we are God's work of art, created to live the good in Christ Jesus.

As we live, so shall we die. We must be ever prepared. If we store up treasure in heaven, we will be prepared.

Tuesday   **Ep 2:12-22 Lk 12:35-38**

St Paul is continuing his great treatise. You were once without hope, you were no part of God's revelation, you were immersed in the world without God. But now through Jesus Christ you have been brought together, Jews and Gentiles, and made one in Christ Jesus. You are no longer aliens, but citizens of God's household. You are all being built into the Lord's house.

Be ready for the call of the Lord – dressed for action with your lamps lit.

Wednesday   **Ep 3:2-12 Lk 12:39-48**

St Paul is full of awe that God would choose him. I have been entrusted by God with the grace he meant for you. You are all parts of the one body of Christ. Even though you despised one another, Jews and Gentiles, Greeks and barbarians, you are all to be one, as revealed through the power given me by God. Through that power I am proclaiming and explaining the mysteries.

Again, we are reminded that we must be ready for the call of the Lord – he will come on a day you do not expect and at an hour you do not know.

Thursday   **Ep 3:14-21 Lk 12:49-53**

The prayer of St Paul for his readers. May God give you the power to grow strong, so that Christ may live in your hearts through faith, be planted and built on love. May God help you to know the breadth and length, the height and depth of his mystery, and be filled with the utter fullness of God.

My message is tough, so tough that it may divide families.

Friday   **Ep 4:1-6 Lk 12:54-59**

We begin the second half of St Paul's letter to the Ephesians. Just remember, he says, you are all called to the one Lord, one faith, one baptism. Do all in your power to lead a life worthy of your calling.

Try to read the signs and interpret the times. Be careful about how you judge others.

Saturday   **Ep 4:7-16 Lk 13:1-9**

We are all part of the mystical body. Each of us has been given certain gifts – all to build up the body of Christ. If we live by the truth and in love, we shall grow in all ways into Christ. We won't be tossed around like children.

A common message from Jesus. Repent and produce good fruit – the parable of the fig tree. It was given just one more chance.

Thirtieth Week in Ordinary Time – 2

Monday   **Ep 4:32-5:8 Lk 13:10-17**

Paul sets the highest standards for his readers. They must be imitators of God. They must imitate the love and forgiveness of God. They must imitate the great obedience of Jesus who gave his life for their salvation. They must be so far from shameful conduct that they don't even mention it. This was important at a time when there was so much sexual immorality – the Christians were to set a new standard.

We see the healing power of Jesus – both a physical and spiritual healing; we see the hypocrisy of the synagogue official. We are not made for the sabbath, but the sabbath for us. Isn't it good to heal on the sabbath?

Tuesday   **Ep 5:21-33 Lk 13:18-21**

Today we have the great treatise of St Paul on marriage. It is regarded as the perfect union of body, mind, and spirit between a man and a woman. In doing this, St Paul was putting forward an ideal which shone with radiant purity in an immoral world. Divorce was rampant, women had very few rights. The love that a husband should have is to be a sacrificial love, a purifying love, a caring love, and the whole relationship should be in the Lord.

The kingdom of God begins in a very small way, but grows to have a great influence.

Wednesday   **Ep 6:1-9 Lk 13:22-30**

The Christian faith did a lot for women. It did even more for children. Often a baby daughter was just thrown out. The father had absolute power over the son – even when he had grown up and was married. He even had the power of life and death over him. St Paul obliges children to honour their parents. The fathers were to discipline their children, but not to provoke them. As someone has said, 'spare the rod and spoil the child – but keep an apple at hand when the child does well'. He gives similar instructions to slaves and their masters.

Many will try to come into the kingdom, but will find it very difficult. Just knowing the Lord is not sufficient, one has to do his works.

Thursday **Ep 6:10-20 Lk 13:31-35**

We end this letter today. We can imagine Paul in prison, chained to a soldier, complete with armour. He describes the Christian as having the spiritual armour of truth and righteousness, ready to preach the gospel, with the shield of faith and the Spirit like a sword. Above all, pray, pray, pray.

We see the great sadness of Jesus when Jerusalem, the city he is so proud of, keeps its ears closed to his teaching.

Friday **Ph 1:1-11 Lk 14:1-6**

Philippi was a city in Macedonia, just to the north-east of present-day Greece. It was founded by Alexander the Great. Paul's visit to this town took place during his second missionary journey – the details are in the Acts (chapter 16). He had to leave after a storm of persecution and illegal imprisonment. He wrote the letter from Rome while in prison. The opening, which we had today, sets the tone of the letter – the letter of a friend to a friend. He was very close to these people. Grace and peace are his wish for his friends. He is full of Christian joy. May you never stop improving your knowledge, so that you can become pure and blameless.

For the second time this week we have the account of Jesus healing someone on the sabbath – an example of the people never learning. No wonder he was sad about the future of Jerusalem.

Saturday **Ph 1:18-26 Lk 14:1. 7-11**

He continues with his joyful theme. Christ is proclaimed and that makes me happy. Living is Christ in me. Christ is the beginning of life, the continuing of life, the end of life, the inspiration of life, the task of life. I am caught in this dilemma. I want to depart and be with Christ, but I must remain and stay with them. My desire is not to live for my own sake, but for the sake of those whom he can continue to help.

Jesus reminds his listeners that they must know their true selves. Don't put yourself in a higher place. Go where you belong. Then the Lord may call you to a higher place.

Thirty-First Week in Ordinary Time – 2

Monday   **Ph 2:1-4 Lk 14:12-14**

Avoid all ambition, seeking personal prestige, concentrating on self. Instead, there should be unity among us because we are all in Christ, we have Christian love, we share in the Holy Spirit, we are compassionate. If for nothing else, have this unity among yourselves because of Paul.

Jesus continues in the vein of Saturday's reading. Don't invite those to a party who can return the invitation. Ask those who have no way of repaying you.

Tuesday   **Ph 2:5-11 Lk 14:15-24**

This is one of the greatest and most moving passages in all of St Paul's writings. Christ Jesus was, by very nature, God; by right he was equal to God. Yet he emptied himself, he poured himself out completely in sacrifice for us. He took the form of a slave – he became one of us. He humbled himself, he became obedient to death, even death on a cross. As a result he has been given a name above all names. Jesus is Lord and everyone should bend their knees and proclaim the glory of God.

Jesus tells the parable of the unjust guests, who made many excuses not to come to the party. Instead people from the rough areas of life were invited. So the non-Jews were invited to hear the Good News as well.

Wednesday   **Ph 2:12-18 Lk 14:25-33**

Keep on doing what I have asked you to do. It is God who brings all this to fruition in you. Without any murmuring, show yourselves to be blameless and pure, the spotless children in this warped world of ours. You will shine like stars as a result.

Be realistic if you want to be a follower of mine, because it is not easy. But once committed you must not turn back, but keep your hand to the plough.

Thursday   **Ph 3:3-8 Lk 15:1-10**

We are not a people who believe in mere external ritual. Unlike the Jews, circumcision for the Christian is the internal eradication of any evil that is in us. Paul then reminds his readers that he knows all about the Jewish faith and even went so far as to persecute the Christians until he got to know Jesus Christ the Lord.

Jesus goes on to tell the parable of the lost sheep and the lost silver pieces. There is rejoicing in heaven over one repentant sinner. That should help us keep up the effort.

Friday   **Ph 3:17-4:1 Lk 16:1-8**

Keep your priorities in order and be careful not to follow those who are too materialistic. Remember, if we persevere, God will make our bodies into wonderful copies of his own glorious body. Our true citizenship is in heaven.

Be as energetic and as resourceful in looking after spiritual things as the unjust steward was about his position.

Saturday   **Ph 4:10-19 Lk 16:9-15**

I have full contentment. Through the power of Christ I can control all earthly desires – there is nothing I cannot master with the help of the One who gives me strength. Paul thanks the people of Philippi for the gift they sent him – it touches my heart and makes me very glad. With this note he ends his letter.

Use the goods of this world properly – don't let them lead you away from the spiritual. If money becomes your master, then the Lord can mean nothing to you.

Thirty-Second Week in Ordinary Time – 2

Monday   **Tt 1:1-9 Lk 17:1-6**

This letter to Titus is one of the so-called pastoral epistles. It was written against the background of Judaic legalism and a philosophy called gnosticism which regarded all matter as being evil. So the human body is evil. Even though it was a personal letter to Titus, it seems to have been addressed to the Christians in Crete. It was a bad place to live because of the immorality. 'The Cretans are always liars, wild and evil beasts, lazy gluttons.' Titus was his faithful henchman and he gives him instructions about how to organise the Church. The priest must not be self-willed, angry, given to drunken conduct, ready to come to blows, etc. He must be hospitable, prudent, just, pious and self-controlled.

Have faith and you won't cause scandal to the little ones. Learn how to forgive – forgive whenever and however often the other says sorry.

Tuesday   **Tt 2:1-8. 11-14 Lk 17:7-10**

Paul continues to give instructions to Titus, who is organising the Christians in Crete. The senior men must speak what befits sound teaching. The older women, who have a great standing in the community, must teach and train the young. The younger men must learn prudence. The grace of God brings salvation to all. It will purify us as a special people for himself.

We must do our duty without question – 'we are merely servants; we have done no more than our duty.'

Wednesday   **Tt 3:1-7 Lk 17:11-19**

Today we have rules for the citizens. Be law-abiding, active in service, careful in speech, tolerant, kind and gentle. We have been given a new relationship with God, who will give us love and grace. He will forgive our sins.

Always include a prayer of thanks when we are praying.

Thursday   **Phm 7-20 Lk 17:20-25**

This is the only private letter of St Paul that we possess. It seems that a slave of Philemon – slavery was part of life in those days – had escaped and found his way to Rome, where he became a Christian. Paul tries to send him back, and asks Philemon to realise that he now had great assets, so he should be generous to Onesimus.

The Son of Man must suffer grievously and be rejected by his generation.

Friday   **2 Jn 4-9 Lk 17:26-37**

As well as writing his gospel, John wrote three short letters. Today's extract is from the second. Love is the central theme, so live according to the Commandments. This love is the best weapon for combatting heresy.

We have a reference to the last day. Always be ready.

Saturday   **3 Jn 5-8 Lk 18:1-8**

We have the last extract from the New Testament letters for the moment, taken from the very short third letter of John. This was written to Gaius, a Christian in the church of Asia Minor. He praises his faith and charity.

We try to have persistence in our prayer – like that of the old lady with the judge.

Thirty-Third Week in Ordinary Time – 2

Monday   **Rv 1:1-4. 2:1-5 Lk 18:35-43**

We begin the book of Revelation. This was written during the persecution of the Christians – they were expected to treat the Emperor publicly as a god. It uses a style found in the Old Testament – apocalyptic writing. This described the chaos of the present, referred to terrible calamities falling on the people, but declared that eventually there would be peace in the Day of the Lord. In the New Testament, the Day of the Lord refers to the day of Jesus Christ. After the calamities and tragedies there will be great peace. In this first extract we are told that this is God's revelation to humanity – a revelation of truth. This revelation is given through Christ to John, who is God's slave and servant. This itself is a great honour. The first 'letter' is to the Church of Ephesus. It was one of the great cities, but notorious for its pagan superstition. Christ praises those who were strong in upholding the Christian principles.

We have the beautiful story of the blind man being cured near Jericho, the very ancient city. 'Your faith has saved you.'

Tuesday   **Rv 3:1-6. 14-22 Lk 19:1-10**

John continues his letters to the main churches. We have two today, one to Sardis and the other to Laodicea. Sardis was a wealthy city built on the top of a steep rock or hill. But it was a degenerate city, spiritually dead. Everyone is told to 'watch'. The other city was Laodicea. They were lukewarm. 'Because you are neither hot nor cold, I will vomit you out of my mouth.'

Zacchaeus becomes the special host for Jesus. He overcame his physical size to look for Christ, an example of faith. Faith saved him from his sins.

Wednesday   **Rv 4:1-11 Lk 19:11-28**

Today we have a glimpse of heaven. The description is full of symbols and needs little elaboration. All life is praising Jesus Christ.

We are all given some talents in life. The reward we get will depend on the effort we put into using them positively.

Thursday   **Rv 5:1-10 Lk 19:41-44**

We have another great heavenly vision. When the seal was opened there were great beasts, but all were subject to the Lamb, the Lamb who was sacrificed. 'You bought men for God to serve our God and rule the world.'

Jerusalem did not take the opportunity offered to it – it will be destroyed.

Friday   Rv 10:8-11 Lk 19:45-48

The idea of eating the scroll and prophesying comes from Ezekiel. When the Jews were learning the alphabet, they used a mixture of flour and honey to make the letters. If the child got the sound correct he was allowed to lick the letter off the slate. 'You are to prophecy about the different nations.'

We must have respect for the Temple of the Lord.

Saturday   Rv 11:4-12 Lk 20:27-40

The antichrist is the power of the universe against God, the one who tries to lead people astray. This is the beast who comes from the Abyss to destroy those who are witnessing to Christ in the sinful Jerusalem. But they will rise. This is the story of the Cross and Resurrection. Good will triumph over evil.

Jesus confounds the Sadducees who said there was no resurrection. We are all going to rise on the last day.

Thirty-Fourth Week in Ordinary Time – 2

Monday   Rv 14:1-5 Lk 21:1-4

We have still more visions of heaven. Today we see the Lamb, or Christ, with a huge number of people around him, all stamped with the name of the Father. This indicated that they were his, that they were loyal, that they had security and were safe. The sound they made was like the sound of many waters, of thunder, of harpists, and they sang the song of praise to the Lord, because they were without blemish.

The woman is praised because she gave a large proportion of what she had to help the poor.

Tuesday   Rv 14:14-19 Lk 21:5-11

Today we have the vision of the Last Judgment. There are two ideas of a harvest – the harvest of grain and the harvest of grapes. Those who have persevered will be with the Lord.

Jesus reminds his listeners that even the things that seem to be most permanent will disappear. The end of the world will come with much chaos.

Wednesday   Rv 15:1-4 Lk 21:12-19

We have another vision of heaven – it is like a sea of glass with flashes of flame like lights going through it. Those who were martyred, those who persevered in their fight with the powers of evil, are the ones who sing the great song of praise: 'You alone are holy, all nations will come and worship before you...'

As the years go by, those who are loyal to Christ must suffer much persecution at the hands of the wicked.

Thursday   Rv 18:1-2. 21-23.19:1-3. 9 Lk 21:20-28

Babylon will be destroyed. It is believed that Babylon refers to the Rome of Nero. She has become the dwelling-place of demons and a stronghold of every unclean spirit. Just like a big millstone, when thrown into the sea, this Rome will just disappear. But the great multitudes who persevered in spite of persecution will be in the Lord's presence to sing Alleluia – Praise God.

More desolation will occur as the world comes to an end. Eventually the Son of Man, Christ, will come in his power and glory. Stand with your heads high, because your liberation is near at hand.

Friday   **Rv 20:1-4. 11-21:2 Lk 21:29-33**

The power of Satan is being chained and confined to the abyss or to hell. The souls of the just, especially the martyrs and those who suffered for their faith, are brought into the presence of the Lord. Their names are written in the book of life. We will have written our own destiny – both the good deeds and the bad deeds will be opened up. Those names not blotted out will rise and share in God's glory.

Use nature, for example, the changes in the life history of the fig tree, to help you see that the kingdom of heaven is at hand.

Saturday   **Rv 22:1-7 Lk 21:34-36**

We reach the end of the Book of Revelation and the end of the Church's liturgical year. We have yet another description of heaven, this time more understandable. It is like the Garden of Eden, only much better. There will be no evil, only good things. The Lord God will be a light to them and they will reign with him forever. For us, let us accept and believe the word of God.

For the past week we have been looking at those teachings of Jesus just before his arrest and crucifixion. Watch and pray. Stay awake, praying at all times for the strength to survive all that is going to happen, and to stand with confidence before the Son of Man.

Proper of the Saints
January Feasts

2 January SS Basil the Great and Gregory Nazianzen
Bishops and Doctors of the Church
Memorial

These were two great saints of the early Church. Basil was born in 330 and at forty became the Bishop of Caesarea, after spending a number of years as a hermit. He wrote much of value, especially the monastic rules, many of which are still followed by the monks of the Eastern Church. He was outstanding in helping the poor.

Gregory was born in the same year and joined Basil in undertaking a life of solitude. In 381 he became Bishop of Constantinople. He was a man of great wisdom and eloquence.

4 January St Elizabeth Seton
Widow
[USA: Memorial]

Elizabeth was born in New York of a very distinguished Episcopalian family in 1774. She had three daughters and two sons, but her husband died while the family were in Italy in 1803. During her stay there after his death she became interested in Catholicism and was eventually received into the Church in 1805. As a result she was estranged from her family. She spent her years establishing a school for girls in Baltimore, Maryland, and setting up groups of women to look after the poor. Out of this came the Congregation of the Daughters of Charity of St Joseph which grew rapidly throughout the States. The Congregation was very influential in building up the parochial school system. Elizabeth died in 1821 and was the first native-born North American to be canonised (1975).

5 January St John Neumann
Bishop
[USA: Memorial]

John was born in Bohemia in 1811. After he finished his studies in Prague he went to the New World as a missionary. He was ordained in New York and later joined the Redemptorists. In 1852 he became Bishop of Philadelphia where he promoted the system of parochial schools. He encouraged large numbers of teaching brothers and sisters to help in this work. Among his written works were two catechisms which were widely used in the US for the rest of the century. He died in 1860 and was canonised in 1977.

13 January St Kentigern
Bishop
[Scotland: Feast]

Kentigern (or Mungo) was a missionary in Strathclyde and eventually became their bishop. He had to leave due to persecution and then preached in north-west England and Wales. He returned to Scotland later and died in 603. He is buried in Glasgow.

17 January St Anthony
Abbot
Memorial

Anthony was born near Memphis in Upper Egypt in 251. Before he was twenty he inherited a large estate when his parents died. He was impressed with the Christian message to 'go sell what you have and give to the poor'. He did that and spent the rest of his life as a hermit in various parts of Egypt. He founded a number of monasteries – most consisting of scattered cells. At one stage he was asked by the bishops to preach against the Arians, who did not believe in the divinity of Christ. All were very impressed by his character and words. He was over a hundred when he died.

21 January St Agnes
Virgin and Martyr
Memorial

When she was twelve years of age St Agnes suffered martyrdom at Rome, either in the second half of the third century or, more probably, at the beginning of the fourth century. Pope Damasus embellished her tomb with sacred verses, and many of the Fathers, including St Ambrose and St Augustine, spoke of her with great praise. She is mentioned in the Eucharistic Prayer I.

24 January St Francis de Sales
Bishop and Doctor of the Church
Memorial

Francis was born prematurely in 1567 near Savoy, in France. As he grew up he became very religious and wished to consecrate himself to God. His father was not keen on this, but he persisted and after a brilliant few years in university became a doctor of law and later a priest. He spent much of his time working as a missionary near Lake Geneva. At first he met with much hostility, but his determination and excellent preaching eventually brought great numbers into the Church. He spent a lot of time writing and distributing short religious papers. Later he became a bishop and was much in demand as a preacher all over France. His best known work is the *Introduction to the Devout Life.*

25 January Conversion of St Paul
Apostle
Feast

Saul, a Roman citizen from Tarsus in Cilicia, was brought up a very strict Jew. Highly educated and a scrupulous observer of the Law, he joined the Pharisees. He persecuted the early Christians and took part in the murder of Stephen. After the incident on the road to Damascus he became an ardent Christian. His story is found in Acts, read during the Easter season.

The first reading from Acts tells the great and well-known story of Saul's conversion. With his new life he was given a new name, Paul.

Go out to the whole world and proclaim the Good News. How well Paul carried out that task.

26 January SS Timothy and Titus

Bishops
Memorial

These were two of Paul's most loyal workers. Timothy was a convert from Lystra and accompanied Paul on his second missionary journey. He left him at Ephesus and continued his work there. Titus was put in charge of the Church in Crete. Paul wrote two letters to Timothy and one to Titus. These are often called the pastoral letters.

[II Tm 1:1-8. Tt 1:1-6]

Fan into a flame the gift that God gave you when I laid my hands on you. It is not a spirit of timidity, but one of power.

You are left in charge of the Church in Crete, so that the knowledge of the truth and the hope of eternal life that was promised by God would be given to its people.

28 January St Thomas Aquinas

Priest and Doctor of the Church
Memorial

Thomas spent his early years at the monastery of Monte Cassino in Italy, studied at the university of Naples, and joined the Dominican Order. This caused some trouble with his family, who captured him and held him prisoner for two years. He studied later under St Albert the Great. He taught in the university at Paris and there began his writing career. He produced many famous books and treatises – his devotion to the Blessed Eucharist gave rise to the great hymns we now have. He died at the age of fifty in 1274.

31 January St John Bosco

Priest
Memorial

John Bosco was born in 1815 near Piedmont in Italy. He lost his father when he was two and was brought up by his saintly mother. From his early years he wanted to be a priest and work with destitute boys. Some time after his ordination he managed to set up a training school for poor boys. By 1856 there were 150 resident boys, with four workshops, including a printing-press, some Latin classes and five hundred children in nearby oratories. At first he had a number of priests helping him, but later he founded a religious order to carry on his work. These became known as the Salesians, after his patron saint, St Francis de Sales. John Bosco died in 1863.

February Feasts

1 February St Brigid   Virgin
[Ireland:Feast; Secondary Patron]
It is generally believed that Brigid was born in Faughart, Co. Louth. She spent much of her early years doing farm work – milking and making butter. She was an attractive girl and her father wanted to make a good match for her in marriage. She wished to consecrate her life to God, and it was with difficulty that she persuaded her father to let her go. She first went to the monastery of St Mel in Ardagh. Her reputation for genuine holiness grew and many more young women joined her. She founded a second monastery in Kildare. She often travelled outside the monastery for evangelisation and charitable purposes. She was mainly concerned with hospitality, alms-giving, and care of the sick. She died in 524. She became known as Mary of the Gael, and is venerated in parts of Europe.

2 February Presentation of the Lord   Feast

This is a feast both of Jesus and his mother Mary – the feast of Candles or Candlemas. We go to meet the Lord as Simeon did, to acclaim him as 'a light to reveal God to the nations'. Let us walk as children of the light to bear witness through our Christian lives to Christ the saviour of the world.

Mal 3:1-4 Heb 2:14-18 Lk 2:22-40
Centuries before the coming of Christ a prophet foretold that the Lord would visit his Temple and purify his people.

God visited us in a special way through his Son Jesus who became human in all things like us. He redeemed us by becoming like us.

For a Jew this was an ordinary event, but through the eyes of faith this particular presentation was the fulfilment of God's promises to his people.

3 February St Blaise   Bishop and Martyr
Optional Memorial
Very little is known about St Blaise. It seems that he was born of a rich and noble family, received a Christian education and was made a bishop when quite young. During persecutions he spent much of his time in a cave. Many people came to him for cures. There is one story of how he cured a boy who had a fishbone stuck in his throat. Hence the practice of the blessing of throats grew.

5 February St Agatha

Virgin and Martyr
Memorial

Agatha suffered martyrdom at Catania in Sicily in the year 250. She was venerated throughout the Church from the earliest times and her name was inserted into the Roman Canon. It is believed that through her intercession Catania was miraculously saved from an eruption of Mount Etna. Consequently, she is invoked against any outbreak of fire.

6 February SS Paul Miki & Companions

Priest and Martyrs
Memorial

St Frances Xavier planted Christianity in Japan after he arrived there in 1549. By 1587 there were said to be over two hundred thousand Christians. At this stage the regent Hideyoshi ordered all missionaries out of his dominions, but many stayed behind in disguise. In 1597 26 Christians, mostly Japanese, were crucified in different ways over a period of time. Paul Miki was a high-born Japanese and an eminent Jesuit preacher

10 February St Scholastica

Virgin
Memorial

It is traditionally held that she was the twin sister of St Benedict. She is believed to have been in charge of a convent near Monte Cassino, where Benedict was the abbot. She could visit her brother only once a year, so strict were the rules under which they bound themselves. She died about 543 when she was sixty-seven years old.

11 February Our Lady of Lourdes

Optional Memorial

At Lourdes in 1858, when Mary appeared to St Bernadette, she appealed to sinners to do penance. As a result a great spirit of prayer and charity to the sick and poor grew up in France. Today Lourdes is probably the premier place of devotion to our Lady.

14 February SS Cyril and Methodius

Monk and Bishop
Memorial

These were two brothers from Thessalonica who are venerated as the apostles of the Slav peoples. Cyril studied philosophy in Constantinople and became a lecturer there. His elder brother Methodius became a monk in Greece. In 862 an ambassador from Moravia came to Constantinople looking for suitable missionaries and the two brothers were sent. They ran into much opposition from the German-speaking Church for using the Slav language in their preaching and liturgies. But their knowledge of the language brought many people to the Church. Cyril died on a visit to

Rome in 869. Methodius was made bishop and returned to the Slav countries. Here he met with much more opposition from the German-speaking bishops, and even spent some time in prison. He was often accused of teaching unorthodox doctrine and had to defend himself before the Pope. For the last few years before he died in 884 he translated most of the Bible into the Slav language.

22 February The See of St Peter the Apostle   Feast

This is a very old feast, going back to the fourth century. It has been kept on this day ever since as a symbol of the unity of the Church founded on the Apostle Peter. Peter realised the importance of preaching the Good News to all nations and not just to the Jews. Rome was the centre of the world in those days, with good communications everywhere. It was through this Roman system that the Good News was passed on so quickly.

I Pt 5:1-4 Mt 16:13-19

Peter is anxious to make sure that the Good News is preached in its entirety to the people. He gives practical advice to those who are looking after the various churches. Be like a shepherd and have an interest in your people. Do the work eagerly and gladly.

Today we have the very important and well-known account of the confession of Peter. 'You are the Christ, the Son of the living God,' he said. He was given a new name – Peter, coming from the word, rock. He is given the keys of authority in the new Church, built upon the rock.

23 February St Polycarp   Bishop and Martyr
                                          Memorial

St Polycarp was believed to have been a disciple of St John the Evangelist. He trained many of his own disciples, including St Irenaeus. His letter to the Philippians is still extant. He was Bishop of Smyrna for a number of years, and was highly venerated. He was martyred by being burned around 155.

March Feasts

1 March St David   Bishop
[Wales: Solemnity; England: Feast]
David was born in Cardigan and trained under St Illtyd. He founded a
number of monasteries and attracted many postulants to them. Later he
was consecrated bishop and established the diocese of Menevia. He was
abbot at the monastery there. He died about 588. He is the principal patron
of Wales.

7 March SS Perpetua and Felicity   Martyrs
Memorial
These two martyrs died during the persecution of Septimus Severus in
203, at Carthage. With others they were thrown to various animals in the
amphitheatre in the city, with the crowds crying out for their blood, before
they were killed off with a sword through their throats.

8 March St John of God   Religious
Optional Memorial
John was born in Portugal in 1495. He had a varied youth, spending many
of his years in the army. When he was forty he resolved to amend his
wayward life and began to consider how best he could spend the rest of it
in God's service. St John of Avila inspired and directed him and, eventually,
after many ups and downs, including a stay in a lunatic asylum (his
fasting practices made people think he was insane), he hired a house in
Granada where he looked after the sick and poor. He astonished the city
with the extent and success of his work. This was the foundation of the
order of the Brothers of St John of God, but it was only after his death in
1550 that his followers actually set up the order.

8 March St John Ogilvie   Priest & Martyr
[Scotland: Memorial]
John was born in 1580 near Keith and was brought up a Calvinist. After
he was received into the Catholic Church he became a Jesuit. He worked
in Edinburgh and Glasgow, bringing many back to the faith. He was
betrayed, imprisoned, tortured and hanged in Glasgow in 1615.

17 March St Patrick   Bishop
[Ireland, Australia, England, Scotland: Solemnity
Wales: Feast]
Patrick's father Calpurnius was a deacon and his grandfather was a priest.
When he was in his teens he was captured and brought from his home in
Roman Britain to Ireland. There his faith deepened and he developed a
great love of prayer, praying a hundred times in the day and night, no
matter what the weather was like. He escaped and eventually felt called to
come back after his ordination to convert the people of Ireland in 432. He

set out to evangelise the local leaders and then their people followed. He worked in many parts of Ireland and was responsible for establishing churches all over the country. He died around 461.

19 March St Joseph   Husband of the blessed Virgin Mary
                                                          Solemnity

Very little is known about Joseph, beyond what we find in scripture, as most of the legends can be disregarded. He was of royal descent, as we know from the genealogy in Matthew and Mark. Joseph was described as a just or godly man. He was betrothed to Mary when he discovered she was pregnant, but his fears were set at rest by the angelic vision. As well as being the foster-father of Jesus, he is seen as his protector and early educator.

II S 7:4-5.12-14. 16 Rm 4:13.16-18. 22 Mt 1:16. 18-21. 24 [Lk 2:41-51]
David was the greatest king of the chosen people. The prophet assures him that his dynasty will last forever. Joseph was descended from David and was to be the protector of the Messiah.

Even though Abraham was an old man with a wife who was barren he still believed in the promise that he would be the father of many nations.

Joseph is a man of great faith and undertakes the responsibility of looking after the child conceived by the Holy Spirit. He is to name the child Jesus.

[Joseph undertook the responsibility of looking after Jesus, even though at times he did not understand him. He was his foster-father and protector. Jesus had to be busy about his real Father's business.]

25 March The Annunciation of the Lord   Solemnity

This feast commemorates the real beginning of the Incarnation. Mary was told that she was to become the mother of one who was to be called the Son of the Most High. It is important to remember, that she was not coerced into this position. She gave her free consent when she said: 'Behold the handmaid of the Lord, be it done to me according to your word.' At that time she probably did not fully realise the implications of her undertaking, but she had a great faith and trust in God. Throughout her life we see her keeping her word and committing herself to the service of her son, who was the Word of God.

Is 7:10-14 Heb 10:4-10 Lk 1:26-38

A promise made by the prophet Isaiah to Ahaz, one of the last kings of Judah before the deportation, is applied to the virgin Mary and her son, Jesus – who is really Immanuel or God-with-us.

The old sacrifices were imperfect – they could never bring humankind into a close relationship with God. Christ was fully obedient to the Father and so his sacrifice was perfect. 'Here I am! I am coming to do your will.'

Mary too gave her consent in spite of her fears and questions. 'Behold the handmaid of the Lord. Be it done to me according to your word.'

April Feasts

7 April St John the Baptist de la Salle   Priest
                                                                    Memorial
St John the Baptist de la Salle is the patron saint of schoolteachers. He
was born in 1651 at Rheims. He was inspired by his very devout mother
and eventually became a priest and worked in a parish in the city. He first
became interested in schooling when two schools were set up under his
care by a layman. Eventually he gathered a group of teachers together and
they formed a new community, the Brothers of the Christian Schools. The
numbers grew throughout France and he eventually opened a teacher
training college. Towards the end of his life he retired and wrote many
books. He died in 1719, when he was sixty-eight.

23 April St George   Martyr
                                                      [England, Wales: Feast]
St George is the Protector of the kingdom of England. Very little is known
about his life. It seems that he was martyred in Palestine, probably before
the time of Constantine. Legend tells us that he fought with a powerful
dragon, which had been terrifying the people, and then led it into the city.
There he told the people he would kill it if they believed in Jesus Christ
and be baptised.

25 April St Mark   Evangelist
                                                                        Feast
Mark is probably the person mentioned in the Acts as 'John surnamed
Mark'. He was a kinsman of Barnabas and worked with him when he
travelled with Paul on his missionary journey and later when he went to
Cyprus. He was also closely associated with Peter and is spoken of as
being the mouthpiece of Peter. He was responsible for the second gospel.
He is venerated as principal patron of Venice, though tradition says he
was Bishop of Alexandria.
                                                   I P 5:5-14 Mk 16:15-20
Peter gives encouragement to Mark and the other Christians. Be calm but
vigilant – the enemy is like a prowling lion. The suffering will last only
for a little while: God will support you and bring you to his glory.

   The last action of Jesus was to commission his apostles to go out to the
whole world and proclaim the Good News. Mark did this by writing his
gospel.

29 April St Catherine of Siena   Virgin
                                                                    Memorial
Catherine was an unusual woman. She was the youngest of twenty-five

children and from her early years wished to become a nun. Her father opposed this for a long time, but eventually she joined the Dominicans. Throughout her short life she had a number of very significant visions. These gave her the courage to act as intermediary in many ecclesiastical and political disputes. Her holiness was renowned and she was responsible for the conversion of many people. Her great achievement was persuading the Popes to return to Rome after their seventy-four-year exile in Avignon, France. She wrote a number of books and died in 1378, when she was only thirty-three.

May Feasts

1 May St Joseph the Worker   Optional memorial

This feast in honour of St Joseph the Worker was instituted by Pope Pius XII in 1955. It falls on the first day of the month that is dedicated to the Blessed Virgin Mary. 'May Day' has long been dedicated to labour and the working person. The Pope expressed the hope that the feast would accentuate the dignity of work and bring a spiritual dimension to trade unions.

2 May St Athanasius   Bishop and Doctor of the Church
Memorial

Athanasius was born in 297 at Alexandria. He lived during very troubled times, both politically and within the Church. He was secretary to the archbishop when he attended the Council of Nicaea – we get the Nicene Creed from this. This Council condemned the priest Arius, who taught that Jesus was not divine. After Athanasius became bishop of the city, he had great trouble with the followers of Arius. At times the political leaders supported him, but often they supported his opponents. In all he was banished from his city five times and lived for seventeen years in exile – where he probably got to know St Anthony, the Hermit. His last seven years were quiet and he wrote a life of St Anthony. He died in 373.

3 May SS Philip and James   Apostles
Feast

Philip was a follower of John the Baptist, but accepted Christ's call immediately. He persuaded his friend Nathanael to come and see Jesus for himself. He seems to have been an amiable type of character who did not make decisions quickly. He is named as being present at the coming of the Holy Spirit.

James – the Less, or Younger – may have been a cousin of Jesus. He was present at the Council of Jerusalem, where they decided that Gentiles who wished to become Christians did not have to become Jews as well. It is commonly held that he wrote the Letter of St James in the New Testament.

I Co 15:1-8 Jn 14:6-14

Paul speaks of the resurrection of the dead. This is possible because Christ died for our sins, was buried and was raised to life. Afterwards he appeared a number of times to the apostles, including James.

Jesus uses Philip's question to show that he is in the Father and the

Father is in him. He is going to the Father and will do anything that they ask for in his name.

4 May The Beatified Martyrs of England and Wales

Martyrs
[England: Feast]

Many men and women from England and Wales were persecuted for their faith during the sixteenth and seventeenth centuries. Forty-two of these have been canonised (25 October) and one hundred and sixty have been declared blessed.

14 May St Matthias

Apostle
Feast

Matthias was chosen as the replacement for Judas. Not very much is known about him. He is said to have been martyred in Colchis.

Ac 1:15-17. 20-26 Jn 15:9-17

Peter takes the lead in deciding on a replacement for Judas to bring the apostolic group back up to twelve. Such a person had to know Jesus from the beginning of his public ministry and have seen him after his resurrection. After much prayer among the community they choose Matthias.

Jesus is giving special encouragement to his faithful followers. The primary commandment is to love one another. In that way they will remain in both his and the Father's love. He then tells them that they are not servants but friends – friends for whom he would lay down his life. They were chosen by him to go out and continue his work.

24 May Our Lady Help of Christians

[Australia: Solemnity]

Mary cares for the brothers and sisters of her Son while they are making their spiritual journey on earth, just as she cared for her own Son. She is forever a mother to us. In 1844 she was chosen as the patroness of Australia.

25 May St Bede the Venerable

Priest & Doctor of the Church
[England: Memorial]

Bede was born in 673 near Wearmouth. He joined the monastery there, where he was ordained and spent his time teaching and writing. He wrote many historical and theological works and did much study of Scripture and the early Fathers of the Church. He died in 735.

26 May St Philip Neri

Priest
Memorial

Philip was born in Florence in 1515. After a mystical experience in his late teens he went to Rome and spent two years in prayer. During this time his only outside work was teaching lessons to his host's two sons. Then, after three years study, he went on an apostolate among the people, whose religion was at a low ebb. He was ordained in 1551 and became a great confessor. Later he was helped by a number of priests and the group came to be known as the Oratorians. This society was given formal approbation in 1575. He continued to work very hard until his death in 1595, when he was eighty.

27 May St Augustine of Canterbury   Bishop
[England: Feast]

In 596 Pope Gregory the Great sent about thirty monks under the leadership of Augustine to evangelise England. On their way they were warned that the English would not receive them, and they returned to Rome. Gregory persuaded them to try again. One of his first convert s was King Ethelbert of Kent. Augustine purified and consecrated many pagan temples for Christian worship and rebuilt the ancient church in Canterbury. He died seven years after his arrival, about 605.

31 May Visitation of the blessed Virgin Mary   Feast

Zp 3:14-18 Rm 12:9-16 Lk 1:39-56

This great hymn of praise is taken from the prophet Zephaniah and is applied to the presence of the Lord among his people. Mary brings God-made-man in her womb when she visits Elizabeth.

Paul is very insistent that Christians show sincere love towards all and be persistent in being hospitable to one another, no matter what it costs.

The source of Mary's love and hospitality in this account can be summed up in the first line of her beautiful hymn of praise: 'My soul glorifies the Lord, and my spirit rejoices in God my saviour.'

June Feasts

1 June St Justin Martyr
Memorial

Justin was born in the Holy Land. He was converted from paganism to Christianity and then settled in Rome, where he opened a school. He wrote a number of philosophical works. He also addressed the emperor in his books, known as the *Apologies*. He was martyred about 165.

3 June SS Charles Lwanga and companions Martyrs
Memorial

The first Catholic missions were established in Central Africa in 1879. In Uganda, some progress was made until Mwanga became the ruler. He was addicted to unnatural vice and was determined to root out Christianity among his people. Joseph Mkasa and a young page, Denis, were butchered by him and eventually he had seventeen of his own household, including Charles Lwanga, slaughtered in 1886.

5 June St Boniface Bishop and Martyr
Memorial

Boniface was born in England and became a teacher and later a priest. His wish was to do missionary work and eventually he was commissioned by the pope to go to what is now southern Germany. He worked here for most of his life, establishing many churches and getting rid of clerical abuses. He became Archbishop of Mainz in 747. In his later years he went back to Friesland to convert the pagans. It was here that he was martyred in 754.

9 June St Columba (Colmcille) Abbot
[Ireland: Feast; Scotland: Memorial]

Columba was born in Gartan, Co. Donegal, in 521, into a family of royal lineage. He became a monk and founded monasteries in Derry, Durrow, and possibly Kells in Ireland, and at Iona in Scotland. The latter was his principal foundation and from here the monks carried out the conversion of Northumbria. He died in 597. He was the most popular saint in literature.

11 June St Barnabas Apostle
Memorial

Barnabas, whose original name was Joseph, was not one of the original twelve apostles, but has always been called an apostle because of the work he did for the early Church. He was a Jew, born in Cyprus, and became one of the early converts living at Jerusalem. It was he who first welcomed Paul into the community. He worked in Antioch, where he brought Paul – it was there that the followers were first named 'Christians.' He went with Paul on his first missionary journey and later went back to work in Cyprus with Mark. He is said to have been stoned to death at Salamis.

Ac 11:21-26; 13:1-3 Mt 10:7-13

Barnabas was sent to Antioch. There he took Paul under his care and instructed him for the year. When Paul was ready, both were called by the Lord to go out on their first missionary journey.

Jesus commissions his disciples to go out and preach about the kingdom of God, and to do it without counting the cost. This was Barnabas' attitude.

13 June St Anthony of Padua

Priest and Doctor of the Church
Memorial

Ferdinand was born in Lisbon, Portugal in 1195. He changed his name to Anthony when he joined the Friars Minor. He was a very learned man and was much inspired by a visit to Assisi where he met St Francis. He became famous for his preaching in Italy and especially in Padua, where he lived for his last few years. He was only thirty-six when he died.

20 June Bl Dermot O'Hurley and Companions

Martyrs
[Ireland: Memorial]

Between 1579 and 1681 seventeen people gave up their lives rather than forsake their faith. Dermot O'Hurley was Archbishop of Cashel and was hanged in Dublin in 1584 after being tortured. At Kilmallock two Franciscan priests, Patrick O'Healy and Conn O'Rourke, were hanged in 1579. In Wexford four men, Matthew Lambert, a baker, and three sailors, Robert Meyler, Edward Cheevers and Patrick Cavanagh, were hanged, drawn and quartered in 1581. In Clonmel Maurice McKenraghty was hanged in 1585, and John Kearney, a Franciscan priest, in 1653. A Jesuit lay brother, Dominic Collins, was hanged in his home town of Youghal in 1602. In Dublin Conor O'Devany, Bishop of Down and Connor, and Patrick O'Loughran, a chaplain to the O'Neill family, were hanged, drawn and quartered in 1612. Also in Dublin, Francis Taylor, who was once mayor of the city, was hanged in 1621, Peter Higgins, a Dominican priest, was hanged in 1642, and Margaret Bermingham Ball, from Corballis, Co. Meath, died in prison in 1584. William Tirry, an Augustinian priest from Cork, was hanged in Tipperary in 1654. In 1681 Terence O'Brien, a Dominican and Bishop of Emly, was hanged in Limerick.

20 June St Alban [Julius & Aaron]   Martyrs
[England & Wales: Memorial]
Alban was the first martyr in Britain. His martyrdom occurred in the third
century during the persecution of Diocletian. There was popular devotion
to him from early times and his ancient shrine is in St Albans.

      In this same persecution many others suffered martyrdom,
including Julius and Aaron from Caerleon in Monmoutshire. All three are
honoured in Wales.

21 June St Aloysius Gonzaga   Religious
Memorial
He was born in Lombardy to a family with royal connections. He studied in
Florence and spent some time in Spain. His father wanted him to become a
great soldier, but from his very early years Aloysius wanted to work for
God. He undertook a routine with much prayer, fasting and penitential
exercises. His father tried desperately to get him away from his desire to be a
Jesuit, but eventually, in 1585, he succeeded in becoming a novice in Rome.
Later he worked very hard with the sick and dying during a plague in Rome.
He was a man of great prayer and devotion to the Eucharist. He died later in
1891 when he was only twenty-three. He is the patron of youth.

22 June SS John Fisher & Thomas More   Martyrs
[England: Feast; Wales: Memorial]
John Fisher was born in 1469 and after his studies in Cambridge
University was ordained priest. Later he became Bishop of Rochester and
was an outstanding pastor. He wrote against the doctrinal errors of the
time. Thomas More was born in 1478 and studied at Oxford and at
Lincoln's Inn. He was called to the Bar in 1501 and three years later
entered Parliament, where he was very successful. He married twice and
had four children from his first marriage. Under Henry VIII he became
Lord Chancellor. He opposed many of the King's measures against the
Catholics and was imprisoned in the Tower of London. On 15 June 1535
John Fisher was beheaded and Thomas More suffered the same fate on 6
July.

24 June Birth of St John the Baptist   Solemnity

This feast dates from the fourth century and at one time was preceded by a
day of fasting. St Augustine and some other theologians saw something
symbolic in the fact that John was born in the summer when the days were
getting shorter and Jesus in the winter when the days were getting longer.

Vigil   **Jr 1:4-10 I P 1:8-12 Lk 1:5-17**
The account of the call of the prophet Jeremiah is applied to the call of John

– 'before I formed you in the womb I knew you...... I am putting my words into your mouth.'

Peter speaks about the prophets longing and searching for the joy and salvation that comes from Jesus Christ. This was not for them, but for those to whom the Good News has now been preached.

Zechariah's wife is infertile and he found it difficult to accept the words of the angel in his vision. This son, whom he is to call John, will be very special and will have the spirit of Elijah.

Feast   **Is 49:1-6 Ac 13:22-26 Lk 1:57-66.80**

Isaiah was called before he was born to bring back the wayward people. These words are applied to John who was to go out and prepare the way for the Lord.

Paul makes a reference to the work of John – to herald the coming of Jesus and to preach repentance. When his work was done, he would hand over to Jesus.

Because of his doubts, Zechariah had lost the power of speech. This came back to him in a dramatic way when he was called on to name his son John. John was to be someone very special – 'What will this child turn out to be?'

28 June St Irenaeus

Bishop and Martyr
Memorial

Irenaeus was born about the year 125 in Asia Minor. He received a very wide education and acquired a great knowledge of scripture and Greek philosophy. Many of his teachers would have known the apostles. As a young priest he went on missionary work to Lyons, France, where he eventually became its bishop. He argued very successfully against the Gnostics, who had great influence there at the time. He wrote many books contrasting the doctrines of the various sects with the teaching of the Apostles and the Holy Scripture. He was also involved in solving disputes between the Eastern and Roman Churches.

29 June SS Peter and Paul

Apostles
Solemnity

We know from the gospels that Peter was from Galilee, that his brother was Andrew, that he was married, and that he was a fisherman. Jesus changed his name from Simon to Kephas, the Greek version of the Aramaic for 'rock' and translated from the Latin to Peter. He seems to have been a very impetuous man – as can be seen from his impulsive statement that he would never betray Jesus. But he was a man of great faith and determination. He ended his days as first Bishop of Rome around 64.

Saul came from Tarsus in Cilicia and was brought up a very strict Jew. He was also a Roman citizen. He was highly educated, receiving his instruction in Jerusalem. He was a scrupulous observer of the Law and joined the Pharisees. He became a persecutor of the early Christians and took part in the murder of Stephen. After the incident on the road to Damascus Paul became an ardent Christian. When he had completed his training he set off on a number of missionary journeys and wrote many epistles. His story is found in the Acts of the Apostles, which is read during the Easter season.

Vigil   **Ac 3:1-10 Ga 1:11-20 Jn 21:15-19**

Peter cures the lame man, and does it in the name of Jesus of Nazareth. This needed faith and faith was strengthened by their prayers.

In spite of the times when he persecuted the early Christians, Paul was chosen to be a preacher of the Good News, especially to the pagans.

Peter is commissioned to look after Christ's flock. He is asked three times – once for each of the times he denied him. Eventually, he would die for him.

Feast   **Ac 12:1-11. II Tm 4:6-8.17-18 Mt 16:13-19**

Peter was imprisoned because he preached about Jesus Christ. God looked after him and freed him from the prison, because he still had a lot more work to do.

Paul too realises that the Lord has been with him, and helped him 'fight the good fight'. He stood by him and rescued him from the evil powers.

Simon, after his confession of faith in Jesus, was given a new name – Peter, coming from the word for rock. He is now given the keys of authority in the new Church, built upon the rock.

July Feasts

1 July St Oliver Plunkett   Bishop and Martyr
                                                                  [Ireland:Feast]

Oliver was born into a Catholic family of nobility in Co. Meath, Ireland, in 1629. He went on for the priesthood, studied in Rome in the Irish College and was ordained in 1654. He was unable to return to Ireland because of the political difficulties there, so he taught theology in Rome for twelve years. In 1669 he was appointed Archbishop of Armagh and was consecrated in Ghent. He had to return secretly to Ireland – most of the bishops had been expelled at the time. He worked very hard building up the Church and trying to correct abuses. During the 1670s there were further persecutions of the Catholics and eventually Oliver was arrested. He was tried for treason, first in Dublin and later in London. In 1681 he was hanged, drawn and quartered at Tyburn.

3 July St Thomas   Apostle
                                                                  Feast

Little is known about Thomas other than what we find in the gospels. He was a Jew and probably a Galilean. His name is Syriac and means the 'twin' – as does Didymus, which was his Greek name. He is chiefly remembered for his incredulity after Jesus had risen from the dead – 'unless I see the print of the nails in his hands .... I will not believe'. According to various traditions he did his missionary work in India.

Ep 2:19-22 Jn 20:24-29

All followers of Christ are part of God's household – like a temple with the prophets and apostles as foundations and Jesus as the cornerstone.

Thomas would not believe that Jesus had risen until he saw him in the flesh for himself. Jesus praises those who believe in him without seeing him.

4 July Independence Day   [USA]

In the midst of the national celebrations it is important to recognise the hand of God in our lives. We pray for peace in our country and throughout the world.

Dt 32:7-12 Ga 5:1,13-18 Jn 8:31-36

This is part of the song of Moses used at the end of his days. He recounts all the good deals that the Lord has done for each of his people. He is not protecting him at all times – 'like an eagle watching its nest, hovering over its young, he spreads out its wings to hold him'.

St Paul reminds us that Christ freed us and we are called to liberty. This involves obeying the commandment 'love your neighbour as yourself'. If the Son makes you free, you are free indeed.

11 July St Benedict

Abbot
Feast

Benedict is the patriarch of western monks. He was born in Norcia and was sent to Rome to be educated. He was appaled by the lack of morals there and disappeared to Subiaco in the mountains. After three years of solitude some disciples began to gather and he set up a number of monasteries there. Later he went down south of Rome to Monte Cassino, where he established his principal monastery. As well as looking after the monks, he ministered to the sick and poor of the area. He died in 547. He is one of the patrons of Europe.

Pr 2:1-9 Mt 19:27-29

The prerequisites for discovering the knowledge of God and an understanding of the fear of the Lord are listed – take my words to heart, set store by my commandments, tune your ear to wisdom, apply your heart to truth. The Lord himself is the giver of wisdom and keeps watch on the way of his devoted ones.

Those who give up the things of the world for the sake of Jesus' name will receive a hundred times more.

14 July Bl Kateri Tekakwitha

Virgin
[USA: Memorial]

Kateri was born in 1656 beside the Mohawk River in present-day New York State. Her mother was a Christian Algonquin who, after capture, was married to a Mohawk chief. Her parents died in an outbreak of smallpox when she was four and Kateri was brought up by her aunts who hated Christianity. She was baptised by the French Jesuit missionaries on Easter Sunday 1676. The following year she moved to a Christian village near Montreal where she led a very austere life of hard work, prayer, and mortification. She had great devotion to Christ crucified in the Blessed Eucharist and to Our Lady. Many of her people came to talk and pray with her. In 1679 she made a private vow of perpetual virginity. After her death on 17 April 1680, during Holy Week, she became known as the Lily of the Mohawks.

15 July St Bonaventure

Bishop and Doctor of the Church
Memorial

Bonaventure was born near Viterbo, Italy, and became a member of the Friars Minor. He studied in Paris and become known as the Seraphic

Doctor. He received his degree with St Thomas Aquinas. He preached with great energy and wrote many books on Catholic doctrine. He was a successor of St Francis and managed to sort out serious disputes within the Franciscan order. Later he was appointed bishop of Albano. He died in 1274 while carrying out his work of helping to effect the reunion between the Greeks and Rome.

22 July Mary Magdalene   Memorial

Mary Magdalene was one of the disciples of Jesus. She was one of the first to see the risen Christ, as today's gospel tells us. Pray for a taste of her love and commitment to Jesus. The feast has been celebrated in the east since the tenth century. From the twelfth century in the west, Mary Magdalene was identified as Mary of Bethany, and this is now disputed. In the east they have a separate feast for Mary of Bethany on 18 March.

Sg 3:1-4 II Co 5:14-17] Jn 20:1-2.11-18
In this beautiful poem the bride is looking earnestly for her husband. Mary Magdalene's love was as intense and became more spiritual through her contact with Jesus.
[The love of Christ overwhelms us all, because he has died for us and brought us new life.]
    Mary Magdalene was ever faithful to Jesus – she was the one who stayed last at the tomb. She was rewarded by being the first to see the risen Christ.

25 July St James   Apostle
                                                                Feast
James the Greater was the son of Zebedee and brother of St John. He was a Galilean by birth and by trade a fisherman with his father and brother. Jesus referred to the brothers as Boanerges, or 'Sons of Thunder' – possibly because they were fiery and impetuous. With Peter and John he formed the special trio among the Apostles – they witnessed the transfiguration and the agony in the garden. He was the first of the apostles to die for his faith. According to Spanish tradition he visited Spain.

II Co 4:7-15 Mt 20:20-28
Paul says that we are only earthenware jars that hold the great treasure of God's grace. No matter what problems arise, the power of God will overcome all. 'We have difficulties on all sides, but are never cornered; we see no answer to our problems, but never despair; we have been persecuted, but never killed.' We carry the crucified Jesus in our lives. Life comes for us when we join our sufferings with those of Christ. The power of the

resurrection is taking place among us. Jesus tells James and John that they will suffer for his sake. In the meantime, they must serve one another, just as he, Jesus, served them.

26 July SS Joachim and Anne

Parents of the blessed Virgin Mary
Memorial

Details about Joachim and Ann are found only in apocryphal literature. One of these dates back to 165 and it states that Mary's birth was miraculous because her parents were sterile. Originally there were two feasts, but these were combined in 1969.

Si 44:1. 10-15 Mt 13:16-17

This is a hymn in praise of the piety of Israel's ancestors. Those who were heroes and who followed the law of the Lord are now remembered. Their good works will not be forgotten. Thanks to them the glory of their children will remain forever. Joachim and Anne are included among these good people.

'Happy are you because you see and hear what the prophets of old longed for.' Maybe Joachim and Anne lived to see their daughter's child grow up.

29 July St Martha

Memorial

Martha was the sister of Mary and Lazarus. She is the patroness of innkeepers and hostels. Originally, St Martha and St Mary were honoured on the same day, before people thought that Mary Magdalene and Mary of Bethany were the same person.

Jn 11:19-27 [Lk 10:38-42]

Jesus raises Lazarus the brother of Martha from the dead. Jesus comes to give life, if people receive him. 'I am the resurrection.'

When Martha and her sister asked Jesus into their house for a meal, Martha was the fussy one. She was so over-anxious that she forgot to listen to Jesus.

31 July St Ignatius Loyola

Priest
Memorial

This is a big feast day for the Jesuits, as St Ignatius was their founder. He was born in 1491 in northern Spain. He worked in the castle and in the army. While he was convalescing after being shot in the leg, he read the lives of the saints. As a result he was converted to a life of holiness. He tried to set up a mission in Palestine, but was thrown out. Back at home he was regarded with suspicion by the Church authorities. Eventually, he studied theology in Rome and later formed the Society of Jesus. The Jesuits put themselves directly under the Pope – the Pope's Army – and were outstanding in the reform of the Church. Ignatius died in 1556, aged sixty-five.

August Feasts

1 August St Alphonsus Liguori   Bishop and Doctor of the Church
                                          Memorial
St Alphonsus was born in Naples in 1696. He studied law and by the age of seventeen had acquired doctorates in both civil and canon law. At thirty he became a priest and later founded the Redemptorist Order. He spent most of his time preaching and writing, especially on moral matters. He was a bishop for a while, but went back to his own order and died in 1787 at the age of ninety-one.

4 August St John Mary Vianney, the Curé of Ars   Priest
                                                           Memorial
Most priests in parishes regard this man as their patron. He was a great example of preaching, mortification, prayer and charity. He was tremendous in the confessional. Toward the end of his life, thousands of people came to the little village every week to hear him preach and to talk to him in the confessional.

6 August Transfiguration of the Lord   Feast

This is the feast when we get a glimpse of the glory of Christ – the glory that we are promised a share in.

   Dn 7:9-10.13-14 II P 1:16-19 A: Mt 17:1-9 B: Mk 9:2-10 C: Lk 9:28-36
Daniel's vision in the first reading is full of a sense of the great majesty of the heavenly court with people of all languages and cultures being at the service of him who has eternal sovereignty and whose sway no evil can destroy.
   The three disciples were overawed by the vision they saw. It remained very vivid in their minds for the rest of their lives. They took away this message: 'This is my beloved son, listen to him.' In the second reading Peter speaks of this experience.

7 August St Dominic   Priest
                                Memorial
Dominic was born in Spain in 1170. When he was forty-six Pope Honorius entrusted to him and his companions the mission to preach the Word of God. This was the beginning of a new religious order – the Dominicans. Because of the nature of his work, the members of his order would not be confined to large monasteries, but would work from smaller houses, adapted

to life in the towns that were developing in Europe at the time. Their main work was preaching. Dominic was about fifty-two when he died.

10 August St Lawrence

Deacon and Martyr
Feast

St Lawrence was martyred in 258. He was a deacon and as such gave great service to the Christian community. It is believed that he was martyred by being slowly burned on a gridiron. He has been one of the most venerated martyrs of Rome since the fourth century.

II Co 9:6-10 Jn 12:24-26

St Paul has some beautiful ideas for us today. Be generous with yourself, the Lord loves the cheerful giver.

The wheat grain produces only if it dies in the ground. We can only produce spiritual fruits if we die to ourselves. We may not be asked to die as Lawrence was, but remaining a Christian in this pagan society needs many sacrifices.

11 August St Clare

Virgin
Memorial

Clare was of an aristocratic family. She met St Francis a number of times during her teens and was influenced by him to lead a life of poverty. She was the founder of the Poor Clares, that great religious order which worked in a parallel way with the Franciscans. She wanted a group of people who owned nothing and spent their time in prayer.

14 August St Maximilian Kolbe

Priest and Martyr
Memorial

He was born near Lodz in Poland in 1894. He had great devotion to Mary and after he was ordained he founded a number of Marian communities and produced Marian magazines. During the war he was imprisoned in the concentration camp at Auschwitz and there offered to take the place of a married man who was condemned to die.

15 August The Assumption of the Blessed Virgin Mary   Solemnity

After her great life of service Mary died, but immediately afterwards her body was assumed into heaven. The body that carried Jesus would not undergo corruption. She is now in heaven with a different task. She is our spiritual mother, and is now serving us as she looked after Jesus while on earth. The feast is found in early lectionaries. Pope Pius XII officially promulgated the dogma of Mary's Assumption on 1 November 1950.

Vigil   **I Ch 15:3-4.15-16.16:1-2 I Co 15:54-57 Lk 11:27-28**

The ark of the covenant was very sacred because it represented the presence of God among the Chosen People. When David and his men brought it back to their land, they had a great celebration.

Through the power of the resurrection of Christ we have overcome death. 'Death, where is your victory? Death, where is your sting?'

Happy those who hear the word of God and keep it.

Feast   **Rv 11:19.12:1-6.10 I Co 15:20-26 Lk 1:39-56**

In this great vision we have the powers of evil trying to destroy good. Mary was able to bring forth her child who triumphed over the power of death.

Just as Christ was raised from the dead, so will all people be brought to life through him. Death came through one man, Adam; but life comes through the man, Jesus Christ.

Mary's first act of service was to visit her cousin, Elizabeth. She continued this service for the rest of her life. She still sings the beautiful hymn of praise: 'My soul glorifies the Lord, and my spirit rejoices in God my saviour.'

20 August St Bernard

Abbot and Doctor of the Church
Memorial

St Bernard came from a large, successful family near Dijon in France. When he was twenty-two he felt called to be a monk – and brought many of his family and friends with him to the Cistercians. Eventually he became the abbot of the monastery at Clairvaux, where he and his monks led an extremely strict life. It was a very powerful 'powerhouse of prayer'.

21 August St Pius X

Pope
Memorial

Pius X 'was one of those chosen few men whose personality is irresistible. Everyone was moved by his simplicity and his angelic kindness. Yet it was something more that carried him into all hearts: and that "something" is best defined by saying that all who were ever admitted to his presence had a deep conviction of being face to face with a saint' (Baron von Pastor, Papal historian). His aim when he became Pope was 'to renew all things in Christ'. It was because of him that frequent reception of Holy Communion became possible.

22 August The Queenship of Mary

Memorial

It is fitting that the week after the feast of the Assumption, we honour Mary as Queen of Heaven – she shares in a special way in the glory of her Son. She is ever interceding for us, her children. This feast was instituted by Pope Pius XII in 1955, originally for 31 May. It was transferred to the octave of the Assumption to link her queenship with her glorification. There are many hymns in which Mary is saluted as queen, e.g. 'Hail Holy Queen'.

24 August St Bartholomew

Apostle
Feast

St Bartholomew was one of the first of the apostles. The story of his call is given in the gospel today – he was also known as Nathanael. He is supposed to have preached in India, but he most likely went to Armenia, and was martyred there.

Rv 21:9-14 Jn 1:45-51

In the first reading we have a powerful vision of heaven, showing the glory of God and the presence of the twelve apostles.

The gospel describes Nathanael as one without guile. We pray that we can have the same type of faith that he had, so that we too can 'see heaven laid open and, above the Son of Man, the angels of God ascending and descending'.

26 August St Ninian

Bishop
[Scotland:Memorial]

He was born around 360 in Cumbria and was ordained bishop in Rome in 394. He came to Scotland and made Whithorn his base as he preached the gospel in south-east Scotland. He died about 432.

27 August St Monica

Memorial

Monica is a patron for all mothers. She saw her son leading a wild life, with all sorts of illicit sexual liaisons. She did her best to get him to reform and, eventually, some months before she died, he was baptised and became a great saint – Augustine. We celebrate his feast tomorrow. Let all mothers here pray for some of Monica's commitment and perseverance.

28 August St Augustine

Bishop and Doctor of the Church
Memorial

Augustine is a saint for our times. He led a life of debauchery, living with many women. Then he was converted and became a Christian and changed the face of Christianity. His writings have had a tremendous influence on the Church. He was baptised by St Ambrose in 387 when he was thirty-three. Four years later he was ordained a priest and after another four years he became bishop in the diocese of Hippo in North Africa. He campaigned and preached against many heresies in his thirty-five years as bishop. He wrote many books, his *Confessions* being one of the more famous of these. He was seventy-six when he died.

29 August The Beheading of John the Baptist

Martyr
Memorial

This feast has its origin in Samaria, where the Baptist's skull was venerated in the fourth century. By the seventh century the feast was celebrated everywhere.

Jr 1:17-19 Mk 6:17-29

The first reading is aptly applied to John the Baptist: 'I, the Lord, will make you into a fortified city, a pillar of iron and a wall of bronze to confront all this land.'

The gospel brings us the story of our celebration today. Let us pray that we can be men and women of principle, and not count the cost.

September Feasts

3 September St Gregory the Great   Pope and Doctor of the Church
                                                                    Memorial
                                                            [England:Feast]

Gregory came from an educated family in Rome, which had some possessions in Sicily. Rome was in a bad way around this time, having been ravished by barbarians, plagues and earthquakes. When he became Pope he made sure that everyone was treated with justice. He took as his motto, *servus servorum,* the servant of servants. Gregorian chant dates back to him, as does the Gregorian calendar, which is the one we use today. Gregory is also Apostle of the English.

8 September Birthday of Mary   Feast

We know very little of the early life of Mary. Traditionally, we believe that her father and mother were Joachim and Anna. Today we celebrate her birth – the beginning of the instrument of our salvation. She is now our mother, and we can trust in her protection.

Mi 5:1-4 [Rm 8:28-30] Mt 1:1-16.18-23
The first reading from the prophet Micah reminds the Israelites that out of the remnant will come the saviour, who will be born in Bethlehem

[God cooperates with those who love him. He chose them for this. Those he called he will justify; those he will justify, he will share his glory with.]

The gospel gives us Jesus' genealogical table, followed by the story of the annunciation. Joseph was to take care of Mary.

9 September St Peter Claver   Priest
                                                            [USA: Memorial]

Peter was born in Catalonia in Spain and went to university in Barcelona. He volunteered for mission work and went to Cartegenia in present-day Columbia. There he became 'the slave of the Negro slaves forever'. It estimated that during his forty years he instructed and baptised over 300,000 slaves. He taught them how to use the sacrament of confession – and is said to have heard over 5,000 of their confessions in a year. He ran into many difficulties with the authorities – he was taking up too much of the slaves' time. He was ill during his last years and was almost totally ignored until after his death.

13 September St John Chrysostom   Bishop and Doctor of the Church
                                                                    Memorial

John was a tremendous teacher and earned the name Chrysostom – Golden Mouth. He was born in 347 at Antioch. He had a very devoted mother who was widowed at the age of twenty. According to the custom of the time he was not baptised until he was twenty. He was a hermit for a number of years after which he was ordained priest. He became Archbishop of Constantinople in 398. He worked very hard for the poor and for the reform of his clergy. He ran into difficulties with the wife of the Emperor and was banished and died in exile in 407.

14 September Exaltation or Triumph of the Cross   Feast

There have been many examples of the power of the Cross down through the ages. Many battles were won under its protection. It is most important for our spiritual battles with the powers of evil.

Nb 21:4-9 Ph 2:6-11 Jn 3:13-17

The scene from the Book of Numbers prefigures the death of Jesus on the cross. Just as the Israelites were freed from the poison of the serpents by looking at the standard with the bronze serpent stuck on it, so would we be saved from the poison of evil by trusting in Jesus on the cross.

This is one of the greatest and most moving passages in all St Paul's writings. Jesus was by very nature, God; by right he was equal to God. Yet he emptied himself, he poured himself out completely in sacrifice for us. He took the form of a slave – he became one of us. He humbled himself, he became obedient to death even to death on a cross. As a result he has been given a name above all names. Jesus is Lord and everyone should bend their knees and proclaim the glory of God.

In the gospel, Jesus speaks of this scene to Nicodemus. It prefigures what is going to happen to him.

15 September Our Lady of Sorrows   Memorial

This is a fitting feast on the day after the Triumph of the Cross. Mary had many sufferings in her life. Think of the terrible anguish she must have experienced when she met her son on the way to his crucifixion.

Heb 5:7-9 Jn 19:25-27

The Letter to the Hebrews reminds us that Jesus obeyed his Father and suffered so that we might share in his glory.

The sequence is a beautiful hymn and prayer to our Lady who suffered. The gospel gives us just one incident where she went through her agony at the foot of the cross. Here, Jesus made her our mother through John, who represented us.

16 September SS Cornelius and Cyprian   Pope, Bishop and Martyrs
                                                        Memorial

Cornelius was ordained Bishop of Rome and Pope in 251 and worked against serious heresies. He was sent into exile by the Emperor.

Cyprian was one of bishops who supported and helped Cornelius in his work. He was Bishop of Carthage in North Africa. He too was exiled by the Emperor and later suffered martyrdom in 258.

20 September SS Andrew Kim Taegon and Companions   Martyrs
Memorial

French missionaries arrived secretly in Korea towards the beginning of the last century – up to that time the Catholics there depended on lay ministers. Shortly afterwards the Church was persecuted and between 1839 and 1867 there were 103 martyrs, mainly lay people. Andrew Kim was the first priest to be martyred, and Paul Chong the first lay apostle.

21 September St Matthew   Apostle and Evangelist
Feast

Matthew began as a tax collector, one of the most despised professions in Israel. The gospel tells us of his call. He was a sinner and accepted the Lord's call to righteousness and repentance. He was responsible for one of the gospels. He was martyred in Ethiopia.

Ep 4:1-7.11-13 Mt 9:9-13

St Paul reminds us that we have all been given a share in the grace of Christ. Through this grace we get different gifts, which we must use for the good of the Body of Christ. Some, like Matthew, are evangelists, others are pastors and teachers. All of us together build up the body of Christ – we make a unity in doing this.

Jesus calls Matthew and asks him to follow him.

24 September Our Lady of Ransom   [England:Memorial]

This is the only feast of our Lady proper to England. Devotion to our Lady of Ransom originated in Spain for ransoming Christians enslaved by the Moors. This devotion reminds us that we are the Dowry of Mary. Pope Leo XIII set up this feast to foster the reconversion of England.

27 September St Vincent de Paul   Priest
Memorial

Vincent was born in 1580 at Gascony in France, and became a priest at the age of twenty. Some years later he was very much influenced by a holy priest and then spent the rest of his life in Paris, trying to persuade people to go to Confession and looking after the poor. In 1633 he gathered a group which would later form the Congregation of the Mission

(Vincentians). They preached parish missions and also worked in seminaries. Vincent died in 1660. Due to his influence the Daughters of Charity were set up in 1633 – these women engaged in works of charity. Today the Vincent de Paul Society looks after the poor of many parishes, and helps those who have run into financial difficulties.

29 September SS Michael, Gabriel and Raphael

Archangels
Feast

Today is really a feast celebrating the care of God for us. He is always looking after us. Traditionally, we believe that angels are his messengers to us. Michael means 'who is like God'. Gabriel means 'God's power'. Raphael means 'God's healing'.

Dn 7:9-10.13-14 [Rv 12:7-12] Jn 1:47-51

We have the second part of Daniel's great vision. The four beasts who emerged from the earth and were pushed back represented the pagan gods which surrounded the Chosen People. Out of all the chaos would come the one of great age, the saviour, whose empire would never be destroyed.

[This is the great vision of John in the Book of Revelation. The power of evil, as represented by the dragon and his angels, was beaten back and driven out of heaven. This was done through the power of the sacrifice of Christ. Let all the heavens rejoice.]

The gospel describes Nathanael as one without guile. Our destiny is that we too can 'see heaven laid open and, above the Son of Man, the angels of God ascending and descending'.

30 September St Jerome

Priest and Doctor
Memorial

Jerome was a great saint but a terrible man to get along with! He had tremendous personal sanctity, but was too outspoken and sarcastic for many. In his early years he was given a very good classical education, was then baptised and later became a monk. He was involved in a number of doctrinal controversies on the side of orthodoxy, but his great work was the translation of the scriptures into Latin, which he did while in Bethlehem.

October Feasts

1 October St Thérèse of the Child Jesus

Virgin
Memorial
[Australia: Feast]

Thérèse grew up in a very happy home. Her two older sisters joined the Carmelite nuns. She fought hard to join also, but was told she was too young. Eventually she had her way and joined at fifteen, and was professed when she was seventeen. She fulfiled her duties, especially that of praying for priests, with great determination. Her writings were full of great spiritual insights. She had a very full life, but died in 1897 at the age of twenty-five.

2 October The Guardian Angels

Memorial

Today is another feast celebrating God's care for us. Traditionally, we believe that each one of us has a guardian angel looking after us. Devotion to the guardian angels dates back to the Middle Ages.

Ex 23:20-23 Mt 18:1-5.10

The account from the Book of Exodus is an example of God's providence: 'My angel will go before you.'

You must be like little children. Be careful never to despise such a one – their angels are continually in the Father's presence.

4 October St Francis of Assisi

Religious
Memorial

Francis was born in Assisi in Italy. He lived a very lavish life until he was about twenty when he was captured by soldiers from a neighbouring city and held prisoner for a year. After some illness and other experiences he decided to live a life of poverty. He ran into severe opposition from his father. After a number of years he was joined by others and eventually he established the order of Friars Minor to live in poverty and look after the poor. He made several unsuccessful attempts to bring his work abroad. He did manage to get to the Holy Land during one of the Crusades, but was horrified by the attitude of the Christians there. The Order spread over Europe during these years. St Francis received the stigmata in 1224. He is also said to be the first person to set up a crib at Christmas Mass. He died in 1226.

7 October Our Lady of the Rosary

Memorial

This feast was instituted by Pope Saint Pius V on the anniversary of the naval battle of Lepanto in 1571. It was said that the Christians were victorious because of the help of the holy Mother of God invoked by the saying of the Rosary. Today's celebration urges us to meditate on the mysteries of Christ with Our Lady. She was very closely associated with all his important actions. In the fifteen mysteries we have the central themes of all our faith. The Rosary is a prayer that involves the full person – the body, as the hands finger the beads, the voice, as we say the prayers, and the mind, as we meditate on these mysteries. October is the month of the Rosary.

13 October St Edward the Confessor

King
[England:Memorial]

Edward, who was of royal stock, was sent to Normandy for safety when he was ten years old. Thirty years later in 1042 he returned when he was called to be King of England. His religious and just administration endeared him to the people. He was generous to the poor and strangers, and a great encourager of monks. Every morning, no matter how busy he was, he attended Mass. He refounded and endowed the Abbey Church of Westminster. He died in 1066, one week after it was opened.

15 October St Teresa of Avila

Virgin
Memorial

Like Thérèse of the Child Jesus, Teresa of Avila was a remarkable woman. Her devotion to prayer all began with her childhood studies of the lives of the saints! More or less against her father's wishes she entered the Carmelite convent at Avila in Spain when she was twenty. She suffered poor health during her first years there – she may have had malignant malaria. After some years she devoted herself to very intense prayer – she had many ecstasies and even wrote books on prayer. However, the convent had relaxed rules, which she felt were not conducive to the serious prayer. She was encouraged to found other convents for the reformed Carmelites. She ran into great difficulties over the years – many did not want to change. But she had great support and founded seventeen new convents during her lifetime. She died in 1582 when she was sixty-seven, physically worn out. She was declared a Doctor of the Church in 1970.

16 October St Margaret-Mary Alacoque

Virgin
Optional Memorial

Margaret-Mary lived in Burgundy in France. After a tough childhood, she joined the convent of the Poor Clares. She had great devotion to the Blessed Sacrament and had many visions of the Lord. It was through her that the First Friday devotion and the Holy Hour grew up. She was instrumental in getting the Feast of the Sacred Heart established. She died in 1690 when she was fifty-three.

17 October St Ignatius of Antioch Bishop and Martyr
Memorial

Ignatius was surnamed Theophorus, God-bearer. It seems that he took charge of the Church in Antioch in 69AD. Some years later, during the persecution of Trajan, he was arrested and brought to Rome. That was a long journey and he visited many Christian communities on the way and wrote many letters to other communities. He was martyred in 107 — he was eaten by two lions in the Roman amphitheatre during the Emperor's public games.

18 October St Luke Evangelist
Feast

Luke was a Gentile, a fellow worker of Paul, and a medical man. He may have been a Greek from Antioch. He seems to have spent most of his time with Paul, and was with him during his imprisonment in Rome. He wrote one of the gospels and the Acts (probably while in Greece or Asia Minor).

II Tm 4:10-17 Lk 10:1-9

Luke stood by Paul when many others deserted him. The Lord also stood by him when he presented his defence.

The Lord sends out his disciples – they are to be bearers of peace.

19 October SS John de Brébeuf and Isaac Jogues (priests) and companions

Martyrs
[USA: Memorial]

These were French Jesuits and lay missionaries who brought the mission to the Hurons and Iroquois Indians of North America. Isaac was tomahawked to death by the Iroquois in 1647 near Albany. John was mutilated and slain in 1648 near Georgia Bay. These are the secondary patron saints of Canada.

25 October Forty English Martyrs Martyrs
[England & Wales: Feast]

During the sixteenth and seventeenth centuries Cuthbert Mayne, John Houghton, Edmund Campion, Richard Gwynn, and thirty-six companions (in all seven lay men and women, thirteen secular priests and twenty religious) suffered martyrdom. Pope Paul VI canonised these in 1970 for two reasons: 'They will assist in advancing ecumenism worthy of the name. They will be a true safeguard of those real values in which the genuine peace and prosperity of human society are rooted.'

28 October SS Simon and Jude

Very little is known about these two apostles. Simon was called the zealous apostle and according to tradition he preached in Egypt. Jude was called Thaddeus and according to tradition joined Simon when he came back from Egypt and both went to preach in Persia. His name is associated with one of the epistles in the New Testament.

Ep 2:19-22 Lk 6:12-16

All followers of Christ are part of God's household – like a temple with the prophets and apostles as foundations and Jesus as the cornerstone.

Only after a night of prayer did Jesus choose his apostles.

November Feasts

1 November All Saints   Solemnity

This feast is probably of Celtic origin, where it was celebrated on 17 April (martyrs) and 20 April (saints). In the eighth century it was celebrated on 1 November and became a universal feast. The feast applies not only to all the canonised saints, but to all the souls that are in glory. There are three themes – belief in the combined intercession of the saints, hope of sharing in their glory in heaven, and faith in the Eucharist as the pledge of the eternal banquet.

Rv 7:2-4.9-14 1 Jn: 1-3 Mt 5:1-12

The Book of Revelation is full of visions. Today we have the great number of those who were saved by the blood of the lamb – those redeemed by Jesus Christ. They are from every nation, race, trib, and language.

John gives us beautiful words of hope. We are already children of God. But what we are to be is even more wonderful. For then we shall be like the Father, because we will see him as he really is.

Jesus gives us the real Commandments. If we try to keep these we can be sure of our place in glory with him.

2 November All Souls   Commemoration of all the Faithful Departed
Solemnity

'It is a holy and wholesome thought to pray for the dead, that they may be loosed from their sins.' Today, we pray in a special way for those who have died. All this month we pray for them, especially those we knew personally.

3 November St Martin de Porres   Religious
Optional Memorial

Martin was born in Lima, Peru, in 1579, the natural child of John de Porres, a Spanish knight, and a coloured freed-woman from Panama. He inherited the dark features of his mother. Martin became a lay-brother in the Dominicans. He spent his life looking after the sick of the city, and was instrumental in establishing an orphanage. He took on himself the care of the slaves who were brought to Peru from Africia. He was a close friend of St Rose of Lima. He died in 1639.

4 November St Charles Borromeo   Bishop
Memorial

Charles was born of an aristocratic family. Early in life he became a cleric. He had difficulty in learning, but his doggedness kept him going.

He moved up through the Church ranks fairly quickly and assisted in the for the unity of the Church, and was martyred by his enemies in 1623.

6 November [Ireland: Feast]

This feast was established by indult of Pope Benedict XV.

9 November Feast

This is regarded as the mother church of Christendom. We celebrate the feast as a sign of devotion to and unity with the Chair of Peter, which, as St Ignatius of Antioch wrote, 'presides over the whole assembly of charity'.

Ezk 43:1-2.4-7 I Co 3:9-13.16-17 Jn 2:13-22

The glory of God is present in the Temple. This is where he shall live. You are God's building and the spirit of God is living in you.

Jesus is annoyed at the sellers in the Temple. He makes reference to an even greater Temple of God, his own body – he will die, but be raised in three days.

10 November St Leo the Great Pope and Doctor of the Church
Memorial

Leo was probably born in Tuscany in Italy, but was a Roman in education and mentality. He worked for a while in France. He became Pope in 440 and was a true pastor and father of souls. He worked strenuously to safeguard the integrity of the faith and vigorously defended the unity of the Church. He died in 461.

11 November St Martin of Tours Bishop
Memorial

Martin was born in 316. He gave up the military and was baptised. He founded a monastery in France, was later ordained a priest and became Bishop of Tours. He was an example of a good pastor, founding many monasteries, educating the clergy, and preaching the gospel to the poor. He died in 397.

12 November St Josaphat Bishop and Martyr
Memorial

Josaphat was born in the Ukraine in 1580 and belonged to the Orthodox church. He became a Catholic and joined a Basilian monastery. Later he was ordained and became the Bishop of Polock. He spent his life working for the unity of the Church, and was martyred by his enemies in 1623.

13 November St Frances Xavier Cabrini Virgin
[USA:Memorial]

Frances was born in Lombardy, Italy, in 1850. She founded the Missionary Sisters of the Sacred Heart. She worked for twenty-eight years in the US and South America, establishing schools, hospitals and orphanages. She died in Chicago in 1917. She is the first US citizen to have been canonised (1946).

16 November St Margaret of Scotland

Matron
[Scotland: Feast]

Margaret was born in Hungary about 1046. She was a relative of King Edward the Confessor .When she was twenty-four she married Malcolm III, the King of Scotland, and bore him eight children. She was an excellent wife and served her adopted country well. She promoted the arts of civilisation and encouraged education and religion, doing her best to get good priests and teachers for all parts of the country. In her own private life she was very austere and made time for her devotions each day. She died in 1093, four days after her husband. Margaret is the secondary patron of Scotland.

17 November St Elizabeth of Hungary

Religious
Memorial

Elizabeth born in 1207, the daughter of King Andrew of Hungary. She was married and had three children. After the death of her husband she embraced poverty and spent her days caring for the sick in a hospice which she had built. She died in 1231, aged twenty-four.

21 November Presentation of Our Lady

Memorial

This feast goes back to 543, when a church, built near the Temple of Jerusalem, was dedicated to Our Lady. With the Eastern Christians we celebrate the dedication of herself which Mary made to God from her childhood under the inspiration of the Holy Spirit.

22 November St Cecilia

Virgin and Martyr
Memorial

Very little is known about Cecilia. She seems to have been martyred in the second century and is venerated in the catacomb of St Callistus in Rome. She is the patron saint of music and musicians.

23 November St Columbanus

Abbot
[Ireland: Feast]

Columban was born somewhere in Leinster and from an early age wished

to become a monk. He went to Bangor and worked there for many years. Eventually he was given permission to go abroad and set up monasteries in France, where religion was at a low ebb. His main foundation was at Luxeuil. He ran into many problems with the civil authorities and was eventually banned. He ended up in Italy where he founded the monastery at Bobbio. Many did not like his brand of Celtic Christian discipline – his monastic rule was similar to that of the East, and much more severe than that of Benedict. He died in 615. His followers set up monasteries in France, Germany, Switzerland and Italy.

Last Thursday Thanksgiving   [USA]

This day is not a holy day of obligation, but it is good to make it a holyday. We have much to thank God for at the end of the year. Let's thank God in the company of our families and look after the poor.

Dt 8:7-18 I Tm 6:6-11.17-19 Lk 12:15-21

Moses promises the people that they were being brought into a land filled with all the good things of nature. He reminds them not to forget to give God thanks when they have eaten their fill.

We brought nothing into the world, we can bring nothing out of it. Use the good things of life well, share with those who have not. This will give us a secure foundation in the future.

Avoid greed in all its forms. Remember that what you have, you have from God, and use it well. Be sure to grow rich in the sight of God.

30 November St Andrew   Apostle
                                                                  Feast
                                                   [Scotland: Solemnity]

Andrew was a follower of John the Baptist. He then saw that Jesus was the person John had often spoken about – he must increase, I must decrease. So he joined Jesus. He then introduced his brother, Peter, to Jesus. Later he brought the message of Christ to the Gentiles and is believed to have preached in many parts of the known world. He died on the cross in Achaia. Andrew is the principal patron of Scotland.

Rm 10:9-18 Mt 4:18-22

If you believe that Jesus is Lord, who rose from the dead, you will be saved. But for people to believe, they must have heard of him; they will not hear unless they get a preacher; the preacher must be sent. The footsteps of those who bring good news is a welcome sound.

The gospel gives us the story of the call of Andrew and others. Later they were sent to preach his message.

December Feasts

3 December St Francis Xavier   Priest
                                                      Memorial
                                              [Australia: Feast]

St Francis was a remarkable man. He was born in Spain, joined the Jesuits and then spent every minute of his life trying to convert people. He did this first in Europe and then set sail for the east. The journey took thirteen months to Goa, but he worked hard there, in India, and also in Japan – the first Christian to go there. He even had a shot at China, but got sick and died on one of the islands on 3 December 1552, at the age of forty-six. Reading his life story is like reading a good adventure story. He was a man of tremendous energy, faith, and kindness.

7 December St Ambrose   Bishop and Doctor of the Church
                                                      Memorial

Ambrose was born in Trier, where his father was some kind of governor. When he died his mother moved the family back to Rome, where Ambrose was educated. At one stage he went to Milan to sort out a row between two opposing factions wanting their next bishop and, even though he was still unbaptised, they wanted him after hearing his speech. Later he received the sacraments and was consecrated bishop. All his life he was threatened by rival heretical groups, and a number of political leaders, even the Emperor himself. He reminded him that 'the emperor is in the Church, not over the Church'. He also wrote many treatises against the many heresies that flourished at this time. He baptised St Augustine at Easter 387. He died in 397, aged fifty-seven.

8 December The Immaculate Conception   Solemnity

It was always believed from early times that Our Lady was spared the stain of Original Sin – she wasn't under the influence of sin like we are. It would not have been fitting for her to have been tainted in any way. It was celebrated as the feast of the conception of Mary in the east as far back as 750. The present feast was established in the last century after the dogma of the Immaculate Conception was defined in 1854. It is of relevance that the tradition states that Mary was free from sin from the first moment of her conception – that was when her life began.

Gn 3:9-15.20 Ep 1:3-6.11-12 Lk 1:26-38

Adam eats from the forbidden tree and blames Eve, who in turn blames the serpent. 'I will make you enemies of each other – you and the woman, your offspring and her offspring.' We have here a reference to Mary, who will crush the serpent, the symbol of evil.

We have a beautiful passage in which Paul praises God, the Father of Our Lord Jesus Christ, who blessed us, chose us before the world was made, chose us in Christ to be holy, spotless and to live in his presence. The first to experience this was Mary.

'I am the handmaid of the Lord,' said Mary, 'let what you have said be done to me.' We pray that we too can have this commitment.

13 December St Lucy
Virgin and Martyr
Memorial

Very little is known about Lucy, except that she was martyred in Syracuse in Sicily. A Greek inscription found there in 1894 testifies to the devotion to the saint in the fourth century. The account of her martyrdom states that she wanted to consecrate herself to God and decided to give the money allocated for her dowry to the poor. Her infuriated fiancé brought her to court. She was tortured and died by the sword.

14 December St John of the Cross
Priest and Doctor of the Church
Memorial

John was born into a very poor family – his father was disinherited because he married beneath his station and his mother died when he was young. From his early years he wanted to be a monk. Eventually he joined the Carmelites and studied at Salamanca in Spain. Later he worked with Teresa of Avila to reform the order. This caused him much suffering and many trials for the rest of his life. He believed in contemplative prayer and wrote many famous works on the subject, including *The Living Flame* and *The Spiritual Canticle*. In *The Dark Night of the Soul*, he writes of the times when he lost the taste for prayer and became spiritually dry. Whenever we find it difficult to pray, St John of the Cross would be the ideal patron. He died in 1591.

26 December St Stephen
Protomartyr
Feast

Stephen was a Jew and probably spoke Greek. He was one of the first deacons. He had great wisdom and a strong faith. He infuriated the Jews because he preached that Jesus had superseded the Jewish law, as was foretold in scripture. False witnesses were brought against him and he was eventually stoned to death.

Ac 6:8-10. 7:54-59 Mt 10:17-22
Stephen was filled with grace and power and worked signs among the

people. His zeal and integrity annoyed many and eventually he gave his life for his faith.

Jesus tells his disciples that many will attack them because they are his followers. The Holy Spirit will enlighten them when necessary.

27 December St John
Apostle and Evangelist
Feast

John was the 'beloved disciple' of Jesus. He wrote his gospel and his three letters after the other three gospels had been written. His descriptions are much more reflective. Little is known about his life. According to tradition he was the only apostle who did not suffer martyrdom.

I Jn 1:1-4 Jn 20:2-8

John gives strong testimony to the fact that he saw and related to Jesus. He wants others to share his joy in this.

John had more faith than Peter – as soon as he saw the empty tomb he immediately believed that Jesus had risen from the dead.

28 December The Holy Innocents
Martyrs
Feast

Herod the Great had a huge influence on Judah, building many cities and palaces. He was also a very violent and unscrupulous person. He was afraid of any threat to his position. When he learned of the birth of a king he was worried and tried to eliminate all possible candidates around Bethlehem. It was only when he died that Joseph brought the young Jesus and his mother back to Nazareth.

I Jn 1:5-2:2 Mt 2:13-18

God is light. If we live in light we will live in union with Jesus Christ. None of us is innocent. If we deny any sin in our lives we are liars. But if we acknowledge our sins, then God will forgive our sins and purify us – he is the sacrifice that takes away our sins.

God in his providence looks after his chosen and saves Jesus from the wickedness of Herod. The children become special martyrs. Good is always being attacked. Today it may be more subtle than in Herod's time, but much of what our Church stands for is being ridiculed and criticised from all quarters. Let us learn to trust God and not count the consequences of standing for Christian principles.

29 December St Thomas à Becket
Bishop and Martyr
{England: Feast]

Thomas was born in London in 1118. He was Chancellor of England and in 1162 became Archbishop of Canterbury. He defended the position of the Church against King Henry II, and was exiled to France for six years. He had further trials when he returned and was murdered in 1170 by the King's men. He is Patron of the English Pastoral Clergy.

Brief Summaries of Biblical Books

All scripture is inspired by God and can profitably be used for teaching, for refuting error, for guiding people's lives and teaching them to be holy. [2 Tm 3:16]

The Bible as we have it today developed from about 2000 BC to the end of the Apostolic era. The earliest writings go back to about 1000 BC. The word Bible comes from the Greek βιβλια meaning 'books'. It has been defined as a collection of religious traditions which are revered as sacred because they are inspired by God. The communities of ancient Israel and the early Christians believed that God had been revealed in their midst through the events of history, and these traditions developed and were later written down. They were cherished as authentic and enduring testimonies of God's revelation.

There is a number of different types of books. In the Old Testament these are the historical books, the wisdom books and the prophets. In the New Testament we have historical books, letters from Paul and other apostles, and a poetic book. Some of the books of the Catholic Old Testament are described as deutero-canonical, from the Greek 'second canon'. These were the books that are not in the Hebrew canon (official list), but are found in the Greek translation (Judith, Tobit, Wisdom, Sirach, Baruch, I and II Maccabees and parts of Daniel and Esther).

The Bible is the inspired word of God and so it cannot teach error. It is important to know the time and place in which a particular book was written, the person who wrote or edited it, his style or teaching method, and the people for whom it was originally intended, before we can attempt to understand the spiritual message. Those books that use historical facts cannot be regarded as history resource books (or for that matter science manuals) in the modern sense: the writer uses historical detail as a means of conveying the spiritual message. In fact, people in that part of the world are generally more interested in the meaning or significance of events rather than in the actual details, or even their accuracy. Another point to remember is that what we read is a translation, which often cannot adequately give us the idiom of the original. As a help to understand the background of the Bible a brief description of each of the books is given below, with a reference to the weeks when they are used in the weekday lectionary.

'Ignorance of the Scriptures is ignorance of Christ' (St Jerome). Therefore let us gladly go to the sacred text itself, whether in the sacred liturgy, which is full of the divine words, or in devout reading, or in such suitable exercises and various other helps which, with the approval and guidance of the pastors of the Church, are happily spreading everywhere in our day. Let us remember, however, that prayer should accompany the reading of Sacred Scripture, so that a dialogue takes place between God and ourselves. For 'we speak to him when we pray; we listen to him when we read the divine oracles'.

– St Ambrose.

The following abbreviations are used:
[Monday= (i), Tuesday = (ii) etc. A = Advent, C= Christmastide, L=Lent, E=Easter 1=Year (i), 2=Year (ii)
Thus: A:1(ii)= Tuesday of the first week of Advent
        L:0(iv)=Thursday after Ash Wednesday
        2:23(iii)=Wednesday 23rd week, second year]

Old Testament

Genesis [Gn]   [17 December L:3(v), 5(iv),1:5-6(v), 12-14]

The Pentateuch is made up of the first five books of the Old Testament. The Book of Genesis is the first of these. The first eleven chapters consist of various traditions that were passed down orally from one generation to the next and eventually written down. They were stories with a spiritual significance – each had a special message about God. It is important to remember that the people at the time had no interest whatever in how things happened in the past. The rest of it deals with early salvation history, beginning with the story of Abraham and concluding with the story of Joseph in Egypt.

Exodus [Ex]   [L:4(iv), 1:14-17(iv)]

This book continues the story of salvation history. It begins well after Joseph when his work is forgotten in Egypt and the descendants of Abraham are being exploited. Exodus – the outward journey – deals with the journey of the Chosen People from Egypt and the details of their years in the desert, including the making of the covenant. It is the story of Moses.

Leviticus [Lv]   [L:1(i), 1:17(v-vi)]

Moses tried to prepare the people for their new life in the Promised Land.

It was important that they would remember the providence of God, so they were to have a number of feasts to commemorate the various events that had occurred to them – much like our holy days. This book was really a priest's book. It is full of Commandments which were binding on the Israelites. The central theme is holiness in the ordinary areas of life, such as food, clothing, sickness, the moral ethics of society, as well as regular worship.

Numbers [Nb] [A:3(i), L:5(ii), 1:18(i-iv)]

The Book of Numbers continues the account of the plight of the Israelites in the desert. It is a combination of narratives and laws, something like Exodus and Leviticus. Each collection of laws relates to the experiences and lessons learned from the past. The book continues their story up to the assault on the Promised Land. It takes its name from the two censuses of the Hebrew people that were taken, one near the beginning of the journey in the desert and the other towards the end.

Deuteronomy [Dt] [L(iv), L:1(vi), L:3(iii), 1:18(v)-19(iii)]

The Book of Deuteronomy contains many of the discourses of Moses. It is the fifth and final book of the Pentateuch and is one of the most important and influential books in the Hebrew Scriptures. The final version was probably written during the Exile to encourage the people to a new beginning. It takes its inspiration from the book of the law found by King Josiah (640-609 BC). It is really a sermon with its urgent appeals to obedience and loyalty to God and its severe warnings of the serious consequences that will occur if the people do not follow its teachings. The Israelites had been influenced by the gods of the Egyptians and Moses was trying to get them to break away from those traditions and believe in the one, true God. He reminded them of the wonders the Lord had worked and of the Commandments that they had been given.

Joshua [Jos] [1:19(iv-v)]

The next set of books is often referred to as the books of Deuteronomistic History, because the Book of Deuteronomy is a sort of preface to them. These books are Joshua, Judges, Samuel, Kings and Ruth. Joshua took over from Moses. The Israelites move into the Promised Land at last, bringing the symbol of God with them, the ark of the covenant, containing the Commandments. God would also be with them when they made their way into the great city of Jericho.

Judges [Jg] [18 December 1:20(i-iv)]

The Book of Judges was formed in the Promised Land. The accounts of the activities of the Chosen People were put into the context of Holy War – a battle believed to be fought by the Lord on behalf of Israel. So the heroes or 'judges' became instruments of the Lord who fought for Israel. These tried to keep the people on the road laid down by Moses and Joshua. But the people went over to the gods of the neighbours – they had a great selection of fertility gods with doubtful sexual practices. Whenever the Israelites sinned the Lord punished them by allowing them to be conquered by an enemy. Then Israel would cry to the Lord for help, and the Lord would send a deliverer (a judge) who freed Israel from the enemy. This process was repeated over and over again.

Ruth [Rt] [1:20 (v-vi)]

Ruth was from the tribe of Moab. When she married one of the sons of Naomi she became a firm believer in the God of her husband's people. After his death she would not go back to the worship of the gods of her pagan people. Her son was Obed who was the father of Jesse, who in turn was the father of David.

Samuel [I & II] [S] [22, 24 December 2:1(i-v);1(vi)-4(iii)]

These Books of Samuel are not history in the modern sense but theological history – narrative accounts of God's dealings with the chosen people. The principal message that the Israelites had been given over the years was that if they were faithful to the laws given by Moses, faithful to the covenant, that they would have prosperity and peace; if they were to disobey, they can expect punishment through natural disaster, invasion, and even exile. This is the Deuteronomistic perspective. The three main characters in these books are Samuel, Saul and David. Samuel was the last of the judges. He first chose Saul as the king of Israel, being inspired by God to do so. He did not live up to his commitment and eventually David was anointed king and took over after Saul's death. He was the greatest of the Israelite kings. The first book of Samuel concerns the establishment of a monarchy in Israel, while the second gives an account of the reign of Saul and David.

Kings [I & II] [K] [L:3(i), 2:4(iv)-5; 2:10-12(v)]

The Books of Samuel dealt with Samuel, Saul and David. The book of Kings deals with David's dynasty. This was initiated with David's son, Solomon, succeeding him. The first book deals with Solomon's reign, the building of the Temple, and the eventual unfaithfulness of Solomon, The second book deals with the later kings. The kingdom was divided into two after Solomon's time – Israel in the north and Judah in the south. Again, their infidelity led to various evils and eventually to the destruction of the Temple and the deportation to Babylon.

Chronicles [1 & 2] [Ch] [2:10(vi)]

These books, along with Ezra, and Nehemiah, form the Chronicler's History. It covers the full history of salvation from Adam down to the restoration of the Temple after the exile. The first part of the book contains many genealogies and details of the activities of David. The second book gives the stories of Solomon's reign and the subsequent history of the southern kingdom, Judah. It gives details of how Joash behaved as last king of Judah before the Exile. It contains information on the division between Jews and Samaritans.

Ezra [Ezr] [1:25 (i-iii)]

This and the book of Nehemiah are the only narrative accounts of the post-Exile period to have survived. Originally these two books formed one book. The final phase of the Babylonian exile took place in 587 BC. One of the first things that King Cyrus did when he came to power was to allow captives in Babylon to go home. The first group went back to Judaea in 537. The first thing they did was bring back the sacred vessels so that they could be used in the Temple they intended to rebuild.

Nehemiah [Ne] [1:26(iii-iv)]

Nehemiah was a cupbearer to the Persian king – he had to taste the wine to make sure it wasn't poisoned. He used his position to appeal to the king to let him go back to Jerusalem and help rebuild it. He took a risk in this, as no courtier was allowed to appear sad. But the king allowed him to go. (Psalm – 'By the rivers of Babylon'...) Nehemiah was instrumental in rebuilding the walls of Jerusalem.

Tobit [Tb] [1:9]

This is a fictional story of a dutiful servant son, Tobias, who is given miraculous help by an angel. It was written among the Jews of the Dispersion, possibly in Egypt around the beginning of the second century BC. Tobit was a very religious and law- abiding Jew. Among his good deeds was the burying of the dead, even in war. The book weaves the story of Tobit with those of Tobias and Sarah. Its primary religious message is simply that God rewards those who are faithful. This is a deutero-canonical book.

Judith [Jdt]

This is a fictional story with some historical background. It is the story of how Judith – meaning 'Jewish woman' – delivered the Jews from their enemies. It affirms belief in the one God, who guides all human events and is present with the weak and the oppressed. This is a deutero-canonical book.

Esther [Est] [L:1(iv-v)]

This book is mainly concerned with the survival of the Jewish minority in a world that is growing more hostile to it. It is the story of a threat to its survival and how that was overcome. Mordechai was a Jewish courtier in the service of the Persian emperor. He was helped by Esther in resolving a serious situation where a pogrom against the Jews was organised. Esther's courage came from her belief that God alone could save her people and her confidence that he would answer her prayers, which were accompanied by fasting and alms-giving. The story shows that God will act to preserve the Jewish community in a hidden and indirect way. Parts of this book are deutero-canonical.

Maccabees [I &II] [M] [1:33]

The two Books of Maccabees were probably written around one hundred years before Christ, telling of events some years before. They depict the confrontation between the traditional Jewish religion and the Greek and Near Eastern culture. It is a story of a particular family, nicknamed the Maccabees, after 'hammer,' who decided to rebel against the forces, including the country's leaders, trying to promote this foreign religious culture. This revolt was led first by the father Mattathias and later by his three sons in turn, Judas, Jonathan and Simon. These are deutero-canonical books.

Job [Jb] [2:26]

The Book of Job is the first of the Wisdom books. It is a very famous poem and tries to deal with the huge problem of human suffering. Why does God allow a good person to suffer? What part has suffering to play in the life of a person? Job was a pious and blameless man, who was perfectly happy and contented. Satan insinuates himself among the angel's of God's court and argues that Job's virtue is not genuine. So God allows Satan to test his virtue – but not to touch Job himself. As a result Job lost everything. 'The Lord gave, the Lord has taken back. Blessed be the name of the Lord.' Even his friends were not able to advise him. It was probably written around the sixth or fifth century BC.

Psalms [Ps]

This is the longest book in the Bible and consists of 150 psalms divided into five books. They were written at different times and put into one collection. They are beautiful poetic prayers. The psalms are of three types: hymns or songs of praise; laments – with pleas for deliverance from some misfortune; and prayers of thanksgiving. Two other types were royal and wisdom psalms. Many of these were used in liturgical celebrations; others were used in processions or on pilgrimages. They generally speak to God rather than about God. Yahweh is the most frequent title of God, though Elohim is sometimes used. He is the creator of the universe and the source of all life: he is enthroned in heaven and yet dwelling in Jerusalem. He is concerned with the well-being of all people, though committed to upholding the Mosaic covenant with the people of Israel. The human person has a special place in creation and God protects them from harm. He rewards those who do good and will punish those who remain in their evil ways. Nature reveals the power and glory of God.

Proverbs [Pr]   [2:25(i-iii)]

The Book of Proverbs is the third of the Wisdom books. One aspect of the relationship between God and the Israelites was what is called 'salvation history', which dealt with the role God played in their history. The other role was that in everyday life – the guides for successful living. The Israelites saw their God as a Creator-God, who was responsible for the order in nature. Wisdom was the ability to perceive how to live in accordance with that order in their ordinary lives. The wisdom books are full of instructions in the proper ways of living. Many teaching techniques are used – story-telling, exhortation, warning and questioning. They use riddles, proverbs, parables and metaphors. The poems are challenges on the problems of evil, the suffering of good people, and God's justice. There are also many hymns or psalms which were used in liturgical celebrations. The style is very poetic and uses much nature imagery.

The book of Proverbs probably best characterises the wisdom tradition. Its primary purpose is to teach wisdom. It speaks to children, young men, citizens and women. The book is divided into eight separate teaching sections. Some of these were from the sayings of Solomon – the wise son of David.

Qoheleth/Ecclesiastes [Qo] [2:25(iv-vi)]

The Book of Ecclesiastes is another Wisdom book. It is more correctly called the book of Qoheleth, the Hebrew word for Preacher. One of the best-known extracts begins 'vanity of vanities, all is vanity'. This refers to the uselessness of human things. The Hebrew word means wind, puff or vapour: as used here it means barrenness, impermanence, and the illusory nature of things. They deceive anyone who puts their trust in them. Other well-known sayings are 'You can't take it with you', and 'There is nothing new under the sun.' It may have been written around the third century BC. Along with the Song of Songs, Ruth, Lamentations and Esther, it made up the 'Scrolls'. These were a special collection of books read during various liturgical festivals.

Song of Songs [Sg] [21 December]

This is probably the most difficult book in the Old Testament to interpret. It is a collection of love poems full of sensuous imagery. It never even mentions God and does not seem, at first sight, to promote any theological or moral values. It is attributed to Solomon, though it was not composed by him. Over the years both Jews and Christians have tended to give the book a symbolic meaning. The marriage of God to Israel or Christ to the Church is often used. In Christian liturgy the girl in the Song becomes the Virgin Mary. Mystics have used it to describe the soul's deep yearning for its lover, Christ. The literal interpretation sees the book as a collection of love songs showing that human love is good and is one of God's beauties.

Wisdom [Ws] [L:4(v), 1:32]

The Book of Wisdom is also full of poetry. It is one of the latest books of the Old Testament – it was written in Greek by a pious Jew, perhaps in Egypt, during the first century BC. He had a very good knowledge of the history of Exodus, Greek philosophy, and the religious practices of Egypt. He was trying to ensure that the Israelites would not be led astray by the Greek culture and would have pride in their own religious heritage. This is a deutero-canonical book.

Sirach/Ecclesiasticus [Si]   [A:2(vi), 1:7-8: 2:4(v),10(iv)]

This was a book of moral guidance, containing many maxims. It is full of short essays addressing such topics as duties towards God, towards one's parents, and towards rulers. Its author was Ben Sira and the book was written some time around 180 BC. It teaches that God is all, the only God, the almighty Creator, who brought both natural and moral order to life. This God is the source of good, who acts justly and forgives sin. Life continues in some way after death, with judgment occurring at death. Obedience to the law and participation in the liturgies is important. This is a deutero-canonical book.

Isaiah [Is]
[A:1-2(v), 3(iii-v), 20 Dec, L(v-vi), L:1(ii),L:2(ii), L:4(i-ii), L:6:(i-iii), 2:14(vi)-15(v)]

Isaiah was one of the major prophets, along with Jeremiah and Ezekiel. After the Psalms, this book is the longest in the Old Testament, and may have been written by a number of people. These are often referred to as First, Second and Third Isaiah. It spans several centuries, from before the destruction of Israel and Judah, through the Exile and return of the remnant, to the efforts to revive the old kingdom (742-500 BC). There are three main themes – the Temple at Jerusalem becomes a symbol of Messianic hopes, there is a gradual change in emphasis to include the Gentiles within Israel's salvation, and there is a great sense of justice. First Isaiah (chapters 1-39) – Isaiah of Jerusalem – was active during the last years of the northern kingdom, when the southern kingdom was under threat. His main message was that God is the Holy One of Israel and his holiness shows up the sinfulness of humanity. One must have faith and trust in God and not in one's own resources. David's line will then continue. Second Isaiah (40-55) was written just after the exile and was an attempt celebrate their deliverance and to reformulate the faith of Israel. God (Yahweh) is all-powerful, the Creator of all, the redeemer of Israel who buys it back from the state of slavery. Within this section are the Suffering Servant poems, which were probably written to explain the Babylonian captivity, but are now referred to Jesus Christ. Third Isaiah (56-66) comes from a later period. The nations of the world are invited into the ranks of Israel as the Lord's chosen people. Isaiah was a very popular book both among the Jews and early Christians. Now it is read mainly during Advent and for some of Lent.

Jeremiah [Jr] [18 Dec, L:2(iii-iv), L:3(iv), L:4(vi), L:5(v), 2:16(iii)-18(iv)]

Jeremiah was the second major prophet after Isaiah. He lived about a hundred years later in very eventful times. During his lifetime there were five kings in Judah and he was there to see the destruction of Jerusalem and the kingdom. He was a rather shy and extremely sensitive person. He was called to be a prophet during his adolescence. 'Before I formed you in the womb I knew you... I have appointed you as prophet to the nations.' Of all the prophets he is the closest model of Jesus Christ. The work is full of Messianic references. His life was as much a message as his words. We see his struggle to know what God wants, how he gets courage to seek it, and eventually the wisdom and peace he gets by choosing the right path.

Lamentations [Lm]   [2:12(vi)]

This is a large prayer book, probably written just after the destruction of Jerusalem to help people cope with grief. Even meaningless suffering can have a good purpose, for God, who is compassionate enough to bear our human outrage, walks us through the dark valleys and onto the plateaux of peace. We see great sadness and an intense cry to God for deliverance. Everything that the people held dear was gone. All they could hold onto was the prophecy that eventually a remnant of the people of David would continue as God's Chosen People. In their misery, their Lord would look after them in his own way. Lamentations is divided into five poems (chapters). Three of them have verses beginning with each letter of the Hebrew alphabet in turn. The others are built on a pattern of twenty-two.

Baruch [Ba]   [1:26(v-vi)]

Baruch seems to have been a contemporary of the prophet Jeremiah, as this work refers to the beginning of the Exile in Babylon.In his prayer he reminds the Israelites that their situation is due to their disobedience and disloyalty. They served alien gods and did what was displeasing to their God. It is one of the few books that speaks to the Israelites who live outside the Promised Land. This is a deutero-canonical book.

Ezekiel [Ezk]   [L:4(ii), L:5(vi), 2:19-20]

Ezekiel was the third of the major prophets. He lived at the time of the destruction of Jerusalem and was among the Israelites who went into exile in Babylon. It is difficult to 'see' the real Ezekiel from the text, as there are few biographical references. He used many literary styles to get his message across. His main themes were the importance of the Temple where the Lord was present, the awesomeness of God, and the responsibility of the individual. He describes many of his visions, many of which have apocalyptic overtones.

Daniel [Dn] $\qquad$ [L:2(i), L:3(ii), L:5(i,iii), 1:34]

The Book of Daniel has two parts. The first of these contains fictional tales of heroes during the Babylonian exile, which were used to encourage the people during the Maccabean revolt. The other section contains accounts of various visions – often called apocalyptical material or the revelations, and generally referring to the Last Judgment. Parts of this book are deutero-canonical.

Hosea [Ho] $\qquad$ [L:3(v-vi), 2:14(i-v)]

The Book of the Twelve is a collection of prophetic oracles over a three hundred-year period. These were written by the Minor Prophets. In chronological order, Hosea came second. He lived around the same time as Amos, some years before the destruction of the northern kingdom. It was a time of great instability and crisis for Israel. His oracles are in the form of very beautiful poetry, and he mainly attacks the idolatry of the people. The people had turned their backs on the God who saved them and made a covenant with them. In the first part Hosea uses his marriage in a metaphorical way. He married one who was a prostitute, who had taken part in pagan fertility rites. She had three unhappy children. Israel had behaved in a similar way and had done evil things . But there is hope. The day will come when his wife – and Israel – will return to the master, away from the despicable pagan rites and back to integrity, justice, love and tenderness.

Joel [Jl] $\qquad$ [L(iii),1:27(v-vi)]

Joel is the last of the books which deal with the period after the Babylonian exile, and gives a real sense of doom and gloom. The Israelites have brought this on themselves because they turned away from their God. This day of darkness and gloom, of cloud and blackness, will cause terror among the people. The day of the Lord is coming. They are called to repentance – 'rend your hearts and not your garments'. Eventually God will restore his people and bring peace and contentment.

Amos [Am] $\qquad$ [1:13]

Amos was the earliest of the minor prophets. He came from the southern kingdom, but preached mainly in the north about forty years or so before its destruction. He was not a member of a guild of prophets, but was a shepherd and a dresser of the fruits of sycamores. Unlike other prophets he did not depend on the king for support, and so could speak independently. He used very strong oracles to condemn different types of social injustice – each one beginning 'It is the Lord who speaks.' Amos lists the crimes the Israelites have committed against their fellow human beings. They did this in spite of the care and attention that God had given them. They broke the covenant that God made with them and for this they would be punished.

Obadiah [Ob]

This is the shortest of the prophetic books with only twenty-one verses. It consists of a series of oracles about some of the neighbouring nations, especially Edom, and a prediction of the restoration of Jerusalem.

Jonah [Jon]   [L:1(iii), 1:27(i-iii)]

The Book of Jonah is another book connected with the Babylonian exile. It is regarded as a sermon in the form of a story. It teaches that the mercy of God extends to all nations and is not restricted to the Chosen People. Jonah was afraid to carry out his mission of preaching repentance to the citizens of Nineveh and tried to travel in the opposite direction. The Lord had other plans and eventually caused Jonah to be brought back, having spent three days and three nights in a great fish. Eventually he goes to the city and the people respond to his preaching.

Micah [Mi]   [L:2(vi), 2:15(vi)-16(ii)]

Micah lived around the same time as Isaiah, Amos, and Hosea. He was a prophet in the southern kingdom. He is preoccupied with issues of social justice and the coming of the Assyrian invasion. He condemns those who plan evil against others in the community, especially by taking the fertile land between the mountains and the sea. Just as they plot, so will the Lord plot against them and they will be stripped of everything.

Nahum [Na]   [2:18(v)]

Nahum lived during the latter years of Jeremiah. He speaks to the people of Nineveh, the capital of the warring neighbour which committed so many atrocities. They have now fallen and he tries to persuade them to repent. He stresses the justice and mercy of God, who always comes to the defence of those who love him and keep his Commandments.

Habakkuk [Hab]   [2:18(vi)]

The prophet Habakkuk lived towards the end of Jeremiah's lifetime. Why is God allowing so much evil and hardship to befall his people? Why do evil people go unpunished? God speaks through him – there is hope for the just and upright man; the others will get their just desserts eventually. The just must live in faithfulness and hope.

Zephaniah [Zp]   [A:3(ii), 21 December]

Zephaniah is looking forward to the day — the Day of the Lord — when the people are taken away from their sins and from sinful people. When

the Messiah comes the insincere, the rebellious, the defiled, those who will not listen to the Lord, will all be taken away. God says, I will give the people lips that are clean; you will do no wrong, will tell no lies. You will be able to rest with no one to disturb you. Then there will be peace and contentment.

Haggai [Hg]   [1:25(iv-v)]

Haggai was the prophet in the years after the return of the remnant to Jerusalem. Among other things he exhorted them to get down to the work of rebuilding the Temple and not to make excuses.

Zechariah [Zc]   [1:25(vi)-26(ii)]

Zechariah was the second prophet for the Israelites after their exile in Babylon. He used oracles and accounts of his visions to encourage the people and build up their morale. He attached great importance to ritual in worship.

Malachi [Ml]   [23 December 1:27(iv)]

Malachi ('Messenger') was a prophet who lived some years after the end of the Exile period. He taught through the use of dialogue. This extract gives us a picture of life in the Jewish community before reforms had taken place. The oracles condemned the abuses of the priests who dishonoured God with blemished sacrifices, and those who married pagans. The people who were doing their best were annoyed that the evil-doers were prospering – God did not seem to be interested in punishing them. Malachi assures them that the good deeds are to be recorded and the time will come when the evil-doers will be burnt up like stubble.

New Testament

Matthew [Mt]
[A:1(i,iii-vi), 2(ii-vi),3(i-ii),17,18,26,28,Dec, 7 Jan, L(iii,v),1(i-ii,iv-vi)2(ii-iii), 3(ii-iii,v), 5(iii),E:1(i), 10-21]

The three gospels of Matthew, Mark and Luke are called the synoptic gospels – 'synoptic' comes from the Greek, 'view together' – as there are many parallels in them. In each Jesus begins his public ministry of teaching and healing in Galilee with his disciples and then sets off on his journey with them to Jerusalem, where he undergoes his passion, crucifixion and resurrection. However, each evangelist has his own specific purpose and viewpoint in mind and it is this that makes the difference between them.

Matthew's gospel was probably written after Mark's and is strongly Jewish in flavour. It is basically in the form of a story or a narrative. It begins with the roots of Jesus' family tree and traces his origin back into the history of Israel. It is a dynamic story which gives the details of the activities of Jesus' public life, enriched with his many sayings. Many of these have been organised into discourses or speeches. There are frequent references to the Old Testament, as the author tries to link the story of Jesus with the history of Israel. He also emphasises that Jesus is the Messiah who was spoken of by the prophets. But he is the Messiah for the whole world and not just for the Jews. The gospel can be divided into six sections – the origin of Jesus, the preparation of his ministry, the Galilean ministry, the way to Jerusalem, the final teaching in Jerusalem, and his death and resurrection. In all there are five speeches – the Sermon on the Mount (on holiness), on Mission and Ministry, on the Kingdom and Church, on Life in the Community, and on Judgment. These are separated from one another by narrative material.

Mark [Mk]   [8,9 January E:1(vi), 1-9]

This was probably the first of the gospels. The evangelist put together the sayings of Jesus and the accounts of his ministry into one single dramatic narrative. He begins with the baptism at the Jordan – the first public act of Jesus, and continues till his death and resurrection in Jerusalem. It is a dynamic story, with Jesus going rapidly from one place to another, without wasting any time. The central theme is the understanding of the mystery of the identity of Jesus – 'Who do you say that I am?' Through the parables, the instruction to the disciples, the healing, the conflicts, and especially his death and resurrection, Mark is showing that Jesus is the Messiah, the Son of God. He is also concerned with discipleship and the service that this involves. It took a long while for his disciples to understand what Jesus was about and that they would also have to suffer. He may have written it for the Roman Christians during the persecution of Nero (64 AD). The gospel can be divided into four parts – Jesus in the desert, his Galilean ministry, the journey to Jerusalem, and his death and resurrection.

Luke [Lk]
[A:1(ii), 2(i), 3(iii-iv), 19-24, 29-30 Dec, 10-11 January, L(iv,vi), 1(iii), 2(i,iv), 2(v), 3(i,iv,vi), E:1(iii-iv), 22-34]

Luke was not an eye-witness to the work of Jesus. He was probably a well-educated person with a Greek background. He may have used Mark's gospel and sources used by Matthew. His account was aimed at the Greek-speaking, non-Jewish converts of the cities in the eastern part of the Roman empire. This can be seen when he ties up some of the gospel events with Roman history – for instance, he links the birth of Christ with Caesar Augustus. Like the other two gospels he uses a narrative style. He gives the details of the teaching and parables of Jesus in a way that serves as instruction for the Church. Throughout the gospel there is evidence of the tragedy of Israel. Israel longed for the Messiah, yet when Jesus was in their midst the people rejected him. Luke is a very good story-teller and gets across the idea that salvation is a joyous surprise – how often there are references to people praising and thanking God for what Jesus has done. There is much about mercy and forgiveness. There is also concern about those who are in need. The gospel can be divided into eight sections – the prologue, the infancy narrative, preparations for the public ministry, the Galilean ministry, the journey to Jerusalem, the ministry in Jerusalem, the passion story, and the resurrection narrative. Luke continues his account in the Acts of the Apostles.

John [Jn] [A:3(vi), 27, 31 December; 8,12 January L:4,L:5, L6(i-ii), E:1(ii,v), 2-7.]

This is very different from the other gospels. Jesus speaks in long symbolic discourses, the order of some of the events is different, and often the miracles have discourses attached to them to show the relationship between Jesus and God. Its primary message is the revelation that Jesus is the unique Son of God, and it uses symbols to present this. While the reader knows this, the characters who interact with Jesus in the

243

story are at different levels of understanding and faith. The disciples have some faith that Jesus is the Messiah, but this has to be developed after the first Easter. The crowds are unclear and fluctuate between partial acceptance and rejection. The Judaeans (or 'Jews', as they are called) continually oppose Jesus and reject all his testimony. But belief in Jesus brings people into unity with him: rejection will bring condemnation. It is our mission to continue the work of revealing the Father. We must persuade the world to believe, and show that God is love by the way we live. To help us in this work we have the Paraclete or Holy Spirit. The gospel can be divided into four main parts, with the second and third being further subdivided – prologue, the book of signs [gathering disciples – confrontation with the world], the book of glory [preparing the disciples for the hour – Jesus' arrest, crucifixion, and resurrection], and the epilogue, with its resurrection accounts.

Acts [Ac]   [26 December, E:1-7]

Acts continues the work that began in the gospel of Luke. It is a great adventure story, the story of God's plan for humankind unfolding, in which the gospel is spread beyond Jerusalem to all the people of the earth. It is part of salvation or biblical history, in which the author takes various incidents to show how God interacted with humankind. As such it does not tell the whole story – in fact it finishes rather abruptly with Paul in prison and no details of what happened to him. It gives the more significant details. We see the disciples trying to understand what God's plan was. They had certain guidelines, but they had to work out the details for themselves. They had to sort out for themselves the significance of the deep experiences they had. For all of this they had to rely on prayer. We also see the crucial turning-points where God intervened through the Holy Spirit, the times when their plans were changed and they realised afterwards that the Holy Spirit had guided them. In the beginning of the story the followers of Jesus consisted of a very small band in Jerusalem. At the end there were large groups of Christians in all the main cities of the known world and especially in its centre, Rome. Acts can be divided into five main sections – preparation for the Christian mission, the mission in Jerusalem, the mission in Judea and Samaria, the inauguration of the gentile mission, Paul's missionary journeys.

Romans [Rm]   [1:28-31]

This is one of the greatest of St Paul's letters. It seems that he wrote this to the new community in Rome, to prepare for his arrival in the city (while in Corinth at the end of his stay there on his third missionary journey). He speaks of the need for the salvation of the gospel, and of the way to and the effects of this salvation. In the introduction Paul states that he is specially chosen as an apostle to bring the good news about Jesus the Son of God, who died and rose for our sins. As with most of his letters, it is divided into three main parts – the address, the main body of the letter, and the conclusion. The main body includes his principal theme, the elaboration of this fundamental doctrine, and some ethical conclusions. All have sinned and are in need of being justified. This justification comes through faith in Jesus Christ.

I Corinthians [1 Co] [2:21(iv)-24]

Corinth was the capital of one of the great Roman provinces at the time, with two ports – it was often described as the gateway between the east and the west. In Paul's time it was a Roman colony and had people of many races living and working there. It was a loose-living city, where there was a religious cult to the goddess Venus. Paul had established his Christian community while on his second missionary journey and had developed a deep and lasting relationship with the Christians. Some two years later a number of Christian Jews came with rather unsound doctrine – false apostles, St Paul called them. Paul's letter was in answer to a letter from some influential Christians asking for guidance on marriage, and offerings to idols. He also gives some practical guidelines about the celebration of the Eucharist.

II Corinthians [2 Co] [1:10-11]

The Christians in Corinth tended to be over-enthusiastic at times, jumping to the support of wrong causes. They had strange ideas about the characteristics of an apostle, and some believed that Paul did not live up to their criteria. So Paul had great difficulty in trying to restrain them and keep them on a steady track. He also encouraged them to subscribe to the collection for the Church in Jerusalem. This second letter may be a compilation of a number of letters.

Galatians [Ga] [2:27-28(iii)]

Paul had visited this Christian community around 53 AD during his third missionary journey. He was surprised to find that they had been led astray by 'false brethren', Judaizers, who made out that Christians should conform to the Mosaic Law of the Jews. He wrote this letter mainly to refute these errors. If anyone preaches a version of the gospel different from the one you have already heard, he is to be condemned.

Ephesians [Ep]   [2:28(iv)-30(iv)]

This is regarded as the greatest of Paul's writings and is often called the queen of his epistles. It is believed that St Paul wrote it while in prison, when he had more leisure than at the times he was writing for the other churches. Paul waxes strongly and poetically about God's dealings with men and women. It is too full of material for a few moments here and there to do it justice. God chose us to be his most perfect adopted children. 'Such is the richness of grace which he showered on us in all wisdom and insight.' Christ is the head of the body, the Church. By his resurrection, Jesus became 'Lord' of all, and has conquered sin and death. The believers must be imitators of God and live in love.

Philippians [Ph]   [2:30(v)-31]

Philippi was a city in Macedonia, just to the north-east of present-day Greece. It was founded by Alexander the Great. Paul's visit to this town took place during his second missionary journey – the details are in the Acts. He had to leave after a storm of persecution and illegal inprisonment. He wrote the letter from Rome while in prison. He speaks again against those who insist that Christians become Jews. This letter includes the beautiful hymn to Christ, which is given as a source of encouragement — he emptied himself, and yet he is Lord.

Colossians [Col]   [1:22(iii)-23(iv)]

Colossae was a town near modern Denizli in Turkey. In Paul's time it was a town on the trade route from Ephesus to the interior. Its main industry was in dyed woollen goods. The Christians here seem to have been converted by a representative of Paul. He is writing this letter to combat some heresies which were being preached in the town. Some of the people had the idea that Christ's work of redemption was incomplete. He includes a beautiful hymn to Christ – he is the image of the unseen God and all things are reconciled through him.

1 Thessalonians [1 Th]   [1:21-22(ii)]

Paul came to Thessalonica, which is modern Salonika, during his second missionary journey. It was one of the most important cities in the Roman province of Macedonia. It had a sizeable Jewish community. St Paul spoke in its synagogue on three occasions, explaining that Jesus was the true Messiah. Some Jews and many Greeks accepted his teaching and became Christians. He was persecuted and had to leave. The letter, the earliest writing in the New Testament, was written later to console the Christians and to clarify some points of doctrine. He reminds them to be on their guard against false prophets and false philosophies. He gave them some guidelines on sexual conduct. He exhorted them to be vigilant in waiting for the 'day of the Lord,' and not to be discouraged by opposition and suffering.

2 Thessalonians [2 Th]   [2:21(i-iii)]

The Thessalonians were very happy with Paul's first letter, but as a result there were other questions to be answered. A number in this city, where there were many idle, began to speculate about the Lord's second coming – why work when you are waiting for him? There was much gossip and confusion as a result. In the opening he encourages his faithful followers, because their faith is continually growing. Continue what you have been doing – in this way the name of our Lord Jesus Christ will be glorified, and you will be glorified because of his grace. This may have been written by a disciple of Paul.

I Timothy [I Tm]   [1:23(v)-24]

Timothy was a convert from Lystra who accompanied Paul on his second missionary journey. He left him in Ephesus to continue his work there. This letter, along with the second letter to Timothy and the letter to Titus are called the Pastoral Letters, since they deal with issues regarding the ongoing care of the communities founded by Paul. This particular letter was written to give Timothy the details of how the community was to be organised, and also to give him advice on his personal conduct.

II Timothy [II Tm]   [2:9(iii-vi)]

This is a more personal letter to Timothy than the first. Paul is warning against false teachings. In this first part Paul is reminding Timothy to fan into flame the gift given to him when he laid his hands on him – there must be no timidity, but only the Spirit of power, love and self-control. Bear the hardships that this fidelity will bring.

Titus [Tt]   [2:32(i-iii)]

This letter to Titus is one of the so-called Pastoral Epistles. It was written against the background of Judaic legalisms and a philosophy called gnosticism which regarded all matter as evil. Thus, the human body is evil. Even though it was a personal letter to Titus, it seems to have been addressed to the Christians in Crete. It was a bad place to live because of the immorality. 'The Cretans are always liars, wild and evil beasts, lazy gluttons.' Titus was his faithful henchman and he gives him instructions about how to organise the Church. The priest must not be self-willed, angry, given to drunken conduct, ready to come to blows, etc. He must be hospitable, prudent, just, pious, and self-controlled.

Philemon [Phm] [32(iv)]

This is the only private letter of St Paul that we possess. It seems that a slave of Philemon – slavery was part of life in those days – had escaped and found his way to Rome, where he became a Christian. Paul tries to send him back, and asks Philemon to realise that he now has great assets, so he should be generous to Onesimus.

Hebrews [Heb] [1:1-4, 6(vi)]

Hebrews was written about 80 AD. It is more a sermon than a letter. It begins with a powerful introduction. The Greeks thought of things as being copies or shadows of the real creation – they looked for the real creation: the Jews saw the need for the perfect sacrifice. Both are now fulfiled in Jesus Christ. God sent his Son – the very expression of his essence – into the world. He was the perfect, faithful and compassionate high priest whose great sacrifice purified humankind. He has now taken his royal seat at the right hand of God's glory in the heights. In the past bits and pieces of this were revealed to people, but now we have it all. Christians are exhorted to faith, loyalty, endurance and hope, and to imitate the many witnesses who went before them.

James [Jm] [2:6-7]

The Letter of St James, which may have been written by some of his followers, is a collection of popular moral teachings, similar in style to the Sermon on the Mount. The main concerns of the document are the perseverance in conversion to God and growth in the living of gospel morality. The author stresses the close relationship between faith in God and love of neighbour. He also stresses that we cannot pick and choose from God's laws. At all times people must try to control the various roots of disorder in their lives. The author is impatient with fine words where there is no action. He criticises those who want to live by two standards at once – God's: and the world's.

1 Peter [1 P] [2:8(i-v)]

Peter's first letter is very pastoral and was written to Christians scattered throughout the provinces of Asia Minor. It aims to encourage these new converts in the face of the real problems and crises that they meet in their daily lives. It reminds them of their election by God, and of the noble and rich life they have in Christ after their conversion. The Christian God cares for them and exalts them, and is far superior to their former pagan gods. It opens with a beautiful prayer, which sums up the Christian teaching. We have been given new birth through the death of Jesus Christ and with it the hope of an everlasting inheritance. In the meantime we are filled with a great joy because we love him.

II Peter [II P] [2:9(i-ii)]

This was probably not written by Peter, but by a devoted churchman many years after Peter's time. But it reflects Peter's teachings and deals with some topics that have great relevance today. The main debate is between living faith and practical atheism. Christians have been given a guarantee of something great and wonderful to come, by which they will be able to share the divine nature. To achieve this they have to work at goodness, self-control, patience and kindness.

I John [I Jn] [27 December-12 January]

This was one of three letters, probably written by disciples of John, to encourage unity in the early Church. There were many divisions in these churches. This letter is very positive and loving in tone. We can be sure that we are in God only when the one who claims to be living in him is living the same kind of life as Christ lived. We are now living in the light and must obey his Commandments.

II John [II Jn] [2:32(v)]

In this second letter love is the central theme. Live according to the Commandments. This love is the best weapon for combatting heresy.

III John [III Jn] [2:32(vi)]

This was written to Gaius, a Christian in the church of Asia Minor. He praises his faith and charity.

Jude [Jude] [2:8(vi)]

This short letter seems to have been written to combat some heresies. It does not mention the heretics, so that they will not get any free publicity. Jude reminds the readers that they must build on the foundation of their holy faith. Pray to the Holy Spirit and keep within the love of God, wait for the mercy of Jesus Christ. He finishes with a poetic prayer of praise to God.

Revelation [Rv] [2:33-34]

The Book of Revelation was written during the persecution of the Christians – they were expected to treat the Emperor publicly as a god. It uses a style found in the Old Testament – apocalyptic writing. This described the chaos of the present, referred to terrible calamities falling on the people, but states that eventually there will be peace in the Day of the Lord. In the New Testament, the Day of the Lord refers to the day of Jesus Christ. After the calamities and tragedies there will be great peace. In the prologue we are told that this is God's revelation to us – a revelation of truth. It is given through Christ to John, who is God's slave and servant, which is itself a great honour. The first 'letter' is to the Church at Ephesus. It was one of the great cities, but notorious for its pagan superstition. Christ praises those who were strong in upholding the Christian principles. The book can be divided into seven sections – prologue, the letters to seven churches of Asia, the vision of God and the Lamb in heaven, the visions of the seven seals, trumpets and plagues, with interludes, the punishment of Babylon and the destruction of pagan nations, the new creation, and the epilogue.

Salvation History

Prehistory and the Patriarchs [c .2000 BC]

The first book of the Pentateuch, Genesis, gives an account of the origin of all created things and acts, as it were, as an elaborate introduction to God's revelation to Israel through Moses. It contains the history of Israel's ancestors, from earliest times until the death of Joseph. It covers the lives of the great family of the patriarchs – Abraham, Isaac, Jacob, and Joseph. The chosen people stemmed from this family. We do not know exactly when they lived, but it was probably shortly after 2000 BC. According to the text Abraham was born at Ur in southern Mesopotamia. He made his way north to Haran and later westward to Canaan. Later Jacob and his family settled in Egypt to escape from famine in Canaan. Here they lived comfortably while Joseph enjoyed the favour of the Pharaoh.

Moses [c.270 BC]

Centuries later Moses appeared on the scene. He liberated his people and led them out to the border of Canaan. This event was the very important Exodus, which is the heart of the Pentateuch. On the way they went by the mount of Sinai, where the Lord gave them the ten Commandments and ratified the covenant with them. The two stone tablets with the law on them were placed in the Ark of the Covenant – this was a reminder to them of the Lord's continual presence. Eventually, after the death of Moses, they crossed over the Jordan from the east and into the land of Canaan (1270 BC).

The Judges (c.1220-1050 BC)

Joshua was Moses' successor and he led the people to conquer the Canaanites. Afterwards, he divided the land between the twelve tribes. Many of them took on the customs of the people around them. Later, under the judges, their tribal heroes, they defended the Israelites against the incursions of the many tribes around them. Their position was still very insecure.

David and Solomon [1003 -922 BC]

The last of the judges was Samuel. He was personally opposed to the setting up of a monarchy for theological reasons, he gave in eventually to the people and anointed Saul as king. He was not too successful and when he died, David was made king (probably 1003 BC). He united the northern and southern tribes and made Jerusalem the new capital. He was a great statesman and military commander, and eventually expanded his small kingdom into an empire. Solomon succeed his father. He was a man of great wisdom, though he lacked the military qualities of David. However, during his forty-year reign, there was great economic prosperity and no war. He carried out many building projects, including the building of the Temple.

The Divided Kingdoms [922-586 BC]

At his death in 922 BC, the northern kingdom broke away from the southern kingdom and they were never again reunited. Now there are two sets of history – one for each of these two kingdoms. The arrogant Rehoboam succeeded to the throne in the southern kingdom and Jeroboam in the rival north. Jeroboam set up sanctuaries at Dan and Bethel to keep the people from going to Jerusalem to worship. The kingdom of Israel in the north was larger and more prosperous than Judah in the south, but Judah was more stable and more secure.

Years later, Omri established an impressive dynasty in the north. He moved the capital to Samaria. He solidified Israel's relationship with Phoenicia by the marriage of his son, Ahab, with Jezebel, the daughter of the king of Sidon. Ahab was a good leader too, but allowed himself to be too influenced by Jezebel.

Under Jeroboam II in the north and Uzziah in the south, the two countries worked well together and the prosperity increased. However, much of the wealth was in the hands of the upper classes, and there was great exploitation of the poor. The prophets Amos and Hosea spoke out very strongly against these abuses.

The Assyrians and the Babylonians [745-539 BC]

In 745 BC the scene changed with the accession to the Assyrian throne of Tiglath-pileser III. He conquered most of the countries around the two kingdoms and Israel eventually fell in 721 BC. His policy was to deport many of the inhabitants and replace them by foreigners.

Hezekiah became King of Judah after the fall of Israel, and carried out many religious reforms under the influence of Isaiah. Assyria collapsed in 612 BC and was replaced by the Neo-Babylonian empire under Nebuchadnezzar. In 586 BC Jerusalem fell, the Temple was destroyed and many of the people were exiled to Babylon. Judah became a Babylonian province.

The Persians and the Greeks [539-142 BC]

In 539 BC Babylonia fell to Cyrus, king of Persia. He allowed the Jews to return to their homeland. The Temple was rebuilt. About 458 BC Ezra, priest and scribe, led a group of Jews from Babylon to Jerusalem, where he reinforced the observance of the Torah.

Alexander the Great conquered Palestine in 332 BC. Through his influence the Greek language became dominant in the Mediterranean area. The Hebrew Bible was now translated into Greek (the Septuagint). When Alexander died, Palestine was ruled by Ptolemy I of Egypt, who was one of his generals. A later king Antiochus defiled the Temple and forbade the use of the Torah. This led to a revolt by the Maccabee family. Judas Maccabee conquered Jerusalem in 142 BC and the Temple was rededicated.

The Romans [63 BC -70 AD]

From 63 BC the Romans controlled Palestine. Herod the Great governed Judea for thirty-three years from 37 BC. He was a great builder and many of his projects are still to be seen, though he was a violent man. After his death his three sons, the Tetrarchs Archelaus, Herod Antipas and Philip, ruled the country. From 6 AD Roman prefects governed Judaea. Among them was Pontius Pilate (26-36 AD). Herod Antipas was Tetrarch over Galilee and Peraea from 4 BC till 39 AD. Herod Agrippa I, grandson of Herod the Great, ruled a unified Palestine from 41 to 44 AD.

The Jews revolted against the Romans in 66 AD and the Emperor Nero sent Vespasian to quell the insurrection. When Vespasian became emperor in 69 A.D. his son Titus continued this work. Jerusalem fell in 70 AD and the Temple was destroyed. After this many of the Jews were scattered throughout the Roman world.

Key Dates

1800 BC	Joseph
1300	Moses
1270	Arrival in Promised Land
1003	David
922	Rehoboam in Judah (S) Jeroboam in Israel (N)
721	Assyrians destroy Israel
587	Babylonians destroy Judah [Nebuchadnezzar] – deportation
539	Persian king, Cyrus allow the Jews to return home
332	Alexander the Great conquers Palestine.
164	Maccabean revolt
63	Rome controls Palestine
4	Death of Herod the Great
70 AD	Destruction of Jerusalem by Romans

Prophets	*Period of prophecy*	*Place*
Amos	786 -746	Israel
Hosea	750 -732	Israel
Isaiah	742 -687	Judah
Micah	740 -680	Judah
Jeremiah	650 -582	Judah and in exile
Zephaniah	630 -610	Judah
Nahum	615 -610	Judah
Habakkuk	605 -597	Judah
Obadiah	600	Judah
Ezekiel	598 -571	Judah and in exile
Baruch	587 -550	Exile
Daniel	580 -538	Exile
Haggai	520	Judah (after exile)
Zechariah	520	Judah (after exile)
Malachi	460	Judah (after exile)
Jonah	450?	Judah (after exile)
Joel	400	Judah (after exile)

Appendix A

Readings for Weekdays

Advent -Christmas

For the first nine days the gospel is chosen to suit the the ancient set of readings from Isaiah.

1-2(v)	Isaiah	1(i,iii-vi), 2(ii-vi)	Matthew
		1(ii), 2(i)	Luke

From the Thursday of the second week the first reading is chosen to suit the gospel, which speaks of John the Baptist.

A:2(vi)	Sirach	A:3(i-ii)	Matthew
A:3(i)	Numbers	A:3(iii-iv)	Luke
A:3(ii)	Zephaniah	A:3(v)	John
A:3(iii-vi)	Isaiah		

From 17-24 December the gospel is about the events that led up to the birth of Christ and the first reading presents Old Testament messianic prophecies.

17 December	Genesis	17/18 December	Matthew
18 December	Jeremiah	19-24 December	Luke
19 December	Judges		
20 December	Isaiah		
21 December	Song/Zephaniah		
22 December	1 Samuel		
23 December	Malachi		
24 December	2 Samuel		
26 December	Acts	26/28 December	
		7 January	Matthew
27 December-			
13 January	1 John	27/31 D 2-7/12 J	John
		29/30 D 10-11 J	Luke
		8 January	Mark

Throughout Lent the gospel and Old Testament readings are related, in presenting the major themes of Baptism and penance. For Easter week the gospels recount the appearances of Christ; for the rest of the season the teachings of Jesus are taken from John. The Acts is used for the first readings throughout the season.

L:0(iii)	Joel / 2 Cor	L:0(iii,v)	Matthew
L:0(iv)	Deuteronomy	L:0(iv,vi)	Luke
L:0(v-vi)	Isaiah		
L:1(i)	Leviticus	L:1(i-ii,iv-vi)	Matthew
L:1(ii)	Isaiah	L:1(iii)	Luke
L:1(iii)	Jonah		
L:(iv-v)	Esther		
L:1(vi)	Deuteronomy		
L:2(i)	Daniel	L:2(i,iv,vi)	Luke
L:2(ii)	Isaiah	L:2(ii-iii,v)	Matthew
L:2(iii-iv)	Jeremiah		
L:2(v)	Genesis		
L:2(vi)	Micah		
L:3(i)	2 Kings	L:3(i,iv,vi)	Luke
L:3(ii)	Daniel	L:3(ii-iii,v)	Matthew
L:3(iii)	Deuteronomy		
L:3(iv)	Jeremiah		
L:3(v-vi)	Hosea		
L:4(i,iii)	Isaiah	L:4	John
L:4(ii)	Ezekiel		
L:4(iv)	Exodus		
L:4(v)	Wisdom		
L:4(vi)	Jeremiah		
L:5(i,iii)	Daniel	L:5	John
L:5(ii)	Numbers		
L:5(iv)	Genesis		
L:5(v)	Jeremiah		
L:5(vi)	Ezekiel		
L:6(i-iii)	Isaiah	L:6(i-ii)	John
		L:6(iii)	Matthew
E:1	Acts	E:1(i)	Matthew
		E:1(ii,v)	John
		E:1(iii-iv)	Luke
		E:1(vi)	Mark

Ordinary Time

Year 1		Year 2		Gospels [Year 1 & 2]	
1-4	Hebrews	1(i-v)	Samuel	1-9	Mark
5-6(i-v)	Genesis	1(vi)-4(i)	2 Samuel	10-21	Matthew
6(vi)	Hebrews	4(iv)-51	Kings	22-34	Luke
7-8	Sirach	4(v)	Sirach		
9	Tobit	6-7	James		
10-11	2 Corinthians	8(i-v)	1 Peter		
12-14	Genesis	8(vi)	Jude		
14-17 (i-iv)	Exodus	9(i-ii)	2 Peter		
17(v-vi)	Leviticus	9(iii-vi)	2 Timothy		
18(i-iv)	Numbers	10-12(v)	2 Kings		
18(v)-19(iii)	Deuteronomy	10(iv)	Sirach		
19(iv-vi)	Joshua	10(vi)	2 Chronicles		
20(i-iv)	Judges	12(vi)	Lamentations		
20(v-vi)	Ruth	13	Amos		
21-22(ii)	Thess	14(i-v)	Hosea		
22(iii)-23(iv)	Colossians	14(vi)-15(v)	Isaiah		
23(v)-24	1 Timothy	15(vi)-16(ii)	Micah		
25(i-iii)	Ezra	16(iii)-18(iv)	Jeremiah		
25(iv-v)	Haggai	18(v)	Nahum		
25(vi)-26(ii)	Zechariah	18(vi)	Habakkuk		
26(iii-iv)	Nehemiah	19-20	Ezekiel		
26(v-vi)	Baruch	21(i-iii)	2 Thess		
27(i-iii)	Jonah	21(iv)-24	1Corinthians		
27(iv)	Malachi	25(i-iii)	Proverbs		
27(v-vi)	Joel	25(iv-vi)	Qoholeth		
28-31	Romans	26	Job		
32	Wisdom	27-28(iii)	Galatians		
33	Maccabees	28(iv)-30(iv)	Ephesians		
34	Daniel	30(v)-31	Philippians		
		32(i-iii)	Titu		
		32(iv)	Philemon		
		32(v)	2 John		
		32(vi)	3 John		
		33-34	Revelation		

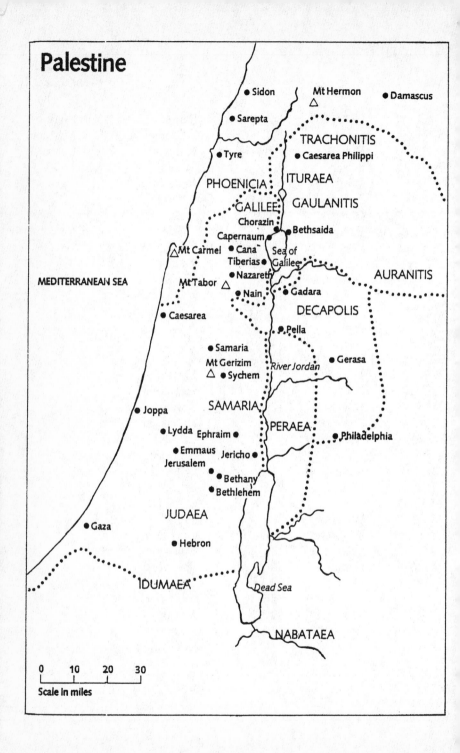

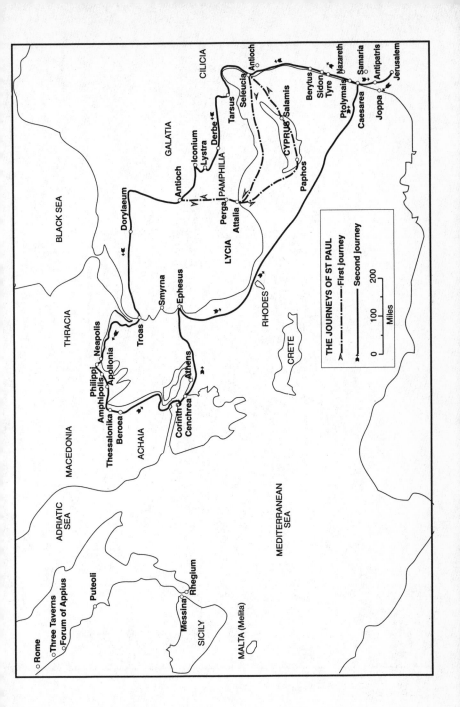

THE JOURNEYS OF ST PAUL

— · — · — First journey
————— Second journey

0   100   200
Miles

259

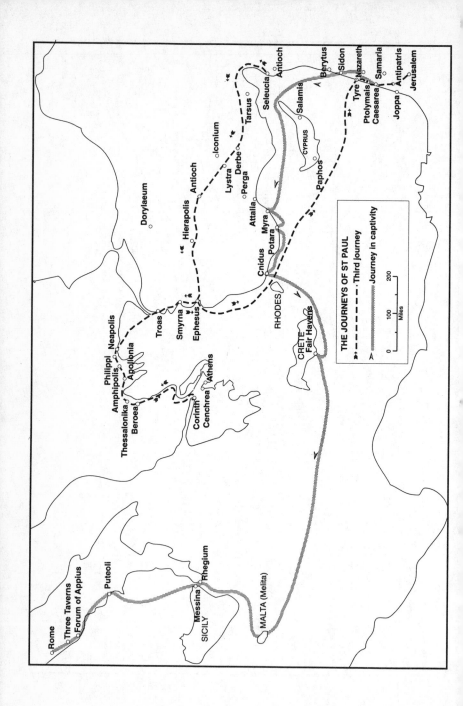

THE JOURNEYS OF ST PAUL

—— ▸▸ —— Third Journey

≈≈≈≈≈ Journey in captivity

Rome
Three Taverns
Forum of Applus
Puteoli
Rhegium
Messina
SICILY
MALTA (Melita)
CRETE
Fair Havens
RHODES
Troas
Smyrna
Ephesus
Neapolis
Philippi
Amphipolis
Apollonia
Thessalonika
Beroea
Corinth
Cenchrea
Athens
Cnidus
Potara
Myra
Attalia
Perga
Derbe
Lystra
Iconium
Antioch
Hierapolis
Dorylaeum
Tarsus
Seleucia
Antioch
Salamis
CYPRUS
Paphos
Berytus
Sidon
Tyre
Nazareth
Ptolymais
Samaria
Caesarea
Antipatris
Joppa
Jerusalem

0   100   200
Miles

Notes

Notes

Notes